W9-BOC-448

LEARN
FRENCH
(FRANÇAIS)
THE FAST AND FUN WAY
Third Edition

by Elisabeth Bourquin Leete
International Language Institute
Northampton, Massachusetts

Heywood Wald, Coordinating Editor
Chairman, Department of Foreign Languages
Martin Van Buren High School, New York

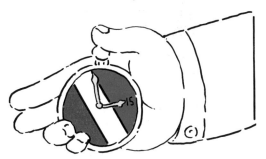

To help you pace your learning, we've included
stopwatches *like the one above* throughout
the book to mark each 15-minute interval.
You can read one of these units each day
or pace yourself according to your needs.

ARTHUR C. MATZ
6602 CAMBRIA TER.
ELKRIDGE, MD 21075

BARRON'S

CONTENTS

© Copyright 2004, 1997, 1985 by Barron's Educational Series, Inc.

All rights reserved.
No part of this book may be reproduced in any form, by photostat, microfilm, xerography, or any other means, or incorporated into any information retrieval system, electronic or mechanical, without the written permission of the copyright owner.

All inquiries should be addressed to:
Barron's Educational Series, Inc.
250 Wireless Boulevard
Hauppauge, New York 11788
http://www.barronseduc.com

Library of Congress Catalog Card No. 2003043702

ISBN-13: 978-0-7641-2559-1 (book)
ISBN-10: 0-7641-2559-1 (book)
ISBN-13: 978-0-7641-7688-3 (cassette package)
ISBN-10: 0-7641-7688-9 (cassette package)
ISBN-13: 978-0-7641-7689-0 (CD package)
ISBN-10: 0-7641-7689-7 (CD package)

PRINTED IN CHINA
9

Cover and Book Design   Milton Glaser, Inc.
Illustrations   Juan Suarez

A Word To The Reader Because exchange rates of foreign currencies against the U.S. dollar vary from day to day, the actual cost of a hotel room, taxi ride, or a meal may be more or less than the amounts in the book. Please consult a newspaper, bank, or currency house for the most up-to-date exchange rate.

Library of Congress Cataloging-in-Publication Data

Leete, Elisabeth Bourquin.
    Learn French (français) the fast and fun way / by Elisabeth Bourquin Leete; Heywood Wald, coordinating editor. — 3rd ed.
        p.   cm.
    ISBN 0-7641-2559-1 (bk.: alk. paper)—
    ISBN 0-7641-7688-9 (bk. & 4 cassettes: alk. paper) —
    ISBN 0-7641-7689-7 (bk. & 4 CDs: alk. paper)
    1. French language—Conversation and phrase books—
English. 2. French language—Textbooks for foreign speakers—English.   I. Title: Learn French the fast and fun way.   II. Title: Learn français the fast and fun way.   III. Wald, Heywood.   IV. Title.

PC2121.L455   2004
448.3'421—dc21   2003043702

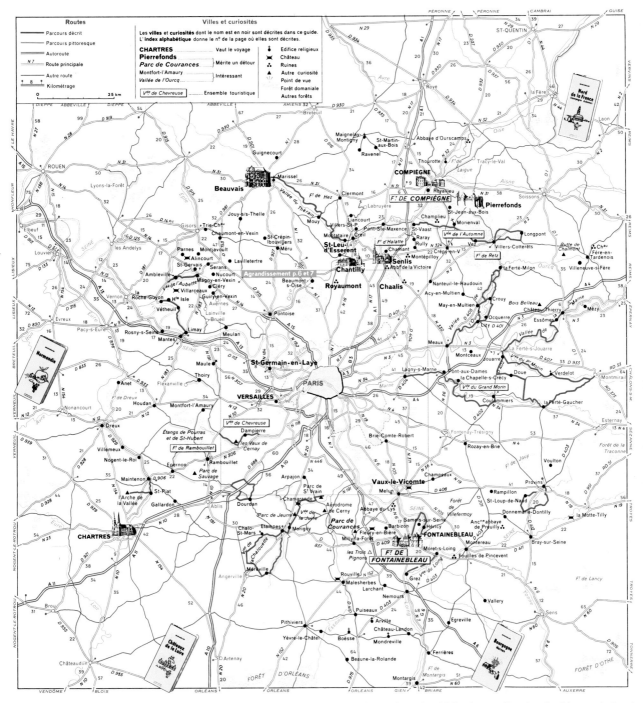

(From Michelin Guide, Environs de Paris, *20th edition. Reprinted with permission.)*

French is a language and culture shared not only by the 55 million people of European France but by many millions more in adjoining Belgium, Luxembourg and Switzerland and in the Canadian Province of Quebec, the Caribbean islands of Martinique, Guadeloupe and Haiti, French possessions in the Atlantic and Pacific, and former French colonies in South America, Asia and, especially, Africa. French is also employed extensively as an international language of diplomatic exchange.

Shaped somewhat like a hexagon, France comprises nearly 213,000 square miles. It is

1

bounded by the English Channel in the north, the Atlantic Ocean in the west, the Pyrénées, Spain and the Mediterranean in the south, and in the east by Italy, Switzerland, the Rhine River, Germany, Luxembourg and Belgium. Its modern history dates to the Roman Conquest of Gaul in the first century B.C.

From Paris, the nation's political and cultural capital, the visitor may strike out in any direction assured that the trip will be rewarding in every sense—historically, culturally, scenically, with the happy bonus of fine wines and cuisine distinctive to every region of France. Paris itself has a concentration of magnificent sightseeing and entertainment opportunities—art museums such as the Louvre and the Musée d'Orsay, echoes of France's days of glory and the Napoleonic era at the Hôtel des Invalides, the Île de la Cité and Notre Dame Cathedral, lovely parks such as the Tuileries and Bois de Boulogne. And, of course, there is the Eiffel Tower.

Public transportation by rail, air and bus is excellent, and France is also blessed with a network of autoroutes together with well-mapped secondary roads, favored by many motorists wishing to gain a more intimate sense of French village and country life. Much of what the traveler may wish to see lies within a day's journey from Paris— Normandy and Brittany to the north and northwest; Marseilles, the Côte d'Azur, the Provence and the Mediterranean beaches to the south; Bordeaux, the Bay of Biscay and the Pyrénées to the southwest; to the southeast, the Alps and Mont Blanc, the Rhône Alps, and the Jura and Vosges mountains; and, to the east, the Rhine River, Champagne, Lorraine and Alsace.

Learning the language adds much interest, pleasure and satisfaction to a trip to France. Of equal importance to many is the access gained to some of the important bases of Western civilization. French philosophers, political theorists, statesmen, artists, writers and scientists have substantially influenced the cultural and political aspects of our world.

Last but not least, you will find in French-speaking countries—as you would in any other part of the world—that your efforts to communicate in the language are rewarded by kindness and offers of friendship.

FRENCH PRONUNCIATION— A FEW SIMPLE RULES

Is French difficult to pronounce? Not at all. French follows a few simple rules, and once you know these, you'll have no problem saying what you want and understanding those who speak to you. There are two basic principles of French pronunciation:
1. Not all letters are pronounced, as they most often are in English. Remember, however, that even in English, we have some silent letters—the *p* in *pneumonia*, for example.
2. The French like to link words. Sometimes a whole sentence may sound to you like one long word, especially in the beginning. For instance, you will find in the dialogue in the first unit, the sentence:
   J'habite aux États-Unis. I live in the United States.
   The sentence should sound like:
   zha-bee-toh-zay-ta-zew-nee

Linking is compulsory in many situations, especially between words that logically belong together, but is optional in other situations. In a few cases, it may seem appropriate to link the words, but it is not permitted (for example, after the conjunction et , which means ''and''). You'll learn the rules for linking up words as you work your way through this book.

The pronunciation tables which follow will help you get started on the road to France and its language. Practice pronouncing the words a few times while you also learn some basic vocabulary. You'll become familiar with how French people pronounce their vowels and consonants, so you'll know how to pronounce a new word when you see it on a road sign or included in an informational brochure. But, to make it all even easier, every time we introduce a new word in this book, we show you how to pronounce it.

VOWELS		
French Letters	Symbol	Pronunciation/Example
a, à	a	This is a short *A*, as in *cat*. Example: *ma* (ma) my.
a, â	ah	A long *AH*, as in *father*. Example: *pas* (pah) step.
é, final er, ez, et	ay	*A* as in *day*. Example *musée* (mew-zay) museum.
e + 2 consonants, e, ê, è	eh	This is a short *E*, as in *ever*. Example: *appelle* (a-pehl) call.
e, eu	uh	*E*, as in English word *the*. Example: *le* (luh) the.
eu	ūh	This sound does not exist in English. The sound is between *UH* and *EW*. Example: *peu* (pūh) little.
i, y	ee	The sound of *EE*, as in *meet*. Example: *valise* (va-leez) suitcase.
o	o	A short *O*, as in *done*. Example: *homme* (om) man.
o, ô	oh	A long *O*, as in *open*. Example: *tôt* (toh) soon.
oi, oî	wa	Pronounced *WA*, as in *watch*. Example: *toi* (twa) you (familiar).
ou	oo	Pronounced *OO*, as in *tooth*. Example: *ouvrir* (oo-vreer) to open.
u	ew	This sound does not exist in English. Say *EE*; round your lips. Example: *tu* (tew) you (familiar).
u + vowel	wee	Pronounced *WEE*, as in *whee*. Example: *huit* (weet) eight.

CONSONANTS

French Letter(s)	Symbol	Pronunciation/Example
b, d, f, k, l, m, n, p, s, t, v, z	—	The corresponding English sound for these French consonants is the same.
c (before e, i, y)	s	This consonant is pronounced *SS*. Example: *merci* (mehr-see) thank you.
ç (before a, o, u)	s	This consonant is pronounced *SS*. Example: *garçon* (gar-sohn) boy.
c (before a, o, u)	k	The *c* without the accent mark is a hard *K*, as in *kind*. Example: *comment* (ko-mahn) how.
g (before e, i, y)	zh	Pronounced like the soft *S* in *pleasure*. Example: *rouge* (roozh) red.
ge (before a, o, u)	zh	Pronounced like the soft *S* in pleasure.
g (before a, o, u)	g	Pronounced like the hard *G* in *go*. Example: *Chicago* (Shee-kah-goh).
gn	ny	Like the sound *NI* in *onion*. Example: *oignon* (o-nyohn) onion.
h	—	The *h* is always silent. Example: *hôtel* (oh-tehl) hotel.
j	zh	Pronounced like the soft *S* in *pleasure*. Example: *je* (zhuh) I.
qu, final q	k	Pronounced like the hard *K* in *kind*. Example: *cinq* (sank) five.
r	r	This sound does not exist in English; roll the *R* at the top of back of mouth, as for gargling. Example *rouge* (roozh) red.
ss	s	The double *s* sound is pronounced *SS*. Example: *poisson* (pwa-sohn) fish.
s (at the beginning of word)	s	Pronounced *SS*. Example: *son* (sohn) his (or hers).
s (next to consonant between vowels)	z	Pronounced *Z*. Example: *poison* (pwah-zohn) poison.
t (before i + vowel)	s	Pronounced *SS*. Example: *nation* (na-syon) nation.
th	t	Pronounced like the short *T* in *top*. Example: *thé* (tay) tea.
x	ks	Pronounced *EKS*, as in *excellent*. Example: *excellent* (eck-se-lahn).
x	s	Pronounced *SS* in these words only: *dix* (dees) ten, *six* (sees) six.

NASAL SOUNDS

These are very common in French and occur when a *single* N or M follows a vowel. The N and the M are not vocalized. The tip of the tongue does not touch the roof of the mouth.

French Letters	Symbol	Pronunciation/Example
an, am, en, em	ahn	This nasal sound is similar to *ON*, as in the English word *on*. Example: *France* (frahns).
in, im, ain, aim, ien, ym	an	This sound is similar to *AN*, as in *can*. Example: *bien* (byan) well, good.
on, om	ohn	Similar to *ON*, as in *long*. Example: *bon* (bohn) good.
un, um	uhn	Similar to *UN*, as in *under*. Example: *un* (uhn) one.

When words LE, LA (''the''), and some pronouns, adverbs and conjunctions which end with an E precede a word that begins with a vowel sound, the final vowel is dropped and replaced by an apostrophe.

EXAMPLE: la + auto = l'auto

le + homme = l'homme

When words merge like this, it is called **elision**.

French syllables all have the same length and approximately the same amount of stress. The last syllable of a word group is slightly emphasized, not by saying it louder, but by making it a little longer.

HOW ENGLISH AND FRENCH ARE SIMILAR

In many ways, French is very much like English. For example, simple French sentences generally follow the same arrangement as English ones:

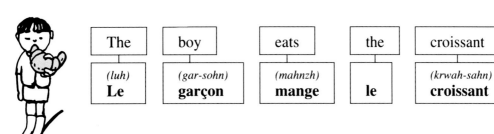

The	boy	eats	the	croissant
(luh) **Le**	*(gar-sohn)* **garçon**	*(mahnzh)* **mange**	**le**	*(krwah-sahn)* **croissant**

We'll also show you some of the differences that exist between the two languages as you become more familiar with French. Let's look at one now.

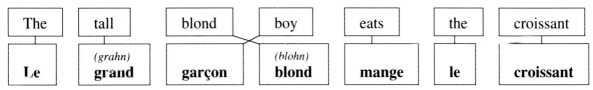

The	tall	blond	boy	eats	the	croissant
Le	*(grahn)* **grand**	**garçon**	*(blohn)* **blond**	**mange**	**le**	**croissant**

5

For now, think about the ways French and English words are alike. You can learn many French words simply by recognizing a few patterns in word endings.

ENGLISH WORDS ENDING IN	FRENCH WORDS ENDING IN
-ION	**-ION**
correction	*(ko-rek-syohn)* **correction**
occasion	*(o-ka-zyohn)* **occasion**
nation	*(na-syohn)* **nation**
station	*(sta-syohn)* **station**
education	*(ay-dew-ka-syohn)* **éducation**
function	*(fohnk-syohn)* **fonction**
-TY	**-TÉ**
city	*(see-tay)* **cité**
sincerity	*(san-say-ree-tay)* **sincérité**
unity	*(ew-nee-tay)* **unité**
possibility	*(po-see-bee-lee-tay)* **possibilité**
-IST	**-ISTE**
dentist	*(dahn-teest)* **dentiste**
violinist	*(vyo-lo-neest)* **violoniste**
pianist	*(pya-neest)* **pianiste**
-OR	**-EUR**
actor	*(ak-tūhr)* **acteur**
sculptor	*(skewl-tūhr)* **sculpteur**
vigor	*(vee-gūhr)* **vigueur**
color	*(koo-lūhr)* **couleur**

Did you realize how much French you already know? In many cases, the only difference is the PRONUNCIATION. In fact, you may not have realized that you've been speaking French for years! Here are just a few expressions which are part of everyday American language.

(foh) (pah)
faux pas

(rahn-day-voo)
rendez-vous

(gaf)
gaffe

(day-zha) (vew)
déjà   vu

(bohn-bohn)
bonbon

(ba-geht)
baguette

(ehs-kar-goh)
escargot

(soop)   (dew) (zhoor)
soupe du jour

(ahn-tray)
entrée

(a) (la) (mod)
à la mode

(zhwah) (duh) (veevr)
joie   de vivre

(pah) (duh) (dūh)
pas de   deux

(or)   duhvr)
hors d'oeuvre

Now you can start building upon what you already know. We don't promise it will be a cinch, but we can guarantee it will be fun, especially when you begin trying to communicate with fluent French speakers. Just put in 15 minutes a day at a pace comfortable for you.

GETTING TO KNOW PEOPLE

(fuh-sohn) *(ko-ne-sahns)*
Faisons Connaissance

	(kohn-vehr-sohn)
1	**Conversons**
	Let's Talk

Knowing how to greet people and how to start a conversation is important, and you should learn those skills first. Read the following dialogue several times, pronouncing each line carefully out loud. The dialogue contains some basic words and expressions that will be useful to you.

Mark Smith, his wife Mary, their daughter Anne, and their son Paul have just arrived at Charles de Gaulle Airport in Paris, and they can't find their luggage. Mark approaches an airline employee:

(bohn-zhoor) *(muh-syúh)*
MARC **Bonjour, Monsieur.**

Hello/Good day, Sir.

(ahn-plwa-yay) *(voo)* *(day-zee-ray)*
EMPLOYÉ **Bonjour. Vous désirez**
(kehl-kuh) *(shohz)*
quelque chose?

Hello/Good day. May I help you? (*lit.* Do you want anything?)

(wee) *(zhuh)* *(shehrsh)* *(may)*
MARC **Oui. Je cherche mes**
(va-leez)
valises.

Yes. I am looking for my suitcases.

(byan) *(ko-mahn)* *(voo)*
EMPLOYÉ **Bien. Comment vous**
(za-play) *(voo)*
appelez-vous?

Well/O.K. What is your name? (*lit.* How do you call yourself?)

(zhuh) *(ma-pehl)*
MARC **Je m'appelle Marc Smith.**

My name is Mark Smith.

(luh) *(new-may-roh)* *(duh)* *(votr)* *(vol)*
EMPLOYÉ **Le numéro de votre vol et**
(o-ree-zheen)
l'origine?

Your flight number and origin?

(trwah)(sahn) *(trahnt)*
MARC **Le vol Air France trois cent trente-**
(trwah) *(duh)*
trois de New York.

Air France flight 333 from New York.

EMPLOYÉ **(uhn) (mo-mahn) (seel) (voo) (pleh)** **Un moment, s'il vous plaît.**	One moment, please.

As the clerk looks through some papers on this desk, Jean **(zhahn)**, a French business friend, sees Mark.

JEAN **(sa-lew) (ko-mahn) (va-tew)** **Salut, Marc! Comment vas-tu?**	Hi, Mark. How are you?
MARC **(zhuh) (vay) (byan) (ay) (twa)** **Jean! Je vais bien, et toi?**	John! I am well. And you?
JEAN **(treh) (tew) (eh) (ee-see) (ahn)** **Très bien. Tu es ici en**	Very well. Are you here on a
(va-kahns) **vacances?**	holiday?
MARC **(zhuh) (tuh) (pray-zahnt) (ma) (fa-mee-y)** **Oui. Je te présente ma famille.**	Yes. Let me introduce my family.
(fam) (fee-y) **Ma femme Marie, ma fille Anne, et**	My wife Mary, my daughter Anne, and
(mohn) (fees) **mon fils Paul.**	my son Paul.
JEAN **(ahn-shahn-tay)** **Enchanté!**	Delighted!
EMPLOYÉ **(ehks-kew-zay-mwa) (voh)** **Excusez-moi, Monsieur. Vos**	Excuse me, Sir. Your
(a-reev) (a-vehk) (luh) (pro-shan) **valises arrivent avec le prochain**	suitcases are arriving on the next
(na-vyohn) **avion.**	plane.

	(zewt)		
MARC	**Zut!**	Darn it!	

MARC   *(zewt)*
Zut!   Darn it!

JEAN   *(pa-syahns)*   *(neh) (pah) (zahn)*
Patience Marc. Tu n'es pas en   Be patient, Mark. You are not in
(na-may-reek)
Amérique!   America!

MARC *(à l'employé)*   **Merci, Monsieur.**   Thank you, Sir.
(oh) (ruh-vwar)
Au revoir!   Good-bye.

EMPLOYÉ   *(voo) (zahn) (pree)*
Je vous en   prie.   You are welcome.

JEAN   *(tool) (mohnd)*
Au revoir, tout le monde!   Good-bye, everybody.

TOUT LE   *(a byan-toh)*
MONDE   **À bientôt!**   See you soon!

Match the French expressions from the dialogue with their English equivalents:

1. Comment vous appelez-vous?
2. Je te présente ma famille.
3. Zut!
4. Vous désirez quelque chose?
5. Je vous en prie.
6. Je vais bien.
7. À bientôt.
8. Je m'appelle . . .
9. Enchanté!
10. Salut. Comment vas-tu?

a. May I help you?
b. My name is . . .
c. What's your name?
d. Hi, how are you?
e. I am well.
f. Let me introduce my family.
g. Delighted!
h. Darn it!
i. You are welcome
j. See you soon.

ANSWERS

Matching   1. c   2. f   3. h   4. a   5. i   6. e   7. j   8. b   9. g   10. d

10

LES GENS ET LES CHOSES
People and Things

One of the first things you need to know is what to call certain things or people—words we call nouns. You will need to know what a French noun looks like, and how to make it plural. Unlike English nouns, all French nouns have a gender (masculine or feminine); like English nouns, they can be either singular or plural. Look carefully at the following examples of nouns given in their singular and plural forms, and write them on the blank line in the space provided.

Singular and Plural

(san-gew-lyay)
SINGULIER

(plew-ryel)
PLURIEL

(gar-sohn)
garçon
boy

_____

(gar-sohn)
garçons
boys

_____

(sha)
chat
cat

_____

(sha)
chats
cats

_____

(pyay)
pied
foot

_____

(pyay)
pieds
feet

_____

(arbr)
arbre
tree

_____

(arbr)
arbres
trees

_____

(pah)
pas
step

_____

(pah)
pas
steps

_____

(nuh-vūh)
neveu
nephew

(nuh-vuh)
neveux
nephews

(sha-poh)
chapeau
hat

(sha-poh)
chapeaux
hats

(zhoor-nal)
journal
newspaper

(zhoor-noh)
journaux
newspapers

These words you have just learned are **masculine nouns**. To form the plural, in most cases, you simply add $\boxed{S}$. If the singular noun ends with an $\boxed{S}$, don't change anything to form the plural. If it ends with $\boxed{EU}$ or $\boxed{EAU}$, add $\boxed{X}$ instead of $\boxed{S}$. If the noun ends in $\boxed{AL}$, the ending becomes $\boxed{AUX}$ in the plural.

Now look at the following nouns:

SINGULIER

PLURIEL

(meh-zohn)
maison
house, home

(meh-zohn)
maisons
houses, homes

(oh-toh-mo-beel)
automobile
automobile

(oh-toh-mo-beel)
automobiles
automobiles

(mehr)
mère
mother

(mehr)
mères
mothers

The preceding words are **feminine nouns.** Simply add an $\boxed{S}$ to form the plural. If the noun ends with an $\boxed{S}$ or an $\boxed{X}$ or a $\boxed{Z}$ in the singular, don't change anything to form the plural. (The final $\boxed{S}$, $\boxed{X}$, or $\boxed{Z}$ is not pronounced.)

Test your knowledge of singular and plural by making these nouns all plural:

(ka-yay)
cahier
workbook

1. _____
workbooks

(stee-loh)
stylo
pen

2. _____
pens

(pehr)
père
father

3. _____
fathers

(shuh-val)
cheval
horse

4. _____
horses

(fees)
fils
son

5. _____
sons

(mahn-toh)
manteau
coat

6. _____
coats

ANSWERS
Plural 1. cahiers 2. stylos 3. pères 4. chevaux 5. fils 6. manteaux

THREE EXCEPTIONS:

1. The following masculine nouns which end in $\boxed{\text{EU}}$ take an $\boxed{\text{S}}$ in the plural:

   (blūh)   *(pnūh)*
   bleus (blue jeans), **pneus** (tires).

2. The following masculine nouns which end in $\boxed{\text{OU}}$ take an $\boxed{\text{X}}$ in the plural:

   (bee-zhoo)   *(ka-yoo)*   *(shoo)*   *(zhuh-noo)*   *(ee-boo)*
   bijoux (jewels), **cailloux** (pebbles), **choux** (cabbages), **genoux** (knees), **hiboux** (owls),
   (zhoo-zhoo)
   joujoux (toys).

3. The following masculine nouns which end in $\boxed{\text{AL}}$ take an $\boxed{\text{S}}$ in the plural:

   (bal)   *(kar-na-val)*   *(fehs-tee-val)*
   bals (balls), **carnavals** (carnivals), **festivals** (festivals).

(uhn)   *(ewn)*   *(day)*

Un, une, des

A (An), Some

When we name something—use a noun—we often precede it in English with the words *a* or *some*. The same is true in French, and here is how to say these words, depending on whether the noun is masculine or feminine.

WITH FEMININE NOUNS

SINGULIER		PLURIEL
(ewn) (fee-y)		*(day)*
une fille		**des filles**
a girl		some girls, girls
(ew) (na-mee)		*(day) (za-mee)*
une amie		**des amies**
a female friend		some female friends

WITH MASCULINE NOUNS

SINGULIER		PLURIEL
(uhn nohnkl)		*(day zohnkl)*
un oncle		**des oncles**
an uncle		some uncles
(uhn na-mee)		*(day za-mee)*
un ami		**des amis**
a male friend		some friends

Note that in English, you often do not use $\boxed{\text{some}}$ in the plural; you'll say: "I have friends in Paris." In French, you **must** say "I have $\boxed{\text{some}}$ friends in Paris": **J'ai des amis à Paris.**

Now test yourself by putting the appropriate indefinite article in front of each noun.
Note: *m.* = masculine noun *f.* = feminine noun *pl.* = plural noun

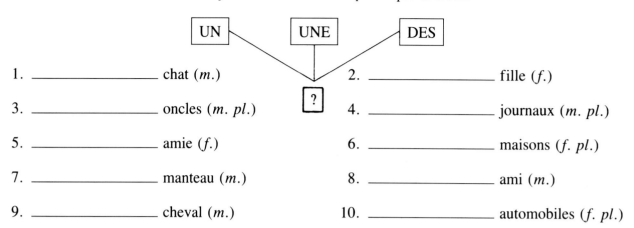

| UN | UNE | DES |

?

1. _____ chat (*m.*)

2. _____ fille (*f.*)

3. _____ oncles (*m. pl.*)

4. _____ journaux (*m. pl.*)

5. _____ amie (*f.*)

6. _____ maisons (*f. pl.*)

7. _____ manteau (*m.*)

8. _____ ami (*m.*)

9. _____ cheval (*m.*)

10. _____ automobiles (*f. pl.*)

Here's another chance to test yourself. Put the correct words on the lines below the pictures using the indefinite articles for "a" (an) and "some" and the French word for what is shown.

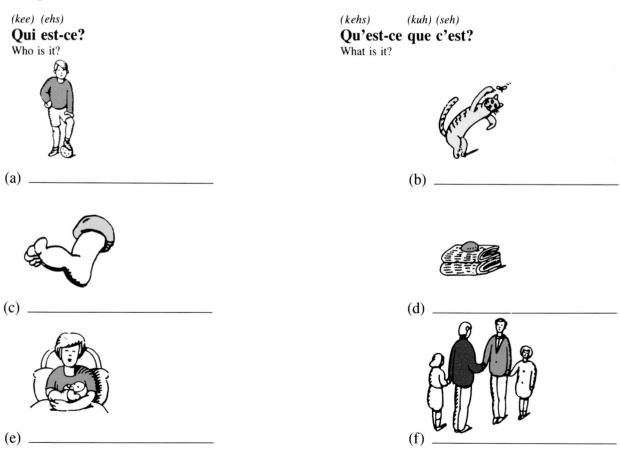

(kee) (ehs)
Qui est-ce?
Who is it?

(a) _____

(kehs) (kuh) (seh)
Qu'est-ce que c'est?
What is it?

(b) _____

(c) _____

(d) _____

(e) _____

(f) _____

ANSWERS

Indéfinite article 1. un chat **2.** une fille **3.** des oncles **4.** des journaux **5.** une amie **6.** des maisons **7.** un manteau **8.** un ami **9.** un cheval **10.** des automobiles
(a) un garçon **(b)** un chat **(c)** un pied **(d)** des journaux **(e)** une mère **(f)** des pères

(zhuh) *(tew)* *(voo)*

Je, tu et vous

"I" and "You"

It is also important to know how to say "I" and "you" in French. These words are called **subject pronouns.**

"I" is simply $\boxed{\text{JE}}$, (but $\boxed{\text{J'}}$ before a vowel).

"You" is given in three ways:

$\boxed{\text{TU}}$	— When addressing one person: a friend, child, family member (familiar address).
$\boxed{\text{VOUS}}$	— When addressing anyone who is not a friend, child, family member.
$\boxed{\text{VOUS}}$	— Plural form of both $\boxed{\text{TU}}$ and $\boxed{\text{VOUS}}$

SUMMARY

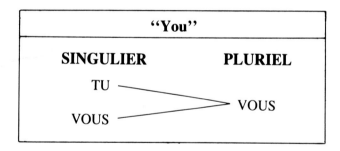

Which would you use—**tu** or **vous**—when speaking to the following? Write your answer in the space provided.

1. the doctor _____

2. your brother _____

3. your sisters _____

4. your child _____

5. the stewardess _____

ANSWERS

Tu or vous 1. vous 2. tu 3. vous 4. tu 5. vous

16

PARLONS DES MEMBRES DE LA FAMILLE

(par-lohns) *(mahn-bruh)* *(fa-mee-y)*

Let's Talk about the Members of the Family

Henriette Dubois
(la) (grahn-mehr)
la grand-mère
grandmother

Pierre Dubois
(luh) (grahn-pehr)
le grand-père
grandfather

Jean-Pierre Dupont
le père
father

Micheline Dupont
(née Dubois)
la mère
mother

(ma-ree)
le mari
husband

(fam)
la femme
wife

Jean Dubois
(lohnkl)
l'oncle
uncle

Marie Dubois
(née Ogier)
(tahnt)
la tante
aunt

Michel Dupont
(frehr)
le frère
brother

Jeanine Dupont
(suhr)
la soeur
sister

le fils
son

la fille
daughter

Philippe Dubois
(koo-zan)
le cousin
cousin (male)

Pierrette Dubois
(koo-zeen)
la cousine
cousin (female)

Note the members of Paul's family.

17

Identify the following members of the family:

1. **Henriette Dubois est la** _____ .

2. **Jean est l'** _____ .

3. **Pierrette est la** _____ .

4. **Jean-Pierre est le** _____ **et le** _____ .

5. **Michel est le** _____ **et le** _____ .

6. **Jeanine Dupont est la** _____ **et la** _____ .

Find the *plurals* of the following nouns hidden in the puzzle, write them down, and then circle them in the puzzle. We've done the first one for you, to show how easy it is.

1. **cousin** cousins _____

2. **cheval** _____

3. **fils** _____

4. **mère** _____

5. **chat** _____

6. **cousine** _____

7. **genou** _____

8. **fille** _____

9. **père** _____

10. **manteau** _____

C	O	U	S	I	N	S	J	E	S	U	F	I	L	L	E	S	X	A
H	U	L	A	L	G	M	A	N	T	E	A	U	X	S	O	U	P	U
E	E	N	M	M	E	O	E	C	H	A	T	S	I	E	O	T	O	P
V	A	U	C	E	D	R	U	N	A	M	D	E	S	N	T	A	I	E
A	L	A	I	R	R	A	C	O	U	S	I	N	E	S	P	O	U	R
U	N	M	O	T	M	E	A	C	H	A	N	G	P	L	U	M	E	E
X	J	A	I	T	U	A	S	I	L	A	N	O	F	I	L	S	O	S

ANSWERS

10. manteaux
Word search 2. chevaux 3. fils 4. mères 5. chats 6. cousines 7. genoux 8. filles 9. pères

Family tree 1. grand-mère 2. oncle 3. cousine 4. père . . mari 5. frère . . fils 6. soeur . . fille

18

Imagine you've begun your trip already. See how well you understand the following situation.

(sewr)

Monsieur Smith et la famille arrivent en France sur le vol 333 de New York. M. Smith

on

(dee)

dit "bonjour" à l'employé. M. Smith dit "merci" et l'employé dit "Je vous en prie."

says

(fee-nahl-mahn)

Finalement, M. Smith dit "Au revoir."

Finally

Are the following true or false?

1. **Monsieur Smith et la famille arrivent à New York.** T
   F

2. **Monsieur Smith dit "Je vous en prie" à l'employé.** T
   F

3. **Monsieur Smith et un ami arrivent en France.** T
   F

4. **Finalement, Monsieur Smith dit bonjour.** T
   F

ANSWERS

True or False 1. F 2. F 3. F 4. F

Have fun with the following crossword puzzle. The clues are English equivalents of French words.

DOWN
1. grandmother
2. some
4. girls, daughters
8. horse

ACROSS
3. I live
5. thank you
6. a, an (fem.)
7. I
9. sister

ANSWERS
DOWN 1. grandmère 2. des 4. filles 8. cheval
Puzzle ACROSS 3. j'habite 5. merci 6. une 7. je 9. soeur

Now study and say aloud these parts of Paul's house.

UNE MAISON
A Home

(ray-free-zhay-rah-tuhr)
le réfrigérateur
refrigerator

(kwee-zeen)
la cuisine
kitchen

(kwee-zee-nyehr)
la cuisinière
stove

(ehs-ka-lyay)
l'escalier
stairway

(sahl) (duh) (ban)
la salle de bain
bathroom

(ay-vyay)
l'évier
sink

(twa-leht)
la toilette
toilet

(sa-lohn)
le salon
living-room

(ban-wahr)
la baignoire
bathtub

(shehz)
la chaise
chair

(ahr-mwahr)
l'armoire
closet

(tahbl)
la table
table

(lee)
le lit
bed

(ka-na-pay)
le canapé
sofa

(shahnbr) (koo-shay)
la chambre à coucher
bedroom

(fuh-nehtr)
la fenêtre
window

(vehs-tee-bewl)
le vestibule
hallway

(zhar-dan)
le jardin
garden

(port)
la porte
door

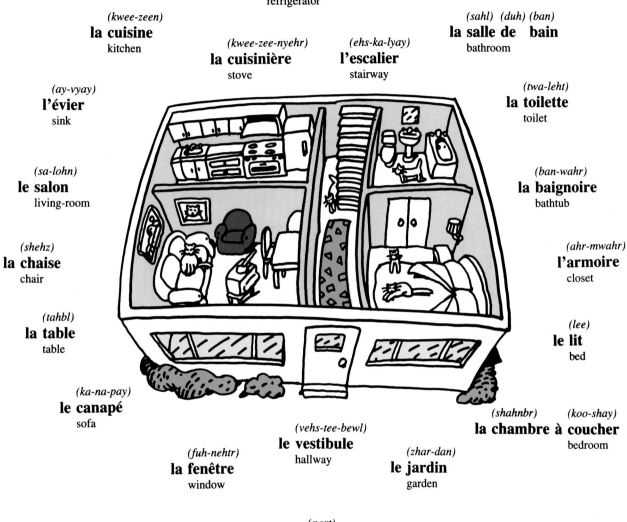

ARRIVAL
(la-ree-vay)
L'arrivée

2	*(a)* *(la)* *(ruh-shehrsh)* *(duhn)* *(ahn-drwah)* *(oo)* *(pa-say)* **À la recherche d'un endroit où passer** *(la)* *(nwee)* **la nuit**

Finding a Place to Spend the Night

You'll probably book your hotel room from home—at least for your first night in France. But whether you have a reservation or not, you'll want to know some basic words that describe the services and facilities you expect to find at your hotel. Learn these words first, and notice how they are used in the dialogue you will read later.

(oh-tehl)
l'hôtel
Hotel

(shahnbr)
la chambre
Room

(pree)
le prix
Price

(sahl) *(duh)* *(ban)*
la salle de bain
Bathroom

(ray-zehr-va-syohn)
la réservation
Reservation

(ray-zehr-vay)
réserver
To Reserve

(pahs-por)
le passeport
Passport

(ahn-plwa-yay)
l'employé/employée
Clerk (m.)/(f.)

(port)
la porte
Door

(fam) *(duh)* *(shahnbr)*
la femme de chambre
Maid

(fuh-nehtr)
la fenêtre
Window

22

Le, la, l', les
The Many Ways of Saying "The" in French

In English we use "the" to precede all nouns. In French, however, there are many ways of saying "the," depending on whether the noun is singular or plural, masculine or feminine.

SINGULIER	PLURIEL
WITH MASCULINE NOUNS	

Before a Consonant

(luh)
Le père
father

Le garçon
boy

Before a Vowel

(lar-br)
L'arbre
tree

L'ami
friend

Les pères
fathers

Les garçons
boys

(lay) (zarbr)
Les arbres
trees

(lay) (zamee)
Les amis
friends

| **WITH FEMININE NOUNS** | |

Before a Consonant

(la)
La maison
house

La fille
girl

La mère
mother

Before a Vowel

(luhr)
L'heure
hour

(la-mee)
L'amie
girlfriend

(lay)
Les maisons
houses

Les filles
girls

Les mères
mothers

(lay) (zhuhr)
Les heures
hours

(lay) (zamee)
Les amies
girlfriends

Here's the same idea presented in a way that will make it easier for you to remember the forms of "the."

SUMMARY: "THE"	
WITH MASCULINE NOUNS	WITH FEMININE NOUNS

Singulier   **Pluriel**
 	
Before a Consonant
    LE
Before a Vowel ⟶ **LES**
    L'
	Singulier **Pluriel**
	
	Before a Consonant
	    LA
	Before a Vowel ⟶ **LES**
	    L'

Let's practice. Put the appropriate form of "the" before each noun listed below. We've done the first for you as an example.

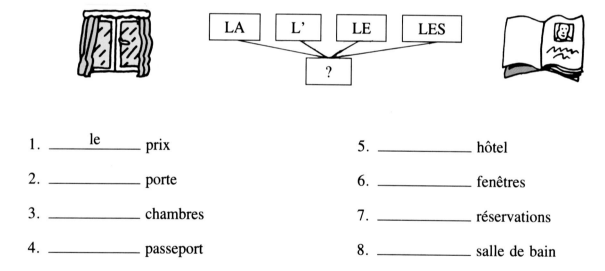

1. ____le____ prix

2. _____ porte

3. _____ chambres

4. _____ passeport

5. _____ hôtel

6. _____ fenêtres

7. _____ réservations

8. _____ salle de bain

ANSWERS

Définite article 1. le prix **2.** la porte **3.** les chambres **4.** le passeport **5.** l'hôtel **6.** les fenêtres **7.** les réservations **8.** la salle de bain

Les pronoms et les verbes

(pro-nohn) *(vehrb)*

Pronouns and verbs

You've already learned how to say "I" and "You" in French. Now it's time to move on to the forms for "he," "she," "we," and "they." Here are your new words:

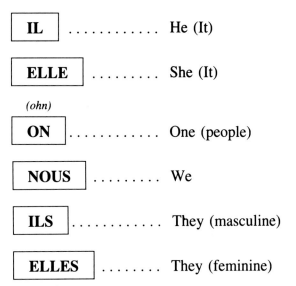

IL . . . . He (It)

ELLE . . . . She (It)

(ohn)

ON . . . . One (people)

NOUS . . . . We

ILS . . . . They (masculine)

ELLES . . . . They (feminine)

Do you remember how to say "I"? And "You"?

JE , **J'** . . . I   **VOUS** . . . . You (polite, singular)

TU . . . . You (familiar, singular)   **VOUS** . . . . You (plural)

Use this table to help you remember the French pronoun:

SUMMARY: PRONOUNS	
je, j'	I
tu	you (familiar)
il	he/it
elle	she/it
nous	we
vous	you (familiar) (pl.)
vous	you (polite)
ils	they (masculine)
elles	they (femine)
on	one

(par-lay)

Now let's conjugate the verb **PARLER**. Conjugating the verb means changing the verb
to speak
ending to agree with the subject. We do this automatically in English when we say "I speak"
but "he speaks." Notice that the verb **PARLER** ends in **-ER**. **PARLER** is called the infinitive
of the verb. The infinitive is the form of the verb corresponding to the English "to —" form.
Many other verbs also end in **-ER**.: **CHANTER**, **ARRIVER**. Watch how to conjugate them:
to sing   *to arrive*
drop the **-ER** and add the appropriate endings.

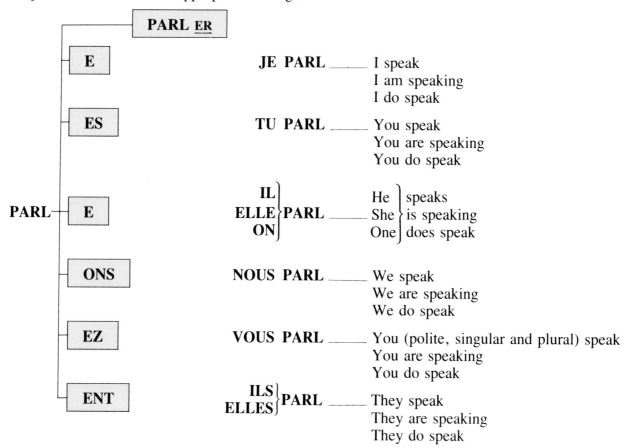

NOTE: that the subject pronouns are **always** necessary, because after JE, TU, IL, ELLE,
ON, ILS and ELLES, the verb sounds exactly the same:
(parl)   *(parl)*   *(parl)*   *(parl)*
je parle, tu parles, il/elle/on parle, ils/elles parlent:

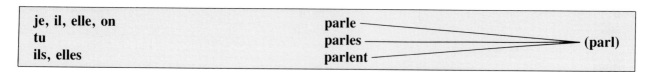

Notice that, exactly as in English, **Il, ELLE, ILS** and **ELLES** replace nouns:

LES GARÇONS	PARLENT	FRANÇAIS.	ILS	PARLENT FRANÇAIS.
The boys	speak	French	They speak	

DON'T FORGET THAT JE becomes **J'** before a vowel sound.

Now try to put the right endings to CHANTER and ARRIVER:

Je chant _____	Nous chant _____	J'arriv _____	Nous arriv _____
Tu chant _____	Vous chant _____	Tu arriv _____	Vous arriv _____
Il chant _____	Ils chant _____	Il arriv _____	Ils arriv _____
Elle chant _____	Elles chant _____	Elle arriv _____	Elles arriv _____
On chant _____		On arriv _____	

Bon! (Good) Now put the right endings on the verbs:

Le garçon parl _____ très bien.

Tu parl _____ et je chant _____ .

Les oncles arriv _____ demain.

Nous chant _____ et vous parl _____ .

Marie chant _____ très bien.

Negatives

NOTE: To make any verb negative, put NE (N' before a vowel sound) before the verb and PAS after the verb:

AFFIRMATIVE	NEGATIVE
JE PARLE I speak	**JE NE PARLE PAS** I don't speak

ANSWERS

Verb CHANTER

Verb CHANTER	
Je chante	Nous chantons
Tu chantes	Vous chantez
Il chante	Ils chantent
Elle chante	Elles chantent
On chante	

Verb ARRIVER

Verb ARRIVER	
J'arrive	Nous arrivons
Tu arrives	Vous arrivez
Il arrive	Ils arrivent
Elle arrive	Elles arrivent
On arrive	

Verb PARLER, verb ARRIVER, verb CHANTER

Le garçon parle très bien.
Les oncles arrivent demain.
Marie chante très bien.
Tu parles et je chante.
Nous chantons et vous parlez.

27

(kee) *(a-teel)* *(dahn)* *(zuhn)* *(nohn)*

Qu'y-a-t-il dans un nom?

What's in a name?

When you are settled in your room, get to know the names of the items there. You might need another towel, or find that your lamp doesn't work. Ask the hotel staff to help you, and explain what you need.

(ewn) *(shahnbr)* *(doh-tehl)*
UNE CHAMBRE D'HOTEL
A Hotel Room

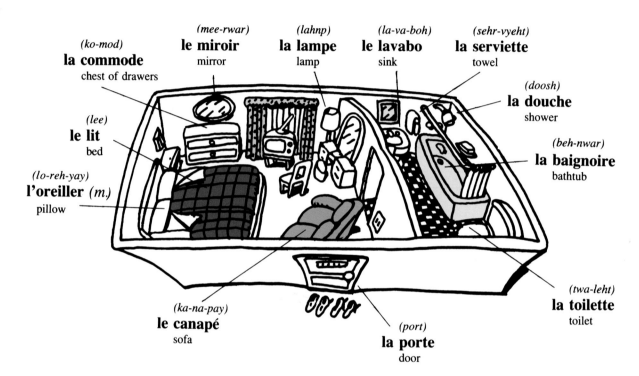

(ko-mod)
la commode
chest of drawers

(mee-rwar)
le miroir
mirror

(lahnp)
la lampe
lamp

(la-va-boh)
le lavabo
sink

(sehr-vyeht)
la serviette
towel

(doosh)
la douche
shower

(lee)
le lit
bed

(beh-nwar)
la baignoire
bathtub

(lo-reh-yay)
l'oreiller *(m.)*
pillow

(ka-na-pay)
le canapé
sofa

(port)
la porte
door

(twa-leht)
la toilette
toilet

1. I need a towel. Il me faut _____ .

2. The lamp doesn't work. _____ ne fonctionne pas.

3. Can you fix the toilet? Pouvez-vous réparer _____?

4. Where is the shower? Où est _____?

5. The bed is too small. _____ est trop petit.

ANSWERS
Hotel room 1. une serviette **2.** la lampe **3.** la toilette **4.** la douche **5.** le lit

Follow the adventures of the Smith family as they check into their hotel. Always read each line of dialogue out loud to practice your pronunciation.

MARC **Excusez-moi, monsieur. J'ai**
(ruh-tuh-new) *(shahnbr)*
retenu deux chambres pour ce soir.

Je m'appelle M. Smith.

Excuse me, sir. I have

a reservation for 2 rooms for tonight.

My name is Smith.

EMPLOYÉ **Bonjour. Oui, nous avons votre**
(ray-zehr-va-syohn)
réservation pour deux chambres à
(lee) *(sahl)* *(duh)* *(ban)*
deux lits avec salles de   bain. Mais il

y a un problème.

Good afternoon. Yes, we have your

reservation for 2 double rooms

with bath. But there is

a problem.

MARC **Qu'est-ce qu'il y a?**

What's the matter?

EMPLOYÉ **Dans une chambre, la douche**
(doosh)

ne marche pas.

The shower in one room is broken.

MARC **Ça ne fait rien. Les enfants peuvent**
(sa) (neh) (fay) (ryan)
(beh-nyay)
se baigner chez nous.

It doesn't matter. The children can use our bath.

EMPLOYÉ **Bon. Mais il y a un autre**

problème. Dans l'autre chambre, on
(oo-vreer) *(fuh-nehtr)*
ne peut pas ouvrir la fenêtre.

Good. But there is another problem.

The window in the other room

doesn't open.

MARC **(à Marie) Qu'est-ce que tu en**

penses? Il n'y a de chambres
(newl) *(fool)*
nulle part. Il y a une foule de touristes
(man-tuh-nahn)
à Paris maintenant.

What do you think?

There are no rooms anywhere.

Paris is full of tourists now.

(shoh)	
MARIE **Il ne fait pas trop chaud. Prenons-**	The weather isn't too hot. Let's take them
(kahn) *(mehm)*	
les quand même.	anyway.
EMPLOYÉ **Bon. Chaque chambre est à**	Fine. The rooms are
(swa-saınt er-ro)	
60 euros par jour.	60 euros each per day.
(puh-tee) *(day-zhŭh-nay)*	
MARC **Est-ce que le petit déjeuner est**	Is breakfast included?
(kohn-pree)	
compris?	
EMPLOYÉ **Mais oui, monsieur.**	Oh yes, sir.
MARC **Bon. Nous les prenons. Voici nos**	Okay, we'll take them. Here are our
(pahs-por)	
passeports.	passports.
(vuh-yay) *(rahn-pleer)* *(feesh)*	
EMPLOYÉ **Veuillez remplir cette fiche.**	Please fill out this form.
(klay)	
Voici votre clé. Les chambres sont	Here is your key. The rooms are
(trwah-zee-ehm) *(ay-tazh)*	
au troisième étage.	on the third floor.
(a-sahn-suhr)	
MARC **Y a-t-il un ascenseur?**	Is there an elevator?
(drwat)	
EMPLOYÉ **Oui, monsieur. À droite.**	Yes. To the right.
MARC **Merci beaucoup, monsieur.**	Thank you very much, sir.
(pree)	
EMPLOYÉ **Je vous en prie, monsieur.**	You're welcome, sir.
(a-mew-zay)	
Amusez-vous bien à Paris.	Have a good time in Paris.

Match these French expressions from the dialogue with their English equivalents:

1. J'ai retenu deux chambres pour ce soir.
2. Il y a un problème.
3. Qu'est-ce qu'il y a?
4. N'importe.
5. Chaque chambre est à 60 euros par jour.
6. Est-ce que le petit déjeuner est compris?
7. Veuillez remplir cette fiche.
8. Amusez-vous bien à Paris.

a. It doesn't matter.
b. What's the matter?
c. Have a good time in Paris.
d. The rooms are 60 euros each per day.
e. There is a problem.
f. Please fill out this form.
g. I have a reservation for two rooms for tonight.
h. Is breakfast included?

ANSWERS

Matching 1. g 2. e 3. b 4. a 5. d 6. h 7. f 8. c

SI VOUS VOULEZ DEMANDER QUELQUE CHOSE
If You Want to Ask for Something

You'll find yourself asking questions every day—of hotel clerks, tour guides, waitresses, and taxi drivers. To form a question from any statement, choose one of the three following methods:

TO FORM A QUESTION FROM ANY STATEMENT:

1. Just raise your voice in the normal way for questions:

(gar-sohn) (mahnzh) (krwah-sahn)
Le garçon   mange le croissant.   Le garçon mange le croissant?
The boy eats the croissant.

2. Put the magical group of words **EST-CE QUE** (**QU'** before a vowel), which means literally

(es) (kuh)

"Is it that," at the beginning of a YES-NO question, or between the interrogative adverb and the rest of the question:

(ehs-kuh)
Le garçon mange le croissant.   Est-ce que le garçon mange le croissant?
                                               Does the boy eat the croissant?

3. You can also invert the subject and the verb and put a hyphen between the two:

(voo) (poo-vay)   *(poo-vay) (voo)*
Vous pouvez.   Pouvez-vous?
You can.   Can you?

NOTICE: The previous inversion is rarely used after **JE**, which means "I." This is one of the times when **Est-ce que** comes in handy—and when the last letter of the verb and the first letter of the pronoun are vowels, you have to put **-T-** between them:

(eel)   *(mahnzh) (teel)*
Il mange.   **Mange-t-il?**
he

(el)   *(mahnzh) (tehl)*
Elle mange.   **Mange-t-elle?**
she

If the subject of the sentence is a noun or a name, the construction is as follows:

Le garçon mange le croissant.
Le garçon mange-t-il le croissant?

Marie mange le croissant.
Marie mange-t-elle le croissant?

BASIC QUESTION WORDS

(kuh)
QUE, QU' (+ vowel) _____ WHAT

(kee)
QUI _____ WHO

(oo)
OÙ _____ WHERE

(ko-mahn)
COMMENT _____ HOW

(poor-kwa)
POURQUOI _____ WHY

(kahn)
QUAND _____ WHEN

(kohn-byan)
COMBIEN _____ HOW MUCH, HOW MANY

NOTICE: When COMBIEN is followed by a noun, the noun is preceded by *(duh)* DE , or D'

(before a vowel):

(dar-zhahn)
Combien d'argent?
money
Combien de garçons?

Combien de filles?

These words can be used to form a question by following one of the two following formulas:

1. Interrogative + EST-CE QUE (EST-CE QU') + Subject + Verb

   Quand est-ce qu'ils arrivent?
   Où est-ce qu'ils habitent?

   Note: QUE becomes QU' before EST-CE QUE
   Qu'est-ce qu'ils cherchent?

2. Interrogative + verb (hyphen) subject (this is called *inversion*):
   Quand arrivent-ils?
   Où habitent-ils?

Try it yourself. Match up each question in the left column with its answer in the right column.

1. **Qu'est-ce que Marie mange?**
   (parl) *(tehl)*
2. **Anne parle-t-elle français?**
   speak
3. **Quand arrivent-ils?**
4. **Où arrivent-ils?**
   (e-may)
5. **Est-ce que vous aimez les**
   like
   croissants?

A. **Oui, j'aime les croissants.**

B. **Marie mange le croissant.**

C. **Oui, elle parle français.**
   (duh-mahn)

D. **Ils arrivent demain.**
   tomorrow
   (a) *(la-ay-ro-por)*

E. **Ils arrivent à l'aéroport.**
   at the airport

The phrase "there is" is useful to know in French. And it is the same in the singular and in the plural:
Il y a une chambre = There is a room.
Il y a des chambres = There are some rooms.

You can use this phrase in another way to ask a question. To form a question, you can either use the inversion or **EST-CE QUE:**

Y a-t-il une chambre? = Is there a room?
Y a-t-il des chambres? = Are there any rooms?

Il n'y a pas de chambre = There is no room.
Il n'y a plus de chambres = There are no rooms left.

Est-ce qu'il y a encore une chambre?
   Is there still a room? (Is there a room left?)

Note: Un, une, des = de in a negative sentence.

(ee-lya) **IL Y A**	*(eel)* *(nya)* *(pah)* **IL N'Y A PAS**	*(ya-teel)* *(ya-teel)* *(pah)* **Y A-T-IL ou N'Y A-T-IL PAS?**
There is	There is not (no)	Is there or Isn't there?
There are	There are not	Are there? Aren't there?

Slow down! If you are getting confused, just ease up on your pace and review what you've learned so far. **Vous comprenez?** (Do you understand?)

See how much French you already know by doing the following "verb" crossword puzzle. These are verbs you have met so far: **parler** (to speak), **chanter** (to sing), **arriver** (to arrive), **habiter** (to live in a place).

ACROSS
5. Elle (arrives)
6. Ils (arrive)
7. J' (live)
8. Nous (sing)

DOWN
1. On (speaks)
2. Tu (are singing)
3. Les garçons (speak)
4. Elles (live)

ANSWERS

Puzzle

ACROSS
5. arrive
6. arrivent
7. habite
8. chantons

DOWN:
1. parle
2. chantes
3. parlent
4. habitent

Now test your comprehension of what you have learned in this unit about requesting a room at a hotel.

Fill in the blanks:

1. M. Smith a une réservation pour _____ .
   two rooms

2. _____ ne marche pas.
   The shower

3. On ne peut pas _____ .
   open the window

4. Le petit déjeuner _____ .
   is included

5. Les chambres sont _____ .
   on the third floor

ANSWERS

Fill in blanks: 1. deux chambres **2.** La douche **3.** ouvrir la fenêtre **4.** est compris **5.** au troisième étage

SEEING THE SIGHTS

(kew-ree-oh-zee-tay)

Allons voir les curiosités

	(a-lohn-zee) *(pyay)*
3	## Allons-y à pied
	Let's Go on Foot

"How do I get to . . . ?" "Where is the nearest subway?" "Is the museum straight ahead?" You'll be asking directions wherever you travel. Acquaint yourself with words and phrases that will make getting around easier. Don't forget to read each line aloud several times to practice your pronunciation. Act out each part to be certain you understand these new words.

(Paul and Anne Smith set out on their first day to visit a museum.)

(duh-mahn-dohn)   *(la-zhahn)*

ANNE **Paul, demandons à l'agent de**
    (pol-lees)   *(e)*   *(mew-zay)*
police où est le musée.

Paul, let's ask the policeman where the museum is.

    (sewr)   *(ray-ew-seer)*

PAUL **Je ne suis pas sûr de réussir . . .**

I am not sure of succeeding . . .

Excusez-moi, Monsieur l'agent,

Excuse me, Sir,

    (deer)
pouvez-vous nous dire où est le

can you tell us where the museum is?

musée?

(sehr-ten-mahn) *(kohn-tee-new-ay)* *(too)* AGENT **Certainement. Continuez tout** *(drwah)(zhews-ka)* *(rew)* *(mo-lyehr)* **droit jusqu'à la rue Molière et** *(toor-nay)* *(drwat)* **tournez à droite. Continuez jusqu'à** *(vol-tehr)* *(ahn-sweet)* **la rue Voltaire, ensuite tournez à** *(gohsh)* *(ra-seen)* **gauche et continuez sur la rue Racine** *(zhews-koh)* *(fūh)* *(la)* *(a)* **jusqu'aux feux. Le musée est là, à** *(koh-tay)* *(lay-gleez)* **côté de l'église.**	Certainly. Continue straight ahead to Molière Street and turn right. Continue to Voltaire Street, then turn left and continue on Racine Street to the traffic lights. The museum is there, next to the church.
PAUL **Merci mille fois.**	Many thanks.
(ryan) AGENT **De rien.**	You are welcome. (*lit.* of nothing.)

After having followed the directions:

(suh) *(nay)* *(pas)* *(luh)* *(mew-zay)* ANNE **Ce n'est pas le musée.**	This building is not the museum.
(post) **C'est la poste.**	It's the post office.
(troh) *(tar)* PAUL **Patience, Anne. Il est trop tard** *(poor)* *(fee-neer)* *(notr)* **pour finir notre sightseeing.** *(ruh-toor-nohn)* **Retournons à l'hôtel.**	Be patient, Anne. It's too late to finish our sightseeing. Let's go back to the hotel.

Can you answer these true-false questions based on the dialogue? Write VRAI (true) next to each true statement. Correct any false statement.

_____ 1. Paul demande à l'agent où est *l'église*.
_____ 2. L'agent dit de tourner *à droite*.
_____ 3. Le musée est à côté de *l'école*.
_____ 4. Ce n'est pas *le musée*.
_____ 5. C'est *l'aéroport*.

ANSWERS
True-false 1. le musée **2.** VRAI **3.** l'église **4.** VRAI **5.** la poste

(oo)   *(a-lay)*   *(voo)*
OÙ ALLEZ-VOUS?
Where Are You Going?

You'll find yourself *going to* a museum, or being *at* a bakery or *in* a theater often if you go abroad, so knowing the following words will come in very handy.

(lom)
L'homme est <u>à</u> Paris.
in

(va)
L'homme va <u>à</u> New York.
goes to

L'homme est à ✗ **le** →
(oh)
<u>AU</u> cinéma.
at the

L'homme va à ✗ **le** →
<u>AU</u> théâtre.
to the

Le garçon est <u>à la</u>
at the
boulangerie.
bakery

Le garçon va <u>à la</u>.
to the
boulangerie

Le garçon est <u>à l'école</u>.
at the school

Le garçon va <u>à l'école</u>.
to the

Madame Dubois est
à ✗ **les** → **<u>AUX</u> États-Unis.**
in the

Madame Dubois va
à ✗ **les** → **<u>AUX</u> États-Unis.**
to the

Des petits mots qui signifient beaucoup

Little words that mean a lot

The preposition | **À** | means "to" or "at" and is used before proper nouns:

    Il parle à Jean.

The definite articles | **LA** | (used before feminine singular nouns beginning with a consonant) and | **L'** | (used before all singular nouns beginning with a vowel) can be placed after | **À** | to express "to the" or "at the":

    Le garçon est | **À LA** | **boulangerie.**   **Le garçon est** | **À L'** | **école.**

The definite articles | **LE** | (used before masculine singular nouns beginning with a consonant) and | **LES** | (used before all plural nouns) contract with | **À** | to form completely new words:

> | **À** | + | **LE** | = | **AU** | (TO, AT THE)
>
> | **À** | + | **LES** | = | **AUX** | (TO, AT THE)
>
> ---
>
> **Il parle** | **AU** | **garçon.**
>
> **Il parle** | **AUX** | **garçons.**

Try this exercise:

Jean va 1. _____ cinéma.

    2. _____ école.

3. _____ États-Unis.

4. _____ Paris.

5. _____ boulangerie.

The same situation occurs with | **DE** |, which means "from," "of" or "about":

    Il parle | **DE** | **Jean.**

    Il parle | **DE** | **la boulangerie.**

    Il parle | **DE** | **l'école.**

But note:

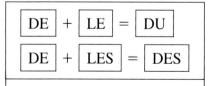

> | DE | + | LE | = | DU |
>
> | DE | + | LES | = | DES |
>
> ---
>
> **Il parle du garçon.**
> **Il parle des garçons.**

ANSWERS
Prépositions 1. au cinéma 2. à l'école 3. aux États-Unis 4. à Paris 5. à la boulangerie

Now do this exercise.

Jean parle 1. _____ école.   4. _____ New-York.

2. _____ théâtre.   5. _____ filles.

3. _____ boulangerie.

The other prepositions are easier. Some are followed by $\boxed{\text{DE}}$ and the rule you just practiced applies.

(dahn)
Le garçon est dans la maison.
         in   house
(sewr)
Le chat est sur la chaise.
       on
(shyan)   *(soo)*
Le chien est sous la table.
         under
(soo-ree) *(lwan)*
La souris est loin du chat.
mouse   far from
         (pwa-sohn)
La souris est près du poisson.
      near   fish
        (gohsh)
Le réfrigérateur est à gauche de la table.
        left
   (drwat)
La table est à droite du réfrigérateur.
    right
    (koh-tay)
La chaise est à côté de la table.
    next to
      (duh-vahn)
Le dîner du chien est devant la chaise.
        in front of
      (deh-ryehr)
Madame Dubois est derrière la porte.
     behind

Can you describe where everything and everybody is in this picture?

1. Le garçon est _____ la porte.
        behind

2. M. Dubois est dans la _____ .
        kitchen

3. Le réfrigérateur est à côté de la _____ .
        stove

ANSWERS

Describe 1. derrière **2.** cuisine **3.** cuisinière

About 1. de l'école **2.** du théâtre **3.** de la boulangerie **4.** de New-York **5.** des filles

40

(ahn-kor)
Encore des verbes
Verbs again

In the previous unit you learned how to conjugate verbs ending in -ER. These are known as verbs of the first conjugation. Now you will learn how to conjugate some common verbs of the second conjugation. These end in -IR. Drop **IR** and add the endings:

FINIR (TO FINISH)		RÉUSSIR (TO SUCCEED)	
je	*(fee-nee)* **fin*is***	je	*(ray-ew-see)* **réuss*is***
tu		tu	
il	*(fee-nee)* **fin*it***	il	*(ray-ew-see)* **réuss*it***
elle		elle	
on		on	
nous	*(fee-nee-sohn)* **fin*issons***	nous	*(ray-ew-see-sohn)* **réuss*issons***
vous	*(fee-nee-say)* **fin*issez***	vous	*(ray-ew-see-say)* **réuss*issez***
ils	*(fee-nees)* **fin*issent***	ils	*(ray-ew-sees)* **réuss*issent***
elles		elles	

Remember that to make verbs negative, you put NE (N') before the verb and PAS after.

Je ne finis pas.   **Je ne réussis pas.**

Can you figure out each verb by unscrambling the letters? The only two verbs used are FINIR and RÉUSSIR.

a. Jean UÉRITSS _____ à parler français.

b. Jean et Anne TNESSINIF_____ leur sightseeing.
(luhr)
their

c. Nous NFIISOSSN _____ le dîner.

d. IRZEEUSSSSS -vous à parler français?

(tra-va-y)
e. Je NIFIS ce travail.

f. Tu RIÉUSSS _____ .

g. On TFINI _____ .

h. Vous EZNIFSSI _____ .

ANSWERS

Unscrambling IR verbs

a. Jean *réussit* à parler français.
b. Jean et Anne *finissent* leur sightseeing.
c. Nous *finissons* le dîner.
d. *Réussissez*-vous à parler français?
e. Je *finis* ce travail.
f. Tu *réussis*.
g. On *finit*.
h. Vous *finissez*.

41

Quelques mots utiles
(kel-kuh) *(moh)* *(zew-teel)*

Some useful words

(see-nay-mah)
le cinéma
movies

(ma-ga-zan)
le magasin
store

(mar-shay)
le marché
market

(bahnk)
la banque
bank

(lay-gleez)
l'église
church

(tro-twar)
le trottoir
sidewalk

(fehr) *(koors)*
faire des courses
to shop

(root)
la route
road

Comment désigner les choses en français
(day-zee-nyay) *(shohz)* *(ahn)*

How to point things out in French

Words like "this" and "that" are important to know, particularly when you go shopping, and want to buy that good-looking pair of gloves in the shop window. The French forms of these words vary, depending on whether the item is masculine or feminine, and whether you are pointing to one item or to many.

"THIS" or "THAT" and "THESE" or "THOSE"	
WITH FEMININE NOUNS	
Singulier	**Pluriel**
(set) **CETTE FILLE**	*(say)* **CES FILLES**
CETTE AMIE	**CES AMIES**
WITH MASCULINE NOUNS	
(suh)(bah-tee-mahn) **CE BÂTIMENT** this building	*(bah-tee-mahn)* **CES BÂTIMENTS** these buildings
(se tay-tew-dyahn) **CET ÉTUDIANT** this student—male	*(say zay-tew-dyahn)* **CES ÉTUDIANTS** these students

NOTE: CE becomes CET before masculine singular nouns which begin with a vowel.

42

(ee-see)
[ICI] means "here" and [LÀ] means "there." So if you want to be more specific or to differentiate *(la)*
between this thing here and that thing over there, you simply add [-CI] or [-LÀ] to the noun.

"HERE" AND "THERE"

[ICI]	[LÀ]
cette fille-ci	cette fille-là
cette amie-ci	cette amie-là
ce garçon-ci	ce garçon-là
cet étudiant-ci	cet étudiant-là
ces filles-ci	ces filles-là
ces étudiants-ci	ces étudiants-là

Now, try the following: Put the appropriate form of "this" or "these" and "that" or "those" in each slot:

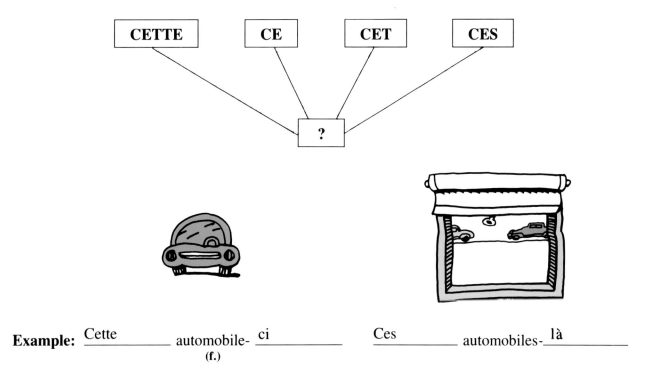

Example: <u>Cette</u> automobile-<u>ci</u>   <u>Ces</u> automobiles-<u>là</u>
            (f.)

43

_____ chat- _____ _____ chats- _____
(m.)

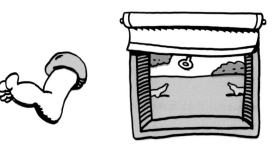

_____ pied- _____ _____ pieds- _____
foot **(m.)**

_____ maison- _____ _____ maisons- _____
house **(f.)**

_____ étudiant- _____ _____ étudiants- _____

_____ église- _____ _____ églises- _____
church **(f.)**

(o-pay-rah)

_____ opéra- _____ _____ opéras- _____
opera **(m.)**

ANSWERS

Demonstrative adjectives

Ce chat-ci	Ces chats-là	Cette église-ci
Ce pied-ci	Ces maisons-là	Cette maison-ci
Ces pieds-là	Cet étudiant-ci	Ces étudiants-là
	Cet opéra-ci	Ces opéras-là

44

Now have fun with the following crossword puzzle:

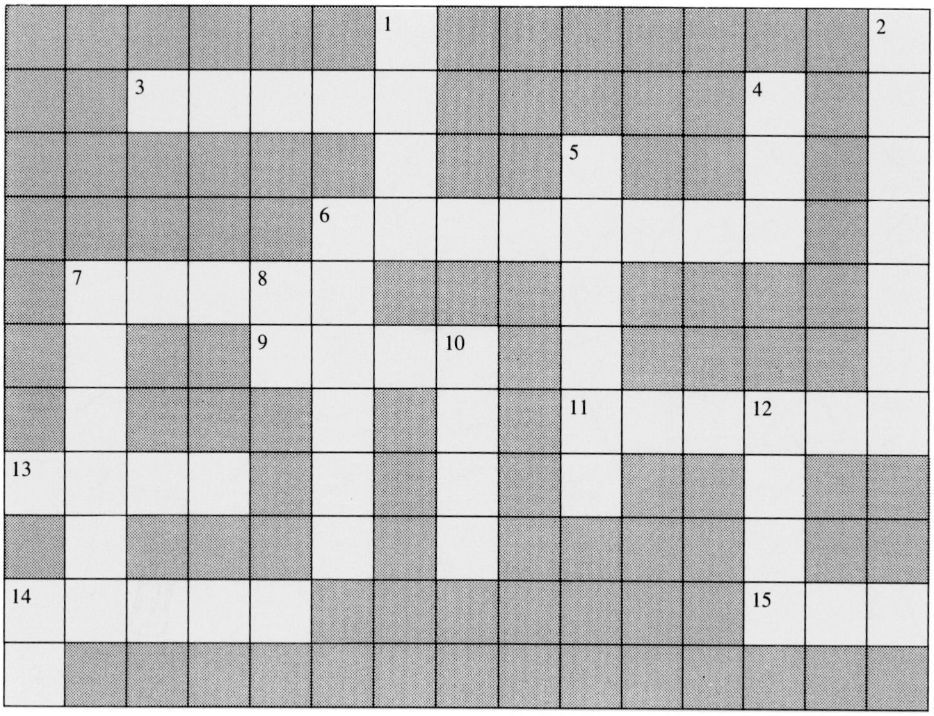

Across
3. Hotel
6. Behind
7. School
9. With
11. House
13. Foot
14. This (f.)
15. On

Down
1. She
2. Store
4. One, a (f.)
5. Movies
6. In front
7. Church
8. The (f.)
10. Cat
12. Under
14. This (m.)

ANSWERS

Across 3. Hôtel 6. Derrière 7. École 9. Avec 11. Maison 13. Pied 14. Cette 15. Sur
Down 1. Elle 2. Magasin 4. Une 5. Cinéma 6. Devant 7. Église 8. La 10. Chat 12. Sous 14. Ce

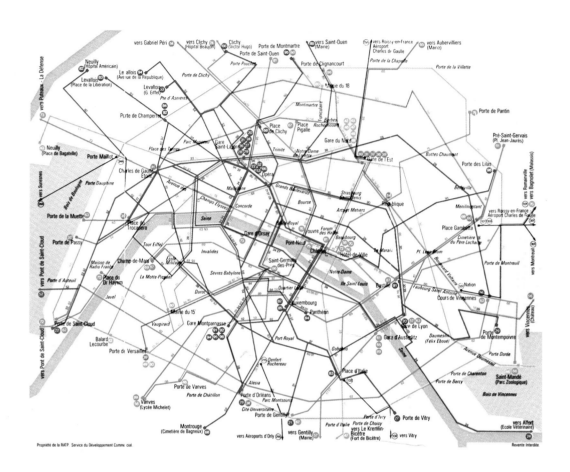

You will certainly want to take public transportation when you are in a foreign city. The following dialogue contains some words and expressions that you will find useful in order to get around easily using public transportation. Always read the dialogue carefully several times out loud to familiarize yourself with the meaning and pronunciation of the words.

	(pruh-nohn) (tak-see) (a-lay)	
MARIE	**Prenons un taxi pour aller au** **cinéma.**	Let's take a taxi to go to the movies.
MARC	(troh) **Non. C'est trop cher.**	No. It's too expensive.
MARIE	**Alors prenons le métro.**	Then let's take the metro.
MARC	(vwa) (vew) **Non. On ne voit pas la vue.**	No. One doesn't see the view.

46

MARIE *(keh) (lom) (ma-va) (ray) (dee-fee-seel)*
Quel homme avare et difficile!

Alors prenons l'autobus. *(o-to-bews)*

What a stingy and difficult man!

Then, let's take the bus.

MARC **D'accord. Notre billet de tourisme** *(bee-yay) (too-reesm)*

est bon pour le métro et l'autobus. *(bohn)*

Okay. Our tourist ticket

is good for the metro and the bus.

Dans l'autobus

On the Bus

MARC **Pardon Madame, où descendons-** *(de-sahn-dohn)*

nous pour aller au cinéma Broadway?

Excuse, me, Madam, where do we get off

to go to the cinema "Broadway"?

LA DAME **À l'arrêt après la Concorde.** *(a-reh) (a-preh) (kohn-kord)*

At the stop after the Concorde.

MARC **Comme les Français sont aimables!** *(kom) (sohn) (teh-mahbl)*

How kind the French are!

Circle the best answer to each question.

1. Marie désire prendre un taxi pour aller
   a. au musée b. au cinéma c. à l'hôtel d. à Paris

2. L'autobus
   a. ne va pas au cinéma b. est trop cher
   c. va directement au cinéma d. ne va pas à la Concorde

3. Marie et Marc décident de prendre l'autobus et d'utiliser
   a. la carte de tourisme b. le billet de cinq euros
   c. le passeport d. le billet de tourisme

4. Le cinéma Broadway est
   a. tout droit b. à la rue Racine c. à côté du musée
   d. à l'arrêt après la Concorde

Qu'est-ce que c'est?

a. un_____

b. un_____

ANSWERS

Qu'est-ce que c'est? a. un taxi b. un autobus

Multiple choice 1. b 2 c 3. d 4. d

47

c. un _____   d. une _____

Encore des verbes
More Verbs

(de-sahndr)
Now, you will learn how to conjugate third conjugation verbs like DESCENDRE and
to go down—to get off

(vahndr)   *(ehtr)*   *(a-vwar)*   *(prahndr)*
VENDRE and the irregular verbs ÊTRE, AVOIR and PRENDRE. Notice that third conjugation
to sell   to be   to have   to take

verbs end in ⬚ -RE . Drop the ⬚ -RE and add the endings.

VEND*RE* TO SELL		DESCEND*RE* TO GO DOWN, TO GET OFF	
je tu	*(vahn)* **vend***s*	je tu	*(deh-sahn)* **descend***s*
il elle on	*(vahn)* **vend**	il elle on	*(deh-sahn)* **descend**
nous	*(vahn-dohn)* **vend***ons*	nous	*(deh-sahn-dohn)* **descend***ons*
vous	*(vahn-day)* **vend***ez*	vous	*(deh-sahn-day)* **descend***ez*
ils elles	*(vahnd)* **vend***ent*	ils elles	*(deh-sahnd)* **descend***ent*

Remember that you are saying "I sell," "I am selling" or "I do sell." In other words, one
French structure can express three different ideas in English.

ANSWERS

Qu'est-ce que c'est?   **c.** un métro   **d.** une automobile

It's wise now to review the conjugations of the three groups of regular French verbs.

SUMMARY: ENDINGS FOR THREE TYPES OF REGULAR VERBS			
	PARL-*ER*	FIN-*IR*	VEND-*RE*
je	-E	-IS	-S
tu	-ES	-IS	-S
il, elle, on	-E	-IT	—
nous	-ONS	-ISSONS	-ONS
vous	-EZ	-ISSEZ	-EZ
ils, elles	-ENT	-ISSENT	-ENT

Do you begin to see a pattern? Now conjugate DESCENDRE:

1. Je descend _____

2. Tu descend _____

3. Il descend _____

4. Nous descend _____

5. Vous descend _____

6. Ils descend _____

7. Le garçon descend _____

8. Les hommes descend _____

COMMENT PARLER AU CONTRÔLEUR . . .
How to Speak to the Conductor . . .

As a tourist in a French-speaking city, you may

wish to communicate with the **conducteur** or
(kohn-dewk-tuhr)
driver

(kohn-troh-luhr)
the **contrôleur** of the bus. Here are some

typical questions.

ANSWERS

Descendre

1. Je descends 2. Tu descends 3. Il descend 4. Nous descendons 5. Vous descendez 6. Ils descendent 7. Le garçon descend 8. Les hommes descendent

	(pŭh) *(ash-tay)*	
Est-ce que je peux acheter mon billet dans l'autobus? buy		Can I buy my ticket on the bus?

Est-ce que je peux acheter mon billet dans l'autobus? *(pŭh)* *(ash-tay)*
buy

Can I buy my ticket on the bus?

Est-ce qu'il faut monter devant ou derrière? *(foh)* *(mohn-tay)*
get on

Should one get on in the front or in the rear?

Combien coûte le billet? *(koot)*

How much does the ticket cost?

Pouvez-vous me dire quand il faut descendre?

Can you tell me when to get off?

Je suis désolé, je n'ai pas de monnaie. *(day-zo-lay)* *(mo-ne)*

I am very sorry, I don't have any change.

(lay) *(vehrb)* *(kee)* *(nuh)* *(suh)* *(kohn-form)* *(pah)* *(zoh)* *(rehgl)*

Les verbes qui ne se conforment pas aux règles
Verbs that don't follow the rules

You've learned how to use some common verbs that end in "er," "ir," and "re." Unfortunately, using verbs isn't that simple! *Naturellement!* There are exceptions to the rules, and we call them "irregular verbs." Here are two common irregular verbs. Notice how they take on different forms, depending upon the subject. It is hard work, but you just have to learn these well, because you will want to use them often.

	(ehtr) **ÊTRE** TO BE		*(a-vwar)* **AVOIR** TO HAVE	
je	*(swee)* suis	j'	*(zhay)* ai	
tu	*(eh)* es	tu	*(a)* as	
il, elle, on	*(eh)* est	il, elle, on	*(a)* a	
nous	*(som)* sommes	nous	*(a-vohn)* avons	
vous	*(eht)* êtes	vous	*(a-vay)* avez	
ils, elles	*(sohn)* sont	ils, elles	*(zohn)* ont	

You may have noticed these verbs in the previous chapters:

Je ne suis pas sûr de réussir.   I am not sure of succeeding.
Demandons à l'agent où est le musée.   Let's ask the policeman where the museum is.
Comme les Français sont aimables!   How friendly the French are!

Now, write down the meaning of the next short sentences in English.

1. Nous sommes à Paris. _____

2. Vous avez une réservation. _____

3. L'hôtel est loin de la banque. _____

4. Marc et Marie n'ont pas de réservation. _____

_____.

5. Est-ce que vous avez de la monnaie? _____

_____?

(prahndr)

There are a few more irregular verbs that you'll need to know. Take a look at **prendre**,
to take

(a-prahndr)   *(kohn-prahndr)*
apprendre, and **comprendre**.
to learn   to understand

	PRENDRE TO TAKE	**APPRENDRE** TO LEARN	**COMPRENDRE** TO UNDERSTAND
je, j'	prend**s**	apprend**s**	comprend**s**
tu	prend**s**	apprend**s**	comprend**s**
il, elle, on	prend	apprend	comprend
nous	*(pruh-nohn)* preno**ns**	*(a-pruh-nohn)* appreno**ns**	*(kohn-pruh-nohn)* compreno**ns**
vous	*(pruh-nay)* pren**ez**	*(a-pruh-nay)* appren**ez**	*(kohn-pruh-nay)* compren**ez**
ils, elles	*(pren)* pren**nent**	*(a-pren)* appren**nent**	*(kohn-pren)* compren**nent**

ANSWERS
English Translation 1. We are in Paris. **2.** You have a reservation. **3.** The hotel is far from the bank. **4.** Mark and Mary have no reservation. **5.** Do you have any change?

This is how they would appear in context.

Prenons l'autobus! Let's take the bus!   **J'apprends le français.** I am learning French.

(too) (ptee) (pūh)
Je comprends le francais un tout petit peu. I understand French a tiny little bit.

Write the meaning in English of the following sentences.

1. Marc et Marie comprennent le français. _____.

2. Est-ce que vous apprenez l'anglais? _____?

3. Jean ne comprend pas très bien le français. _____.

4. Prenons le métro! _____!

5. Prennent-ils un taxi? _____?

Now see if you can remember the regular and irregular verbs by writing in the appropriate forms on the blanks.

	ÊTRE	AVOIR	PRENDRE	DESCENDRE	FINIR
JE	_____	_____	_____	_____	_____
TU	_____	_____	_____	_____	_____
IL, ELLE, ON	_____	_____	_____	_____	_____
NOUS	_____	_____	_____	_____	_____
VOUS	_____	_____	_____	_____	_____
ILS, ELLES	_____	_____	_____	_____	_____

ANSWERS

Verbs,	**être**	**avoir**	**prendre**	**descendre**	**finir**
je, j'	suis	ai	prends	descends	finis
tu	es	as	prends	descends	finis
il elle on	est	a	prend	descend	finit
nous	sommes	avons	prenons	descendons	finissons
vous	êtes	avez	prenez	descendez	finissez
ils elles	sont	ont	prennent	descendent	finissent

English Translation
1. Mark and Mary understand French.   2. Are you learning English?
3. John does not understand French very well.   4. Let's take the metro.   5. Are they taking a taxi?

Revenons aux prépositions
Getting back to prepositions

Earlier we saw how the prepositions $\boxed{\text{À}}$ ("to," "in") and $\boxed{\text{DE}}$ ("of," "from," "about") contract with the definite articles $\boxed{\text{LE}}$ and $\boxed{\text{LES}}$ to become $\boxed{\text{AU}}$, $\boxed{\text{AUX}}$, and $\boxed{\text{DU}}$, $\boxed{\text{DES}}$. But we practiced them mostly before names of places (Paris, le cinéma, etc.). However,

$\boxed{\text{À}}$ **is the equivalent of "to" in a statement such as:**

>   Je parle au garçon.   I speak to the boy.

The indefinite article $\boxed{\text{DES}}$ (plural of $\boxed{\text{UN}}$, $\boxed{\text{UNE}}$) could be considered a contraction of DE + LES, meaning "about the," "of the," "from the." However,

$\boxed{\text{DE}}$ **+ definite article (or proper name) expresses possession:**

>   Le livre du garçon   The boy's book
>   Le livre de Paul   Paul's book

and means "about" in sentences such as:

>   Nous parlons du professeur.   We are talking about the teacher.

A little practice? Try these:

1. Le livre _____ garçon
   of the

2. Le cahier _____ fille
   of the

3. Les amis _____ étudiant
   of the

   (ay-tew-dyant)
4. L'ami _____ étudiante
   of the   _fem. student_

5. Je parle _____ étudiant
   about the

6. Le professeur parle _____ livre _____ étudiants
   about the   _to the_

7. J'ai _____ amis _____ Montréal
   some   _in_
   (don)

8. Je donne le livre _____ garçon
   give   _to the_

   (tay-lay-fo-nohn)
9. Nous téléphonons _____ hôtel
   to the

ANSWERS

DE
1. du 2. de la 3. de l' 4. de l' 5. de l' 6. du aux 7. des à 8. au 9. à l'

53

The following brief passage will let you find out how well you have learned to answer questions and to get around town.

Monsieur Legros et sa femme prennent
        his   (plew)
l'autobus et descendent deux arrêts plus
                two   more
loin. Puis ils prennent le métro. Ils
        (roo-soh)
descendent à la rue Rousseau. Ils arrivent
        (a-shet)   (boh-koo)   (shohz)
au marché et achètent beaucoup de choses.
                many   things

1. Qu'est-ce que les Legros prennent ?

_____

2. Où descendent-ils?

_____

3. Et ensuite, qu'est-ce qu'ils prennent?

_____

4. Où est-ce que les Legros arrivent?

_____

5. Qu'est-ce qu'ils achètent?

_____

ANSWERS

Questions 1. (Ils prennent) l'autobus. **2.** (Ils descendent) deux arrêts plus loin.
3. (Ils prennent) le métro. **4.** (Ils arrivent) au marché. **5.** (Ils achètent) beaucoup de choses.

Comment exprimer l'heure et les nombres

(ko-mahn) *(lūhr)* *(nohmbr)*

Expressing Time and Numbers

Il est 9 heures du matin.

Il est 1 heure du matin.

Il est 3 heures de l'après-midi.

Il est 8 heures du soir.

Il est 3 heures du matin.

Expressing time is easy. Simply state the number of the hour, followed by the word **heure(s)**.

You use *du matin* (A.M.) for the morning and *de l'après midi* (P.M.) for early afternoon; *(ma-tan)* *(duh)* *(la-preh-mee-dee)* *du soir* (P.M.) is used for later afternoon and evening. *(swar)*

COMMENT COMPTER EN FRANÇAIS
(kohn-tay)

How to Count in French

Les nombres cardinaux 1–1000
(kar-dee-noh)

Cardinal numbers 1–1000

1	2	3	4	5	6	7	8
ahún			*(katr)*	*(sank)*	*(sees)*	*(seht)*	*(weet)*
UN	DEUX	TROIS	QUATRE	CINQ	SIX	SEPT	HUIT

9	10	11	12	13	14	15
nœf	*deen*	*(ohnz)*	*(dooz)*	*(trehz)*	*(ka-torz)*	*(kanz)*
NEUF	DIX	ONZE	DOUZE	TREIZE	QUATORZE	QUINZE

16	17	18	19	20
saye				
(sehz)	*(dee-set)*	*(dee-zweet)*	*(deez-nuhf)*	*(van)*
SEIZE	DIX-SEPT	DIX-HUIT	DIX-NEUF	VINGT

Now it's easy . . . until we reach 70.

21 VINGT ET UN	*(san-kahnt)* 50 CINQUANTE	90 QUATRE-VINGT-DIX
22 VINGT-DEUX	*(swa-sahnt)*	91 QUATRE-VINGT-ONZE
23 VINGT-TROIS etc.	60 SOIXANTE	92 QUATRE-VINGT-DOUZE etc.
(trahnt)	70 SOIXANTE-DIX	*(sahn)*
30 TRENTE	71 SOIXANTE ET ONZE	100 CENT
31 TRENTE ET UN	72 SOIXANTE-DOUZE etc.	200 DEUX CENTS etc.
32 TRENTE-DEUX	80 QUATRE-VINGTS	*(meel)*
(ka-rahnt)	81 QUATRE-VINGT-UN	1000 MILLE
40 QUARANTE	82 QUATRE-VINGT-DEUX etc.	

PRONUNCIATION NOTE: Six and ten are pronounced "sees" and "dees" if they are by themselves. When followed by a noun, they become "see" and "dee." Eight is pronounced "weet" by itself, "wee" when followed by a noun:

(see)
six garçons

(dee)
dix filles

(wee)
huit tables

When these numbers are followed by a noun which begins with a vowel, one has to link:

(see) (zamee)
six amis

(dee) (zay-kol)
dix écoles
schools

And when nine is followed by a vowel sound, the final "F" sounds like a "V": **il est neuf heures**
(nuh) *(vuhr)*

(or-dee-noh)
Les nombres ordinaux 1–10
Ordinal numbers 1–10

┌─── First ───┐		
(Masculine) *(pruh-myay)* **PREMIER**	(Feminine) *(pruh-myer)* **PREMIÈRE**	Second *(dūh-zyehm)* **DEUXIÈME**
Third *(trwah-zyehm)* **TROISIÈME**	Fourth *(ka-try-ehm)* **QUATRIÈME**	Fifth *(san-kyehm)* **CINQUIÈME**
Sixth *(see-zyehm)* **SIXIÈME**	Seventh *(se-tyehm)* **SEPTIÈME**	Eighth *(wee-tyehm)* **HUITIÈME**
Ninth *(nuh-vyehm)* **NEUVIÈME**	Tenth *(dee-zyehm)* **DIXIÈME**	

ALARME ... STOP

9ème 10ème
7ème 8ème
5ème 6ème
3ème 4ème
1er 2ème

(rayd) *(shoh-say)*
rez-de-chaussée

NOTE: The "rez-de-chaussée" is the ground floor in the U.S.;
(ay-tahzh)
the "premier étage" is the second floor in the U.S.

(ke) (luh) (reh) (teel)

QUELLE HEURE EST-IL?

What time is it?

1. To add the minutes, simply add the number:

Il est six heures dix du matin.

(dee) (zuhr)
Il est dix heures cinquante du matin.

(se)
Il est sept
(tuhr) (van)
heures vingt.

Il est huit heures
(trahnt) (nuhf)
trente-neuf.

Il est onze heures cinquante-cinq du matin.

(mwan)
2. If the minute hand is close to the next, you can also say the next hour **moins** the number of
minus

minutes to go:
(ohn) (zuhr) (mwan) (dees)
Il est onze heures moins dix.

3. Finally, the quarter hours and the half hours (although not in official time) can be replaced by the following expressions:

(kar)
2:15—deux heures et **quart**
quarter

(duh-mee)
3:30—trois heures et **demie**
half—feminine because HEURE is feminine

2:45—trois heures moins le **quart**.

12:30—midi (minuit) et **demi**
half—masculine because MIDI and
MINUIT are masculine

Easy? In France the 24-hour system is often used, especially in travel schedules and performance times; for example, *quatorze heures* (14 hours) is 2 P.M. To understand this system, subtract 12 from any number more than 12 and add P.M.

A few examples:
Le train part à 22 h 13 = The train leaves at 10:13 P.M.
Le concert commence à 20 h 30 = The concert begins at 8:30 P.M.
L'avion arrive à 17 h 35 = The plane arrives at 5:35 P.M.

Un moment. Now give the following times in French:

2:15	1:10
8:30	3:35
9:45	5:25
7:00	4:55

Express these numbers in French:

14	62
23	71
37	89
46	98
55	116

The following dialogue contains some useful expressions related to the telling of time. Read it out loud a few times.

MARC **Pardon, Monsieur, quelle heure est-il?**

Excuse me, Sir, what time is it?

UN MONSIEUR **Il est minuit.**

It's midnight.

MARC *(ehs)* *(po-seebl)* *(fay)*
Comment est-ce possible? Il fait encore jour. *(tahn-kor) (zhoor)*

How can it be? It is still daytime.

UN MONSIEUR **Excusez-moi. Dans ce cas** *(kah)* **il est midi.**

Excuse me. In that case, it is noon.

MARC *(play-zahn-tay)* **Vous plaisantez?**

Are you joking?

UN MONSIEUR *(mohntr)* **Non. Je n'ai pas de montre.** **Vous êtes touriste?** *(too-reest)*

No. I don't have a watch. Are you a tourist?

ANSWERS

Time deux heures quinze, huit heures et demie, neuf heures quarante-cinq, sept heures, une heure dix, trois heures trente-cinq, cinq heures vingt-cinq, quatre heures cinquante-cinq.

Numbers quatorze, vingt-trois, trente-sept, quarante-six, cinquante-cinq, soixante-deux, soixante et onze, quatre-vingt-neuf, quatre-vingt-dix-huit, cent seize.

58

MARC	**Oui.**		Yes.

UN MONSIEUR   *(voo-lay)*   *(ash-tay)*
Voulez-vous acheter une

montre? Onze euros.

Do you want to buy a watch?

  Eleven euros.

MARC   *(dee)*
Mais vous avez dit que vous n'avez

pas de montre!

But you said that you do

not have a watch!

UN MONSIEUR   **Nuef euros.**

Nine euros.

MARC   **Non, merci.**

No, thanks.

UN MONSIEUR   **Voilà votre montre. Je suis**
(peek-po-keht) *(oh-neht)*
un pickpocket honnête!

Here is your watch.
I am an honest
pickpocket!

Can you write these phrases in French as they appear in the dialogue?

1. What time is it? _____

2. It is midnight. _____

3. It is still daytime. _____

4. It is noon. _____

5. Are you a tourist? _____

6. Here is your watch. _____

ANSWERS

Dialogue 1. Quelle heure est-il? **2.** Il est minuit. **3.** Il fait encore jour. **4.** Il est midi. **5.** Vous êtes touriste? **6.** Voilà votre montre.

(uhn) *(mo-mahn)* *(ahntr)* *(ohtr)*
UN MOMENT ENTRE AUTRES
A Place in Time

Remember the saying, "If it's Tuesday, I must be in . . ."

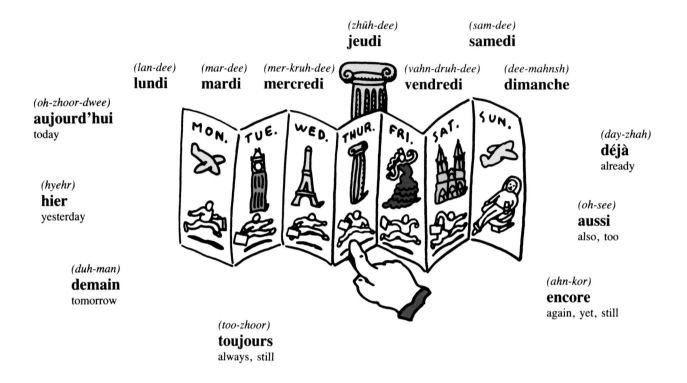

(oh-zhoor-dwee)
aujourd'hui
today

(hyehr)
hier
yesterday

(duh-man)
demain
tomorrow

(lan-dee) *(mar-dee)* *(mer-kruh-dee)* *(vahn-druh-dee)* *(dee-mahnsh)*
lundi **mardi** **mercredi** **vendredi** **dimanche**

(zhūh-dee) *(sam-dee)*
jeudi **samedi**

(day-zhah)
déjà
already

(oh-see)
aussi
also, too

(ahn-kor)
encore
again, yet, still

(too-zhoor)
toujours
always, still

Now, see if you remember the meaning of the following adverbs by matching them up to their English equivalents.

1. **aujourd'hui** A. today
2. **hier** B. yesterday
3. **demain** C. again
4. **toujours** D. tomorrow
5. **encore** E. always
6. **aussi** F. already
7. **déjà** G. also

ANSWERS

Matching adverbs 1. A 2. B 3. D 4. E 5. C 6. G 7. F

(ahn-kor)   *(vehrb)*   *(ee-reh-gew-lyay)*

Encore des verbes irréguliers
More irregular verbs

In a previous unit you learned to conjugate verbs of the second conjugation ending in **-IR**. There is a fairly large group of **-IR** verbs which follow a different pattern and are considered irregular. This table will help you remember these special verbs.

(dor-meer) **DORMIR** to sleep		*(par-teer)* **PARTIR** to leave	
je tu	*(dor)* **DOR***S*	je tu	*(par)* **PAR***S*
il elle on	*(dor)* **DOR***T*	il elle on	*(par)* **PAR***T*
nous	*(dor-mohn)* **DORM***ONS*	nous	*(par-tohn)* **PART***ONS*
vous	*(dor-may)* **DORM***EZ*	vous	*(par-tay)* **PART***EZ*
ils elles	*(dorm)* **DORM***ENT*	ils elles	*(part)* **PART***ENT*

               (sor-teer)   *(ser-veer)*   *(sahn-teer)*   *(mahn-teer)*
Some other verbs in this group are SORTIR,   SERVIR, SENTIR,   MENTIR. Unfortunately,
                   to go out, to exit   to serve   to smell, to feel   to lie
you cannot predict which verbs belong to which group.

Add the endings to the verb stems in the following list.

1. Je sor _____

2. Tu dor _____

3. Il par _____

4. Elle ser _____

5. On sen _____

6. Nous men _____

7. Vous dor _____

8. Ils par _____

9. Elles sor _____

ANSWERS

IR Verb 1. Je sors   **2.** Tu dors   **3.** Il part   **4.** Elle sert   **5.** On sent   **6.** Nous mentons   **7.** Vous dormez   **8.** Ils partent   **9.** Elles sortent

How can you recognize a special **"-IR"** verb that takes these endings? You can't. **Je le regrette.** (I'm sorry!) Let's review all the regular and "semi-regular" verb forms. Now try to put the right endings in the blanks.

a. JE   parl_____

           fin _____

           ven _____

           dor _____

b. TU   parl_____

           fin _____

           ven _____

           dor _____

c. IL/ELLE/ON   parl_____

           fin _____

           ven _____

           dor _____

d. NOUS   parl_____

           fin _____

           ven _____

           dor _____

e. VOUS   parl_____

           fin _____

           ven _____

           dor _____

f. ILS/ELLES   parl_____

           fin _____

           ven _____

           dor _____

(mohn)   *(ma)*   *(may)*

Mon, ma, mes,

(tohn)   *(ta)*   *(tay)*

Ton, ta, tes
Mine and yours

What's "mine" or "yours"? Here's how to tell in French. Note that the forms of these words change, depending on the nouns they describe.

ANSWERS

Regular and Semi-Regular Verbs

a.	b.	c.	d.	e.	f.
Je parle	Tu parles	Il, parle	Nous parlons	Vous parlez	Ils, parlent
Je finis	Tu finis	Elle, finit	Nous finissons	Vous finissez	Elles finissent
Je vends	Tu vends	On vend	Nous vendons	Vous vendez	Ils vendent
Je dors	Tu dors	dort	Nous dormons	Vous dormez	dorment

WITH FEMININE NOUNS	WITH MASCULINE NOUNS

MY

MA	valise		MON	livre
MES	valises		MES	livres

YOUR (familiar)

TA	valise		TON	livre
TES	valises		TES	livres

YOUR (plural and polite)

(votr)

VOTRE	valise		VOTRE	livre

(voh)

VOS	valises		VOS	livres

HIS/HER

SA	valise		SON	livre
SES	valises		SES	livres

OUR

(notr)

NOTRE	valise		NOTRE	livre

(noh)

NOS	valises		NOS	livres

THEIR

(luhr)

LEUR	valise		LEUR	livre
LEURS	valises		LEURS	livres

Notice that the possessive adjective agrees with the thing possessed and not with the person who possesses, as in English.

Notice, as well, that the forms VOTRE, VOS mean ''Your'' (several possessors), and ''Your'' (polite form, singular).

Note that the masculine singular possessive adjective is used before feminine nouns beginning with a vowel. Example: **mon automobile** *(fem.)*.

MA   VALISE

MES   VALISES

MON   LIVRE

MES   LIVRES

Now test your knowledge by putting the appropriate possessive adjective in front of the following nouns:

1. _____ mère
   my

2. _____ maison
   your (fam.)

3. _____ chat
   his

4. _____ chat
   her (BE CAREFUL!!!)

5. _____ ami
   our

6. _____ automobile
   your (polite)

7. _____ valise
   their

8. _____ soeurs
   my

9. _____ maisons
   your (fam.)

10. _____ chats
    his

11. _____ chats
    her

12. _____ amis
    our

13. _____ automobiles
    your (polite)

14. _____ valises
    their

If someone asks you, can you tell him or her the time in French? Read this passage and then answer the questions that follow.

"Quelle heure est-il?" demande le père à sa fille. "Il est trois heures,"
                              asks

dit la fille. "A quelle heure pars-tu pour la France?" demande le père. "À dix-sept

                                    (ray-pohn)
heures vingt," répond la fille. "Bon voyage!" "Au revoir, papa."
                answers   Goodbye

1. Le père demande à sa fille:
   A. quelle heure il est en France;
   B. quelle heure il est;
      (see)
   C. si elle part en voyage;
      if
   D. quand le train de France arrive.

2. Quelle heure est-il?
   A. Il est deux heures.
   B. Il est six heures et quart.
   C. Il est trois heures.
   D. Il est neuf heures moins le quart.

ANSWERS

Possessive Adjectives

1. ma mère	5. notre ami	10. ses chats
2. ta maison	6. votre automobile	11. ses chats
3. son chat	7. leur valise	12. nos amis
4. son chat	8. mes soeurs	13. vos automobiles
	9. tes maisons	14. leurs valises

Paragraph. 1. B 2. C

If you need to take the train, the following dialogue might prove useful to you. Don't forget to read it out loud.

MARIE **Nous voici à la gare.** *(gar)*

Here we are at the train station.

ANNE **Papa, prenons-nous le rapide pour** *(ra-peed)*

aller à Cannes?

Dad, are we taking the express train to go to

Cannes?

MARC **Non, c'est trop cher.**

No, it's too expensive.

ANNE **Alors, nous prenons l'express?** *(ehks-prehs)*

Then we are taking the fast train?

MARC **Oui. (à un employé): Pardon.**

Combien coûte un billet aller et retour *(a-lay) (ruh-toor)*

pour Cannes pour quatre personnes?

Yes. Excuse me,

how much does a round-trip ticket

to Cannes for four people cost?

L'EMPLOYÉ	*(par)* **Par l'express?**	By fast train?
MARC	**Oui.**	Yes.
L'EMPLOYÉ	*(suh-gohnd)* **Première ou seconde classe?**	First or second class?
MARC	**Seconde.**	Second.
L'EMPLOYÉ	**Cent quatre-vingt-huit euros par personne.**	188 euros per person.
MARC	**C'est cher . . .**	It's expensive . . .
L'EMPLOYÉ	*(fa-mee-y)* **Il y a des billets de famille qui coûtent moins cher.**	There are family tickets which cost less.
MARC	**Bon.**	Good.
L'EMPLOYÉ	*(kohn-par-tee-mahn) (few-muhr) (oo)* **Compartiment fumeurs ou non-fumeurs?**	Smoking or nonsmoking compartment?
MARC	**Non-fumeurs.**	Nonsmoking.
L'EMPLOYÉ	**Deux cent trente euros. Voilà vos billets.**	230 euros. Here are your tickets.
MARC	**Merci. À quelle heure est-ce que le train part?**	Thank you. At what time does the train leave?
L'EMPLOYÉ	**À quinze heures trente.**	At 3:30 P.M.

Match these French words or expressions from the dialogue with their English equivalents.

1. la gare

2. un billet aller et retour

3. première classe

4. des billets de famille

5. compartiment non-fumeurs

a. first class

b. family tickets

c. nonsmoking compartment

d. the station

e. a round-trip ticket

European trains are excellent. The **T.E.E. (Trans-Europe-Express)** and the **T.G.V. (Trains à Grande Vitesse)** are two very popular high-speed trains. Here are some examples of the **T.E.E.**:

L'Etoile du Nord: Paris/Bruxelles/Amsterdam in 5 hours (547 km.)
Le Parsifal: Paris/Liège/Cologne/Dortmund/Hambourg in 9¼ hours (954 km.)
Le Cisalpin: Paris/Lausanne/Milan in 7 hours 53 minutes (822 km.)

These trains are more expensive and you must reserve your seat ahead of time. In order to make a reservation or to obtain information, go to any travel agency. You can even put your car on the train and check your bags.

(sheh)
To help you read the *Chaix* here is the explanation for a few signs:
official train schedule

(zhoor) (oo-vrahbl)
jours ouvrables
week days

(va-gohn) (lee)
wagon-lit

(vwa-tewr) (bar)
voiture-bar

(dee-mahnsh)
dimanches et
Sundays
(feht) *(suhl-mahn)*
fêtes **seulement**
holidays only

(rehs-to-rahn)
wagon-restaurant

ANSWERS

Matching 1. d 2. e 3. a 4. b 5. c

Here is a train schedule. Plan a trip from Paris to Nice. Figure out the cities you would like to visit along the way and the timetable you would follow. (Note: each timetable indicates: (1) in left columns, the departure times from the first station, then arrival time; (2) in right columns, departure times, then arrival times at the end of the line; (3) in italics, the schedule that requires changing trains).

SUD-EST

							Station							
6 55	7 44	10 16	11 42	15 10	17 46	18 40	PARIS-Gare de Lyon*	11 33	12 54	13 54	16 58	18 51	21 43	23 33
	9 12						LE CREUSOT TGV*		12 25					22 04
9 48	10 45		14 35	18 05	20 41	22 37	VALENCE*	8 34	9 57	10 51	13 59		18 44	20 28
10 46	11 45	14 12	15 33	19 05	21 43	22 37	AVIGNON*	7 34	8 59	9 49	12 59	14 55	17 44	19 28
11 17	12 13	14 39	16 04	19 33	22 11	23 08	NIMES*	7 04	8 27	9 20	12 29	14 27	17 14	18 58
11 42	12 39	15 05	16 29	19 59	22 36	23 34	MONTPELLIER*	6 39	8 02	8 55	12 04	14 02	16 49	18 33
12 41	13 29	15 30	17 17	20 51	23 05	0 51	SÈTE*	6 01	7 05	8 24	11 06	12 59	16 15	17 43
13 18	13 55	15 58	17 21	21 19	23 35	1 21	BÉZIERS*	5 29	6 31	7 59	10 41	12 25	15 45	17 12
13 43	14 12	16 16	17 39	21 39	23 52	1 41	NARBONNE* (A)	5 12	6 16	7 42	10 24	12 10	15 27	16 50
...	14 47	17 08	18 14	22 42	...	...	PERPIGNAN* (A)	...	5 35	6 40	9 22	11 22	14 24	16 03

							Station							
6 55	7 44	10 10	11 42	12 48	15 10	16 49	PARIS-Gare de Lyon*	6 21	6 25	7 42	8 14	9 29	11 33	12 54
9 48	10 45	13 05	14 35	15 41	18 05	19 52	VALENCE*		0 08			6a15	8 34	9 57
10 46	11 45	14 05	15 33	16 39	19 05	20 52	AVIGNON*		23 01	23 59	15 00	5a14	7 34	8 59
11 48	12 51	15 07	16 35	17 40	20 11	21 54	MARSEILLE*		21 47	22 35			6 29	7 58
13 16	14 00	16 03	17 29	18 37	21 13	22 45	TOULON*	21 48	20 48	21 32	23 03	...	4 35	6 52
14 50	14 50	16 56	18 14	19 29	22 01	23 32	ST-RAPHAEL	20 52	19 25	20 33	22 15	...	...	...
15 17	15 17	17 22	18 37	19 53	22 24	23 56	CANNES	20 28	18 58	20 08	21 49	...	...	...
15 31	15 31	17 38	18 47	20 03	22 36	0 07	ANTIBES	20 13	18 40	19 51	21 32	...	...	...
15 48	15 48	18 00	19 02	20 18	22 52	0 23	NICE*	19 55	18 19	19 30	21 15	...	...	...

							Station							
17 46	18 40	20 00	20 45	21 46	22 17	22 36	PARIS-Gare de Lyon*	13 54	16 58	18 56	19 50	21 43	22 32	23 33
20 41	21 37	23a13					VALENCE*	10 51	13 59		16 51	18 39	19 33	20 28
21 43	22 37	0a15				5 35	AVIGNON*	9 49	12 59	15 00	15 51	17 39	18 29	19 28
22 48	23 40	...	5 06			7 20	MARSEILLE*	8 45	11 54	14 00	14 51	16 39	17 29	18 23
...	1 22	...	6 14		7 00	8 33	TOULON*	7 47	10 53	12 59	13 55	15 31	16 21	16 46
...	...	...	7 16	6 50	8 03	9 27	ST-RAPHAEL	6 52	9 48	12 12	13 06	14 37	15 34	
...	...	...	7 42	7 16	8 29	9 50	CANNES	6 27	9 21	11 49	12 43	14 13	15 10	
...	...	...	8 00	7 35	8 46	9 59	ANTIBES	6 16	9 05	11 39	12 30	14 03	15 00	
...	...	...	8 21	7 55	9 10	10 14	NICE*	6 00	8 47	11 24	12 10	13 48	14 45	

(A) Voir aussi tableau PARIS-TOULOUSE-BARCELONA.
(a) Changement de train à Lyon Part-Dieu.

Courtesy of S.N.C.F., Paris

(voo-lwar)   *(poo-vwar)*

Vouloir c'est pouvoir
To want is to be able to

"To want" and "to be able to" are very useful verbs when requesting and asking for things. The French verbs are VOULOIR and POUVOIR. They are both irregular, but follow a similar pattern.

VOULOIR	POUVOIR

je *(vūh)* **veux**
tu **veux**
il / elle / on *(vūh)* **veut**
nous *(voo-lohn)* **voulons**
vous *(voo-lay)* **voulez**
ils / elles *(vuhl)* **veulent**

je *(pūh)* **peux**
tu **peux**
il / elle / on *(pūh)* **peut**
nous *(poo-vohn)* **pouvons**
vous *(poo-vay)* **pouvez**
ils / elles *(puhv)* **peuvent**

If you want to be really polite—"I would like"—"Could you," the forms are:

(voo-dreh)
JE VOUDRAIS _____ I would like

(poo-ryay)
POURRIEZ-VOUS _____ Could you

Now fill in the blanks with the appropriate form of the verb.

1. _____-vous *(meh-day)* m'aider?
   could   help

2. Je _____ , donc je _____ .
         want   *(dohnk)* therefore   can

3. _____-vous du café? *(ka-fay)*
        want

4. Je _____ une omelette, s'il vous plaît.
        would like   *(om-leht)* *(seel)(voo)* *(pleh)*

5. _____-nous prendre le rapide?
      can, may

6. Anne et Jean ne _____ pas prendre le rapide.
                          can

NOTE: You may have noticed that there is only one verb in French for "can" and "may."

ANSWERS
Fill ins
1. Pourriez 2. veux...peux 3. Voulez 4. voudrais 5. Pouvons 6. peuvent

69

(ahn) *(vwa-tewr)*
EN VOITURE!
All Aboard!

(pa-sa-zhehr)	*(a-swar)*	*(suh luh-vay)*
une passagère	**s'asseoir**	**se lever**
passenger	to sit down	to get up

(sahl) (da-tahnt)	*(o-rehr)*	*(kay)*	*(sha-reht)*	*(par-tuhr)*	*(tran)*
la salle d'attente	**l'horaire** *(m.)*	**le quai**	**la charrette**	**le porteur**	**le train**
waiting room	schedule	railway platform	luggage cart	porter	train

(feht)   (luh) (voo)   (mehm)

Faites-le vous-même

Do it yourself

(ruh-gard)   (ta-bloh)
Il regarde le tableau.

Il se regarde.

Reflexive verbs express actions people do "to themselves": to get up, to sit down, to get dressed, to go to bed, to wake up, to get married, to have fun, to be bored. For example, "to get washed" is a reflexive verb because you wash yourself or "reflect back" the action of the verb upon yourself. This is done by means of reflexive pronouns, like "myself" and "yourself." Here are the reflexive pronouns in French.

REFLEXIVE PRONOUNS

(muh)

ME , **M'** (before vowel)   Myself

(tuh)

TE , **T'** (before vowel)   Yourself (familiar)

SE , **S'** (before vowel)   Himself, Herself, Oneself

NOUS   Ourselves

VOUS   Yourselves, Yourself (polite)

SE , **S'** (before vowel)   Themselves

Now let's conjugate a reflexive verb: LAVER *(la-vay)* can become reflexive "To wash oneself" (SE LAVER) as follows:

JE	ME	LAVE	I wash myself, I am washing myself, I do wash myself
TU	TE	LAVES	You wash yourself, etc.
IL, ELLE, ON	SE	LAVE	He/She/One washes himself/herself/oneself
NOUS	NOUS	LAVONS	We wash ourselves
VOUS	VOUS	LAVEZ	You wash yourselves/yourself (polite)
ILS, ELLES	SE	LAVENT	They wash themselves

Now you try it with the verb AMUSER *(a-mew-zay)*, which in its reflexive form means "To enjoy oneself, to have fun." It begins with a vowel, so the reflexive pronouns become m', t', and s'.

1. je _____ amuse.

2. tu _____ amuses.

3. il, elle _____ amuse.

4. nous _____ amusons.

5. vous _____ amusez.

6. ils, elles _____ amusent.

ANSWERS

Reflexive verbs   1. je m'amuse
2. tu t'amuses
3. il, elle s'amuse
4. nous nous amusons
5. vous vous amusez
6. ils, elles s'amusent

The following passage is about train travel. Read about Marc and Marie, then answer the questions that follow.

(vohn)   *(eel)(za-sheht)*

Marc et Marie vont à la gare. Ils achètent un billet aller-retour Paris-Marseille. Ils voyagent par le T.G.V. de Paris à Lyon. Ensuite, de Lyon à Marseille ils prennent un rapide. Ils arrivent à cinq heures.

1. Où vont Marc et Marie?

_____

2. Qu'est-ce qu'ils achètent?

_____

3. Qu'est-ce que c'est que le T.G.V.?

_____

ANSWERS

Reading   1. Ils vont à la gare.   **2.** Ils achètent un billet.   **3.** C'est le Train à Grande Vitesse.

(peh-yee) *(lahng)*

Les pays et les langues
Countries and Languages

Je parle un peu français. I speak a little French. And so do you! By now you've learned quite a bit of French. Take a look at the rest of the world, too, and learn how to say the names of other countries in French. Note that in French the article "the" is used with the name of a country, a city, or a language. Also note that, except for Le Mexique, countries ending in E are feminine.

COUNTRIES

Masculine		**Feminine**			
(bray-zeel) **le Brésil**	*(por-tew-gal)* **le Portugal**	*(al-ma-nyuh)* **l'Allemagne** Germany	*(ar-zhahn-teen)* **l'Argentine**	*(sheen)* **la Chine**	*(po-lo-nyuh)* **la Pologne** Poland
(ka-na-dah) **le Canada**	*(vay-nay-zew-ay-lah)* **le Vénézuéla**	*(a-may-reek)* **l'Amérique**	*(ohs-tra-lee)* **l'Australie**	*(ehs-pa-nyuh)* **l'Espagne** Spain	*(rew-see)* **la Russie**
(shee-lee) **le Chili**	*(mehk-seek)* **le Mexique**	*(ahn-gluh-tehr)* **l'Angleterre** England	*(oh-treesh)* **l'Autriche** Austria	*(uh-rop)* **l' Europe**	*(sew-ehd)* **la Suède** Sweden
(dan-mark) **le Danemark**	**Plural**		*(bel-zheek)* **la Belgique** Belgium	*(frahns)* **la France**	*(swees)* **la Suisse** Switzerland
(zha-pohn) **le Japon**	*(ay-ta) (zew-nee)* **les États-Unis**	*(grahnd)* *(bruh-ta-nyuh)* **la Grande Bretagne**		*(grehs)* **la Grèce**	*(tewr-kee)* **la Turquie**
				(o-lahnd) **la Hollande**	
				(ee-ta-lee) **l'Italie**	

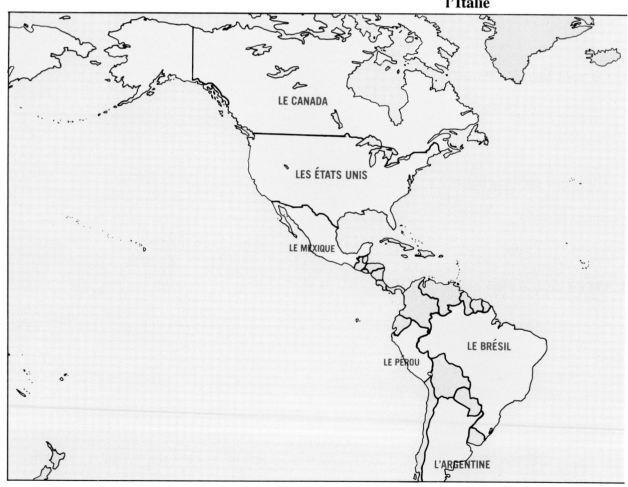

LE CANADA

LES ÉTATS UNIS

LE MEXIQUE

LE PÉROU

LE BRÉSIL

L'ARGENTINE

Je parle
I speak

(zha-po-nay)
Je parle japonais.

(al-mahn)
Je parle allemande.
German

(ehs-pa-nyol)
Je parle espagnol.

(shee-nwah)
Je parle chinois.

(ahn-glay)
Je parle anglais.
English

(frahn-say)
Je parle français.

(rews)
Je parle russe.

Names of languages are masculine and are not capitalized. After verbs other than parler
(eh-may)
(comprendre, apprendre, aimer, and so on), the definite article LE is used: J'aime le français!
to like, love

Nationalities are not capitalized when they are used as adjectives. They *are* capitalized when
used as nouns. Example: **un homme français arrive,** but le **Français arrive..**

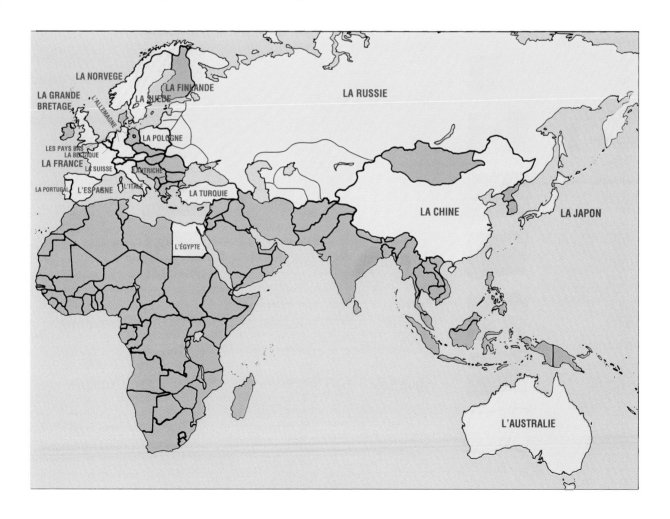

(zhuh) (swee)

Je suis

I am

Many of us are combinations of several nationalities. Which are you? Use **Je suis** . . . (I am . . .)

MASCULIN	FÉMININ	MASCULIN	FÉMININ
(al-mahn) **Je suis allemand**	*(al-mahnd)* **allemande**	*(frahn-say)* **français**	*(frahn-sehz)* **française**
(a-may-ree-kan) **américain**	*(a-may-ree-kehn)* **américaine**	*(o-lahn-day)* **hollandais**	*(o-lahn-dehz)* **hollandaise**
(ahn-glay) **anglais**	*(ahn-glehz)* **anglaise**	*(ee-ta-lyan)* **italien**	*(ee-ta-lyehn)* **italienne**
(ohs-tra-lyan) **australien**	*(ohs-tra-lyehn)* **australienne**	*(zha-po-nay)* **japonais**	*(zha-po-nehz)* **japonaise**
(oh-tree-shyan) **autrichien**	*(oh-tree-shyehn)* **autrichienne**	*(mehk-see-kan)* **mexicain**	*(mehk-see-kehn)* **mexicaine**
(behlzh) **belge**	*(behlzh)* **beige**	*(nor-vay-zhyan)* **norvégien**	*(nor-vay-zhyehn)* **norvégienne**
(ka-na-dyan) **canadien**	*(ka-na-dyehn)* **canadienne**	*(po-lo-nay)* **polonais**	*(po-lo-nehz)* **polonaise**
(shee-nwah) **chinois**	*(shee-nwahz)* **chinoise**	*(rews)* **russe**	*(rews)* **russe**
chinois	**chinoise**	*(swees)* **suisse**	**suisse**
(da-nwa) **danois**	*(da-nwaz)* **danoise**	*(sew-ay-dwah)* **suédois**	*(sew-ay-dwahz)* **suédoise**
(ehs-pa-nyol) **espagnol**	*(ehs-pa-nyol)* **espagnole**	*(tewrk)* **turc**	*(tewrk)* **turque**
		(rih-ro-pay-an) **européen**	*(ah-ro-pay-ehn)* **européenne**

(zhuh) (vay)

Je vais

I am going to

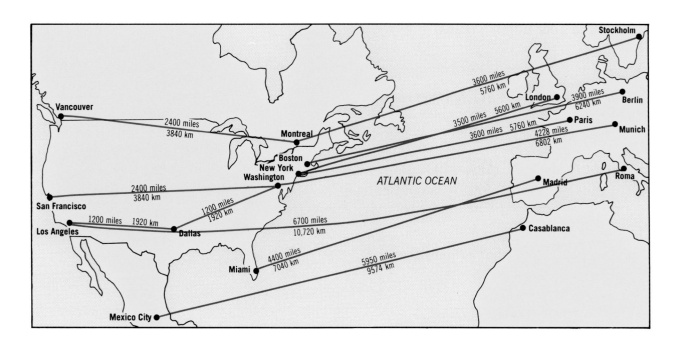

à + CITIES	en + FEMININE COUNTRIES & COUNTRIES STARTING WITH A VOWEL *	au + MASCULINE COUNTRIES	aux + PLURAL COUNTRIES
(pa-ree) **Paris**	France	Canada	
(ma-dreed) **Madrid**	Espagne	Portugal	
(ber-lan) **Berlin**	Allemagne	Chili	États-Unis
(rom) **Rome**	Italie	Brésil	Pays-Bas
(brew-sel) **Bruxelles**	Belgique	Mexique ⎫ exceptions Zaïre ⎭	
(zhuh-nehv) **Genève**	Suisse		
	(ee-rahn) **Iran**		
	Alaska		

*****En** *is also used with continents, and subdivisions, such as states and provinces.*

Now, **répondez aux questions**, using the correct **préposition** as in the following example:

(ark)(duh)(tree-yohnf)
Où est l'Arc de Triomphe? *L'arc de Triomphe est à Paris.*

(toor) (eh-fehl)
1. Où est la Tour Eiffel?   (Paris)

_____

2. Où est New York?   (États-Unis)

_____

3. Où est Acapulco?   (Mexique)

_____

(bah-tohn) (roozh)
4. Où est Bâton   Rouge?   (Louisiane)
   red   stick

_____

5. Où est Berlin?   (Allemagne)

_____

(ko-lee-zay)
6. Où est le Colisée?   (Rome, Italie)

_____

(prah-doh)
7. Où est le Prado?   (Madrid, Espagne)

_____

(ran)
8. Où est le Rhin?   (Allemagne)

_____

ANSWERS

Prépositions: 1. à Paris **2.** aux États-Unis **3.** au Mexique **4.** en Louisiane **5.** en Allemagne
6. à Rome, en Italie **7.** à Madrid, en Espagne **8.** en Allemagne

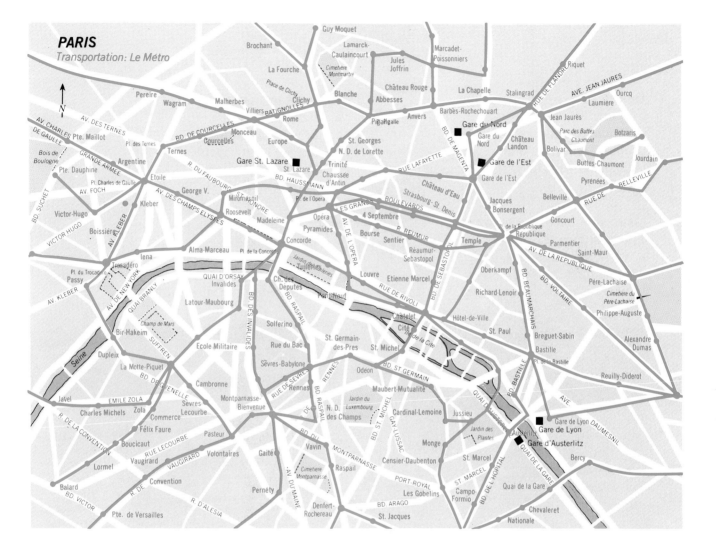

Read the following brief passage and try answering the questions.

(gar) *(lyohn)* *(sahntr)* *(pohn-pee-doo)*

Anne part de son hôtel près de la Gare de Lyon pour aller au Centre Pompidou. À la

(shah-tlay)

station du Châtelet, une jeune fille française commence à lui parler. Elle dit qu'elle désire

(a-kohn-pa-nyay) *(sor)* *(oh)* *(ahl)*

l'accompagner voir l'exposition d'art. Quand elle sort du métro aux Halles, Anne est très

leaves

79

(kohn-tahnt)   *(ofr)*

contente d'avoir une amie. La jeune fille française offre aussi de lui montrer quelques

                                                     some

(kew-ryo-zee-tay)

curiosités de la belle capitale et elle l'invite à prendre chez elle un déjeuner typiquement

                                                                        lunch

français.

1. Anne désire
   a. visiter les jardins.
   b. écouter un concert.
   c. aller à un centre d'art.
   d. déjeuner dans un grand restaurant.

2. Anne entre en conversation avec
   a. une Française.
   b. un homme étranger.
   c. un garçon.
   d. une jeune fille américaine.

3. Anne est très contente
   a. d'aller à Nice.
   b. de voyager en métro.
   c. de parler à un garçon.
   d. d'avoir une amie.

4. Anne va prendre
   a. un avion anglais.
   b. un déjeuner français.
   c. une photo de la jeune fille.
   d. une montre française.

ANSWERS

Multiple choice 1. c 2. a 3. d 4. b

(vwa-tewr) *(grahnd)* *(puh-teet)*
Les voitures, grandes et petites
Cars, Big and Small

(see-nya-lee-za-syohn) *(roo-tyehr)*
La signalisation routière
Road Signs

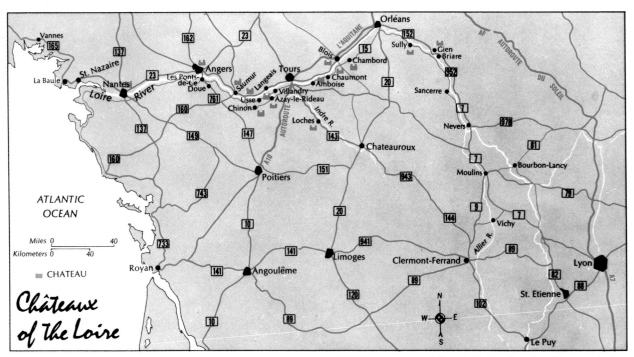

© *Fisher Annotated Travel Guides. Reprinted by permission.*

Mark has decided to rent a car and take his family for an excursion into the French countryside. You may want to rent a car and see the country close up yourself!

(a-zhahns) *(lo-ka-syohn)*
À L'AGENCE DE LOCATION DE VOITURES
At the Car Rental Office

MARC **Bonjour, Monsieur. Je voudrais**   Good morning, Sir. I would like

(loo-ay)

  louer une voiture.   to rent a car.

rent

                         (tahn)

L'EMPLOYÉ **Pour combien de temps?**   For how long?

         (suh-mehn)

MARC **Deux semaines. Ça coûte combien?**   Two weeks. How much does that cost?

     (vwa-yohn)   *(pŭh zhoh)*

L'EMPLOYÉ **Voyons . . . Une Peugeot**   Let's see . . . A Peugeot

pour deux semaines;	for two weeks;
trois cent cinq euros, *(eh-sahns)* *(a-sew-rahns)* *(kohn-preez)* essence et assurance comprises.	305 euros, gas and insurance included.
(pay-yay) *(plews)* Vous payez en plus une taxe *(poor-sahn)* de trente-trois pour cent.	You also pay a tax of 33%.

MARC **C'est cher. Est-ce que vous avez** — That's expensive. Do you have

une **voiture plus petite?** — a smaller car?

(ruh-noh)
L'EMPLOYÉ **Oui, une Renault: deux** — Yes, a Renault:

cent treize euros. — 213 euros.

(kee-lo-may-trahzh)
MARC **Est-ce que le kilométrage est** — Is the mileage included?
(kohn-pree)
compris?

(mehm)
MARIE (à elle-même) **Comme il est avare!** — How stingy he is!
to herself

(a-lay) *(ay-trahn-zhay)*
L'EMPLOYÉ **Oui. Allez-vous à l'étranger?** — Yes. Are you going abroad?
(a-lohn)
MARC **Non. Nous allons voir les Châteaux** — No. We are going to see the castles

de la Loire. — of the Loire valley.

(ram-nay)
L'EMPLOYÉ **Allez-vous ramener la voiture** — Are you going to bring the car back

à Paris? — to Paris?

(pro-bah-bluh-mahn) (see-nohn)
MARC **Probablement. Sinon, est-ce que** — Probably. If not,

nous pouvons la laisser à votre agence — can we leave it at your agency
(or-lay-ahn)
à Orléans ? — in Orléans?

(byan) (sewr)
L'EMPLOYÉ **Bien sûr.** — Of course.

(mohn-tray)
MARC **Pouvez-vous me montrer comment** — Can you show me how

(vee-tehs)
marchent le changement de vitesse et — the gear shift and the
(far)
les phares? — lights work?

L'EMPLOYÉ	*(na-tew-rehl-mahn)* **Naturellement. Voilà la clé et** **les papiers de la voiture. Je viens avec** *(vyan)* **vous.**	Of course. Here are the key and the car's papers. I'm coming with you.
PAUL	*(dyūh)* *(kohn-dweer)* **Mon Dieu! Il va conduire une** *(oh-toh-ma-teek)* **voiture non automatique!** *(koo-rahzh)* **Courage, Anne!**	My God! He is going to drive a nonautomatic car! Be brave, Anne!

Pretend that you wish to rent a car. How would you respond to these questions and statements based on the dialogue?

Vous: Je voudrais louer une voiture.
L'employé: Pour combien de temps?

1. Vous: _____
    L'employé: Quelle voiture prenez-vous?

2. Vous: _____
    L'employé: Ça coûte trois cent cinq euros.

3. Vous: _____
    L'employé: Allez-vous à l'étranger?

4. Vous: _____
    L'employé: Òu allez-vous ramener la voiture?

5. Vous: _____
    L'employé: Bon. Merci. Voici les clés de la voiture.

ANSWERS

Dialogue **1.** Pour deux semaines. **2.** Une Peugeot. **3.** C'est cher. **4.** Non. Nous allons voir les Châteaux de la Loire. **5.** à Orléans.

The procedure for renting a car in France and other European countries is the same as in the U.S. You can rent the car on a daily, weekly, two-week or monthly basis. The insurance is usually included but there is a 33% tax. If you rent from the larger companies, you can drop the car off at another location at no extra charge. As in the U.S., smaller cars are less expensive.

(a-lay)   *(vuh-neer)*

Aller et venir
To go and to come

While traveling, you will do a lot of "coming" and "going." Study carefully these two very important irregular verbs.

ALLER	VENIR
je **vais** *(vay)*	je **viens** *(vyan)*
tu **vas** *(va)*	tu **viens**
il, elle, on **va** *(va)*	il, elle, on **vient** *(vyan)*
nous **allons** *(a-lohn)*	nous **venons** *(vuh-nohn)*
vous **allez** *(a-lay)*	vous **venez** *(vuh-nay)*
ils, elles **vont** *(vohn)*	ils, elles **viennent** *(vyehn)*

ALLER is also used when inquiring about somebody's health:

(ko-mahn)   *(ta-lay) (voo)*
Comment allez-vous?   How are you? How do you feel?

Je vais
- **très bien, merci.**   Very well, thank you.
- **pas mal, merci.**   Not bad, thank you.
- **assez bien, merci.**   Fairly well, thank you.
- *(kom)*   *(see) (kom)*   *(sa)*
  comme-ci comme-ça, merci.   So-so, thank you.
- **mal, merci.**   Not well, thank you.

Et vous?   And you?

Try to answer the questions:

1. Comment allez-vous?

Je_____

2. Comment va votre mère?

Elle_____

3. Comment va votre mari?

Il_____

(ahn-fahn)
4. Comment vont vos enfants?
children

Ils_____

A simple way of expressing an idea in the future is to use **ALLER** + infinitive:
> **Je vais prendre un bateau-mouche.** I'm going to take a bateau-mouche.

In the negative, **NE** and **PAS** are around the conjugated form of **ALLER**:
> **Je ne vais pas prendre de bateau-mouche.** I'm not going to take a bateau-mouche.

With reflexive verbs, the reflexive pronoun comes before the infinitive:
> **Je vais me lever.** I'm going to get up.

And with negative reflexive constructions, **NE** and **PAS** are around the conjugated form of **ALLER**:
> **Je ne vais pas me lever.** I'm not going to get up.

ANSWERS

Verb ALLER (for health) 1. Je vais bien, merci. (et vous?) 2. Elle va . . . 3. Il va . . . 4. Ils vont . . .

Quelques expressions essentielles

(e-sahn-syehl)

Some essential expressions

(pehr-dew)

Je suis perdu(e).　　　　　　　　　　　I am lost.

(ga-rahzh)

Est-ce qu'il y a un garage près d'ici?　　Is there a garage near here?

Qu'est-ce qu'il y a?　　　　　　　　　What's the matter?

(seer-kew-la-syohn)

Il y a beaucoup de circulation.　　　　There is a lot of traffic.

(ray-zohn)

Vous avez raison.　　　　　　　　　　You are right.

(tor)

Vous avez tort.　　　　　　　　　　　You are wrong.

(deesk)

le disque　　　　　　　　　　　　　　the disk (record)

(pehr-mee)　(kohn-dweer)

le permis de conduire　　　　　　　　driver's license

(eh-sahns)

l'essence　　　　　　　　　　　　　　gasoline

(kwan)

au coin de　　　　　　　　　　　　　at the corner of

(boo)

au bout de　　　　　　　　　　　　　at the end of

(nor)

le nord　　　　　　　　　　　　　　　north

(sewd)

le sud　　　　　　　　　　　　　　　south

(lehst)

l'est　　　　　　　　　　　　　　　　east

(loo-ehst)

l'ouest　　　　　　　　　　　　　　　west

(no)　(rehst)

le nord-est, etc.　　　　　　　　　　northeast, etc.

(fūh)

Les feux　　　　　　　　　　　　　　traffic lights

(zohn) (blūh)*

la zone bleue　　　　　　　　　　　　the blue zone

* In large cities, you get *un disque* which enables you to park in the blue zone (downtown).

LA SIGNALISATION ROUTIÈRE

(see-nya-lee-za-syohn) *(roo-tyehr)*

Road Signs

If you're planning to drive while you're abroad, spend some time memorizing the meanings of these signs.

Dangerous intersection

Danger!

Stop

Speed Limit
(in km/hr)

Minimum
Speed

End of limited
Speed

No Entrance

Yield right-of-way

Two-way
traffic

Dangerous curve

Entrance to expressway

Expressway Exit
(road narrows)

Customs

No Passing

End of
No Passing Zone

One-way Street

Detour

Road Closed

Parking

No Parking
(or waiting)

Roundabout

No Parking

No Parking
(or waiting)

No Cyclists

Pedestrian Crossing

Railroad Crossing
(no gate)

Guarded Railroad
Crossing

À LA STATION SERVICE
At the Service Station

CHARTRES

Ballay (R. Noël)	**AY** 3
Bois-Merrain (R. du)	**AZ** 5
Changes (R. des)	**BY** 14
Delacroix (R.)	**AZ** 27
Guillaume (R. Porte)	**CY** 41
Marceau (Pl.)	**BY** 49
Marceau (R.)	**BY** 50
Soleil-d'Or (R. du)	**BY** 70
Alsace-Lorraine (R. d')	**AX** 2
Beauce (Av. Jehan de)	**AY** 4
Bourg (R. du)	**BY** 6

Bourgneuf (R. du)	**BX** 7
Brèche (R. de la)	**BX** 10
Cardinal-Pie (R. du)	**BY** 12
Casanova (R. Danièle)	**AY** 13
Châtelet (Pl.)	**AY** 16
Chauveau-Lagarde (R.)	**AZ** 17
Cheval-Blanc (R. du)	**AY** 18
Clemenceau (R.)	**CY** 20
Collin-d'Harleville (R.)	**AY** 23
Couronne (R. de la)	**AY** 24
Cygne (R. du)	**BY** 26
Drouaise (R. Porte)	**BX** 29
Écuyers (R. des)	**BY** 30
Épars (Pl. des)	**AZ** 32

Félibien (R.)	**AY** 33
Ferrière (R. de)	**CY** 35
Foulerie (R. de la)	**CY** 36
Grenets (R. des)	**BY** 37
Guillaume (R. du Fg)	**CY** 39
Koenig (R .du Gén.)	**AY** 44
Leclerc (R. Mar.)	**AZ** 45
Lelong (R. Gabriel)	**AZ** 47
Massacre (R. au)	**BY** 51
Morard (Pl.)	**CY** 52
Moulin (Pl. Jean)	**ABY** 53
Muret (R.)	**BY** 55
Pasteur (Pl.)	**BZ** 56
Resistance (Bd de la)	**AY** 61
St-Aignan (⊞)	**BY**
St-André (⊞)	**BY** B
St-Maurice (. R.)	**BX** 64
St-Michel (R.)	**BZ** 65
St-Pierre (⊞)	**CZ** Y
Sémard (Pl. Pierre)	**AY** 67
Tannerie (R. de la)	**BY** 71
14 Juillet (R. du)	**AZ** 72

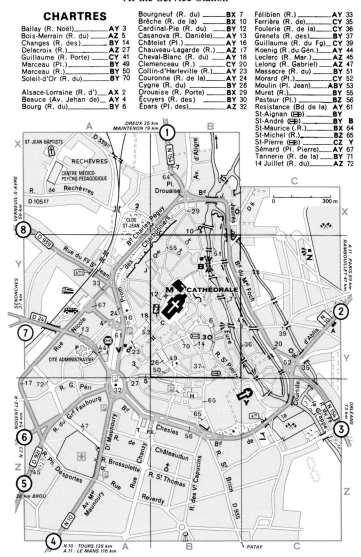

From Michelin Guide, Environs de Paris, *20th Edition. Reprinted with permission.*

	(fehr)	
MARC	**Pardon. Pourriez-vous faire le**	Excuse me. Could you
	(plan)	
	plein?	fill 'er up?
	(or-dee-nehr) *(sew-pehr)*	
LE POMPISTE	**Ordinaire ou super?**	Regular or super?
gas pump attendant		
MARC	**Ordinaire. Et pourriez-vous aussi**	Regular. And could you also
	(vay-ree-fyay) (preh-syohn) (pnūh)	
	vérifier la pression des pneus, et le	check the tire pressure and the
	(weel) *(oh)*	
	niveau d'huile et d'eau?	level of the oil and water?

89

	(ah) (nordr)	
LE POMPISTE	**Tout est en ordre.**	Everything is okay.

	(ka-tay-drahl)	
MARC	**Nous allons a la Cathédrale de**	We are going to the Chartres Cathedral.

(shahrtr)

Chartres. Quelle est la route la plus   Which is the shortest

(koort)

courte?   way?

LE POMPISTE   **Regardez. Vous êtes ici. Allez**   Look. You are here. Go

(drwah)   *(gohsh)*

tout droit, tournez à gauche, puis à   straight ahead, turn left, then

(swee-vay)   *(ay-kree-toh)*

droite. Ensuite suivez les écriteaux.   right. Then follow the signs.

Now write these important words and phrases from the dialogue.

1. Could you fill 'er up? _____

2. Could you also check the level of the oil and the water? _____

_____

3. Everything is O.K. _____

4. Which is the shortest way? _____

5. To the left _____

6. To the right _____

7. Follow the signs. _____

ANSWERS

Dialogue
1. Pourriez-vous faire le plein?   2. Pourriez-vous aussi vérifier le niveau d'huile et d'eau?   3. Tout est en ordre.   4. Quelle est la route la plus courte?   5. A gauche   6. A droite   7. Suivez les écriteaux.

LA VOITURE
(L'AUTOMOBILE)

(vwa-tewr)

The Car

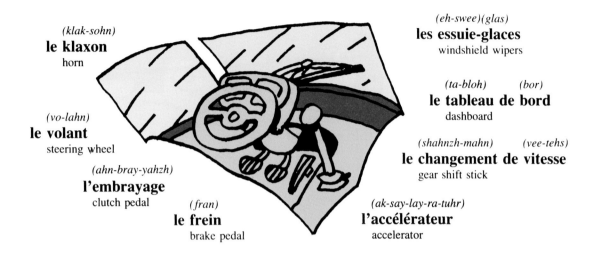

(klak-sohn)
le klaxon
horn

(vo-lahn)
le volant
steering wheel

(ahn-bray-yahzh)
l'embrayage
clutch pedal

(fran)
le frein
brake pedal

(eh-swee)(glas)
les essuie-glaces
windshield wipers

(ta-bloh)   *(bor)*
le tableau de bord
dashboard

(shahnzh-mahn)   *(vee-tehs)*
le changement de vitesse
gear shift stick

(ak-say-lay-ra-tuhr)
l'accélérateur
accelerator

(par) *(breez)*
le pare-brise
windshield

(mo-tuhr)
le moteur
motor

(ra-dya-tuhr)
le radiateur
radiator

(ka-poh)
le capot
hood

(ba-tree)
la batterie
battery

(fahr)
les phares
headlights

(ruh-kewl)
le phare de recul
backup light

(klee-nyo-tahn)
le clignotant
directional signal

(stop)
le stop
brakelight

(kofr)
le coffre
trunk

(lew-neht)
la lunette
rear window

(fūh) (a-ryehr)
le feu arrière
rear light

(plak)   *(ee-ma-tree-kew-la-syon)*
la plaque d'immatriculation
license plate

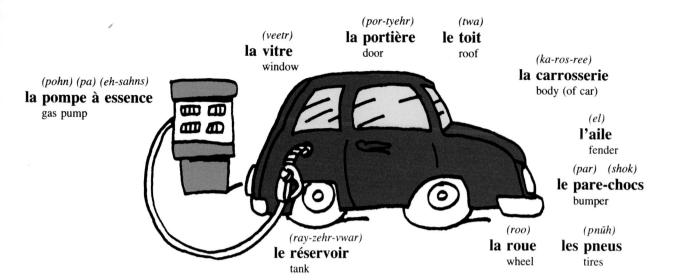

(pohn) (pa) (eh-sahns)
la pompe à essence
gas pump

(veetr)
la vitre
window

(por-tyehr)
la portière
door

(twa)
le toit
roof

(ka-ros-ree)
la carrosserie
body (of car)

(el)
l'aile
fender

(par) (shok)
le pare-chocs
bumper

(ray-zehr-vwar)
le réservoir
tank

(roo)
la roue
wheel

(pnūh)
les pneus
tires

Now fill in the names for the following auto parts.

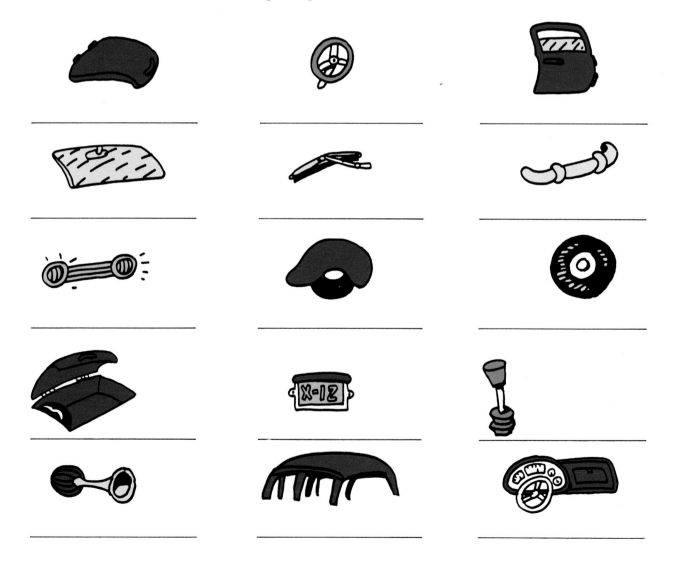

Quelques expressions utiles en cas de difficulté

(ew-teel)   *(kah)*   *(dee-fee-kewl-tay)*

Some phrases useful in case of problems

(meh-day)
Pouvez-vous m'aider?

Can you help me?

(kruh-vay)
J'ai un pneu crevé.

I have a flat tire.

(pan)
Ma voiture est en panne.

My car has broken down.

(day-mar)
Ma voiture ne démarre pas.

My car won't start.

Je suis en panne d'essence.

I've run out of gas.

(marsh)
Mes freins ne marchent pas.

My brakes don't work.

Ma voiture chauffe.

My car is overheating.

(ra-tay)
Mon moteur fait des ratés.

My engine is misfiring.

(day-pah-nūhz)
J'ai besoin d'une dépanneuse.

I need a tow truck.

(kool)
Le radiateur coule.

The radiator is leaking.

(trahns-mee-syohn)   *(kah-say)*
La transmission est cassée.

The transmission is broken.

(pla)
La batterie est à plat.

The battery is dead.

(klee-nyo-tahn)
Les clignotants ne marchent pas.

The signal lights don't work.

(weel)
L'huile coule.

The oil is leaking.

(klee-ma-tee-za-syohn)
La climatisation (le chauffage) ne

The air conditioning (heater)

marche pas.

doesn't work.

93

Fill in the blanks by referring to the dialogue and these new expressions.

1. Je voudrais _____ une voiture.
   to rent

2. Pourriez-vous _____ _____ _____ , s'il vous plaît?
   fill 'er up

3. Mes freins ne _____ pas.
   work

4. Quelle est la route la plus _____ ?
   short

5. Est-ce qu'il y a un _____ près d'ici?
   garage

(fehr)
Faire
To do, to make

Now, here is another common—and irregular—verb:

FAIRE			
je ⟍ *(fay)*		I	do, make
tu ⟋ **fais**		you	do, make
il ⟍ *(fay)*		he ⟍	
elle → **fait**		she →	does, makes
on ⟋		it ⟋	
nous	*(fuh-zohn)* **faisons**	we	do, make
vous	*(feht)* **faites**	you	do, make
ils ⟍	*(fohn)* **font**	they	do, make
elles ⟋			

Fill in the correct form of the verb FAIRE.

1. Je _____ la liste.

2. Que _____-vous?

3. Nous _____ une promenade.

4. Qu'est-ce qu'il _____ ?

5. Elles _____ la queue.
   line

ANSWERS

FAIRE 1. fais 2. faites 3. faisons 4. fait 5. font

Fill in the blanks 1. louer 2. faire le plein 3. marchent 4. courte 5. garage

94

Si vous voulez donner des ordres . . .

If you want to give orders . . .

In order to get people to do things for you, you will have to know how to use verbs in a "command" or "imperative" way. The following chart shows you how to form the imperative of regular verbs. Just keep in mind that the subject of a command is "YOU" (understood). So, simply use the TU form of the verb to be familiar and the VOUS form to be polite, without using the subject pronouns.

THE IMPERATIVE

	Parler	**Finir**	**Attendre**
Familiar	**Parle***	**Finis**	**Attends**
Polite	**Parlez**	**Finissez**	**Attendez**

*Drop the final -s from the "TU" form for -er verbs only.

To say "Let's," use the NOUS form command:

> **Parlons!**   Let's speak!
> **Finissons!**   Let's finish!
> **Attendons!**   Let's wait!

ÊTRE and **AVOIR** have irregular command forms:

	Être	**Avoir**
Familiar	**Sois**	**Aie**
Polite	**Soyez**	**Ayez**
(NOUS)	**Soyons**	**Ayons**

Don't get discouraged. With a little practice, you will become familiar and quite proficient with these verb forms. To make a command negative, put **NE** before the verb and **PAS** after the verb:

> **Ne parlez pas!**   Don't speak!
> **Ne finis pas!**   Don't finish!
> **N'attendons pas.**   Let's not wait.

Now try the following. You are speaking to a person you meet in your travels. Tell him the following:

1. (speak) _____ anglais.

2. (wait for) _____-moi.

3. (finish) _____ vite.
   quickly

4. (be) _____ prudent.

5. (have) _____ _____ du courage.

ANSWERS

Commands   1. Parlez 2. Attendez 3. Finissez 4. Soyez 5. Ayez

Attention! (Watch out!) Driving in a foreign country means watching the road even when the scenery is breathtaking. **Très beau!** Yes, very beautiful! Read the following passage and determine what happened on the trip. Then answer the questions.

(ak-see-dahn)

UN ACCIDENT
An Accident

PREMIER CHAUFFEUR **Sacrebleu! Vous ne** *(sakr-blŭh)*	For heaven's sake! Can't
pouvez pas faire attention? Vous êtes *(a-tahn-syohn)*	you be careful? Are you
aveugle? J'ai la priorité! *(a-vŭhgl) (ay)*	blind? I have the right of way!
DEUXIÈME CHAUFFEUR **Je le sais! Mais** *(say)*	I know! But
vous faites du 150 kilomètres à l'heure	you are driving at 150 km per hour
et la limite de vitesse est 60 kilomètres speed	and the speed limit is 60 km
à l'heure!	per hour!
TROISIÈME CHAUFFEUR **Est-ce que je peux**	May I help you?
vous aider?	
PREMIER CHAUFFEUR **Oui. Demandez à**	Yes. Ask
l'agent là-bas de venir examiner les *(ehg-za-mee-nay)*	the policeman over there to come and look at the
dégâts. *(day-gah)*	damage.
L'AGENT **Qu'est-ce qui se passe?**	What's happening?

	(ee-dyoh) (tahn-po-nay)	
PREMIER CHAUFFEUR	**Cet idiot a tamponné**	This idiot hit
	ma voiture. Il a tort.	my car. He is in the wrong.
	(vreh)	
DEUXIÈME CHAUFFEUR	**Ce n'est pas vrai.**	It's not true.
	(teep) *(foo)*	
	Ce type conduit comme un fou.	This guy drives like a madman.
	(troh) (veet)	
	Il est allé trop vite.	He was speeding.
	(pehr-son) *(bleh-say)*	
L'AGENT	**Personne n'est blessé? Bon. Vos**	Nobody is hurt? Good. Your
	permis de conduire, s'il vous plaît.	driver's licenses, please.
	(au deuxième chauffeur): Est-ce que	(To the second driver): Is this
	c'est une voiture de location?	a rented car?
DEUXIÈME CHAUFFEUR	**Oui.**	Yes.
	(foh) (prayv-neer)	
L'AGENT	**Alors il faut prévenir l'agence et**	Then it's necessary to notify the agency and
	(kohn-pa-nyee) (a-sew-rahns)	
	aussi votre compagnie d'assurance.	also your insurance company.
DEUXIÈME CHAUFFEUR	**Est-ce qu'il y a un**	Is there a
	garage près d'ici?	garage near here?
	(pro-shen)	
L'AGENT	**Oui, au coin de la prochaine**	Yes, at the corner of the next
	(ee)	
	route. Vous pouvez y aller à pied.	road. You can walk there.

(Au garage)

DEUXIÈME CHAUFFEUR	**Est-ce que vous**	Could you repair
	(ray-pa-ray)	
	pourriez réparer vite ma voiture?	my car quickly?
	Je suis touriste.	I am a tourist.
	(may-ka-nee-syan) *(shahns)*	
LE MÉCANICIEN	**Vous avez de la chance.**	You are lucky.
	(vwah-lay)	
	La roue arrière est voilée et le	The rear wheel is bent and the
	(ka-bo-say)	
	pare-choc est cabossé, c'est tout.	bumper is dented, that's all.
	Téléphonez demain après-midi.	Telephone tomorrow afternoon.

Mon numéro est quarante quatre　　　My number is 44-51-17.

cinquante-et-un dix-sept.

DEUXIÈME CHAUFFEUR　**Merci mille fois. (à**　　　Many thanks. (to himself):
　　　　　(kohn-dewk-tühr)
lui-même): Ah, les conducteurs　　　Ah, the French drivers!

français!

Circle the statements which might be appropriate if you had a car accident in France:

1. Je voudrais faire le plein.

2. Demandez à l'agent de venir examiner les dégâts.

3. Je voudrais louer une voiture.

4. Votre permis de conduire, s'il vous plaît.

5. Est-ce qu'il y a un garage près d'ici?

6. Je cherche une agence de location.

Should you get into an accident, do the same things you would do in this country: get the name, address and telephone number of the other person. If you are traveling in a rented car, notify the rental agency. Ask someone to notify the police and, if necessary, to call an ambulance. If it's a minor accident and both persons can drive away, be especially careful to have all the information needed by the insurance company. And try to keep calm!

ANSWERS

Circle statements　2, 4, 5.

(nay-seh-sehr)
LE NÉCESSAIRE
Essentials

(mat-la) *(pnüh-ma-teek)*	*(a-bee)*	*(bwaht)* *(kohn-sehrv)*	*(pa-gay)*
le matelas pneumatique	**les habits**	**les boîtes de conserve**	**les pagaies**
air mattress	clothes	cans	paddles

(koo-vehr-tewr)	*(tahnt)*	*(arbr)*	*(soh-leh-y)*	*(rwee-soh)*
la couverture	**la tente**	**un arbre**	**le soleil**	**le ruisseau**
blanket	tent	tree	sun	brook

(sak) (duh) (koo-shahzh)	*(lahnp) (duh) (posh)*	*(pa-nyay)*	*(bwaht)*	*(ka-noh-ay)*
le sac de couchage	**la lampe de poche**	**un panier**	**une boîte**	**le canoé**
sleeping bag	flashlight	basket	box	canoe

(soh)	*(kan)* *(pehsh)*	*(teer) (boo-shohn)*	*(ews-tahn-seel)* *(kwee-zeen)*
un seau	**une canne à pêche**	**le tire-bouchon**	**les ustensiles de cuisine**
bucket	rod	fishing	corkscrew	cooking utensils

(bot)	*(ar-teekl)* *(twa-leht)*	*(tehr-mohs)*	*(ra-dyoh) (por-ta-teev)*	*(a-lew-meht)*
des bottes	**les articles de toilette**	**le thermos**	**la radio portative**	**des allumettes**
boots	toilet articles		portable radio	matches

If you are planning to go camping in France, a good idea would be to get hold of the *Michelin Guide to Camping and Caravaning*, available in many American bookstores. Conditions and regulations vary from region to region. In general, they are similar to those in the U.S. Road signs tell you which camping grounds are for tents only, for vans only or for both.

In many cities, a good source of information is the Syndicat d'Initiative, the local Tourism Office. If your first stop is Paris, you can go to the Fédération Française de Camping et Caravaning, 78 rue de Rivoli, Paris 75004.

EN ROUTE POUR LE TERRAIN DE CAMPING
(root) *(teh-ran)*

On the Way to the Campground

Now read the following dialogues, which contain some useful words, expressions, and information on camping. Read them aloud, repeating each line several times, so you know how to pronounce the new words.

MARC **Excusez-moi, Monsieur. Est-ce que**
    (poo-ryohn)   *(kahn-pay)*
nous pourrions peut-être camper sur
    (pro-pree-yay-tay)
votre propriété?

Excuse me, Sir.

Could we perhaps camp on

your property?

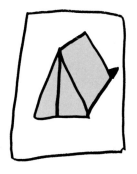

LE FERMIER **Je suis désolé, mais c'est**
(fehr-myay)
farmer
    (tan-po-seebl)   *(kahn-puhr)*
impossible. Les campeurs font trop de
    (ko-shon-ree)
cochonneries.

I am sorry, but it's

impossible. Campers make

too much of a mess.

MARC **Je comprends. Est-ce qu'il y a un**

terrain de camping près d'ici?

I understand. Is there a

campground near here?

LE FERMIER **Oui. À vingt kilomètres.**
    (pa-noh)   *(see-nya-lee-za-syohn)*
Suivez les panneaux de signalisation.
    (mee-lyūh)
Il y a une tente au milieu.

Yes. Twenty kilometers from here.

Follow the signs.

There is a tent in the middle of the signs.

MARC **Savez-vous s'il y a des douches?**

Do you know if there are showers?

LE FERMIER **Pas la moindre idée.**
    (mwandr)   *(ee-day)*

On va vous le dire au camping.
    (pray-fay-ray)
Ou si vous préférez, vous pouvez vous
    (a-reh -tay)   *(san-dee-ka) (dee-nee-sya-teev)*
arrêter au Syndicat d'Initiative au
    (mee-lyūh)   *(vee-lahzh)*
milieu du village.

Not the slightest idea.

They'll tell you at the campground.

Or if you prefer, you can

stop at the Tourist Office in

the middle of the village.

100

SUR LE TERRAIN DE CAMPING
(teh-ran)

At the Campground

MARC   **Est-ce que vous avez de la place**   Do you have room
(plas)

     pour nous?   for us?

LE DIRECTEUR   **Oui. Combien de temps**   Yes. How long
(dee-rek-tühr)   *(tahn)*
manager

     comptez-vous rester?   are you planning to stay?
(kohn-tay)   *(rehs-tay)*

MARC   **Deux ou trois nuits. Est-ce qu'il y**   Two or three nights. Are there
(nwee)

     a des douches?   any showers?

DIRECTEUR   **Oui.**   Yes.

ANNE   **Ouf! Je vais pouvoir me laver la**   Oh! I am going to be able to wash
(oof)

     tête.   my hair!
(teht)

MARC   **C'est combien par jour?**   How much is it per day?

DIRECTEUR   **Pour quatre personnes,**   For four people, 25 euros.

     vingt-cinq euros. Il y a l'électricité dans   There is electricity in
(ay-lehk-tree-see-tay)

     le bâtiment principal. Le soir, la   the main building. In the evening, the
(pran-see-pal)   *(swar)*

     discothèque est ouverte à partir de   discothèque is open from
(dees-ko-tehk)   *(oo-vehrt)*   *(a)*   *(par-teer)*
open

     vingt et une heures.   9 P.M. on.

Fill in the missing word in French:

1. Est-ce qu'il y a _____ près d'ici?
                a campground

2. Savez-vous s'il y a des _____?
                showers

3. Vous pouvez vous arrêter au _____.
                tourist office

4. Combien de temps comptez-vous _____?
                to stay

ANSWERS

Fill in   1. un terrain de camping   2. douches   3. syndicat d'initiative   4. rester

101

J'ai besoin de . . .

I need

Study the vocabulary on page 99, then make a list of items you need to go camping.

EX.: **Pour aller camper, j'ai besoin d'une tente, d'un matelas pneumatique, d'allumettes, etc.** (If the noun is plural, you don't need to use an article; only DE or D'.)

The following puzzle contains seven camping terms in addition to the one circled. Try to find these words: boots, bucket, stream, sun, basket, tree, blankets.

```
T  S  C  O  U  V  E  R  T  U  R  E  S
B  E  A  R  B  R  E  U  X  E  T  I  L
O  R  N  I  A  C  O  I  N  S  T  S  I
T  D  T  T  H  S  U  S  V  U  E  N  T
T  R  O  A  E  E  L  S  O  L  E  I  L
E  X  U  N  O  A  A  E  U  Z  N  U  E
S  D  A  V  O  U  I  A  I  N  N  E  M
P  A  N  I  E  R  S  U  R  E  S  O  N
```

(ay-pees-ree)

À L'ÉPICERIE

At the Grocery Store

(leevr) *(noo-y)*	
MARIE **Je voudrais une livre de nouilles,**	I would like a pound of noodles,
(gram) *(buhr)*	
cent grammes de beurre, quatre	100 grams of butter, four
(trahnsh) *(zhahn-bohn)* *(leetr)* *(leh)*	
tranches de jambon, un litre de lait,	slices of ham, one liter of milk,
(sel) *(boo-teh-y)* *(van)*	
du sel et une bouteille de vin rouge	some salt and a bottle of ordinary red wine . . .
ordinaire . . . et aussi une boîte	and also a box
d'allumettes.	of matches.

ANSWERS

Puzzle (Camping) BOTTES SEAU RUISSEAU SOLEIL PANIER ARBRE COUVERTURES

(lay-pee-syehr)   *(kahn-pūhr)*

L'ÉPICIÈRE   **Vous êtes campeurs? Vous**   You are campers? You
fem. grocer
                             (fūh)

savez qu'il est interdit de faire du feu?   know it's forbidden to light fires?
                      (gahz)

MARC   **Oui, nous avons un réchaud à gaz.**   Yes. We have a gas heater.
          (dwa)

MARIE   **Je vous dois combien?**   How much do I owe you?

L'ÉPICIÈRE   **Quatorze euros.**   14 euros.
          (fee-leh)

Vous avez un filet?   Do you have a string bag?

MARIE   **Non.**   No.
       (tahn) *(pee)*

L'ÉPICIÈRE   **Tant pis. Je vais vous trouver**   Never mind. I'm going to find

un sac en papier.   a paper bag for you.

MARC   (à l'épicière)   **Merci. Au revoir,**   Thank you. Good-bye,

Madame. Bonne journée!   Madam! Have a good day!

Match these French expressions with their English equivalents.

1. une livre   a. a slice
2. cent grammes   b. a bottle
3. une tranche   c. a liter
4. un litre   d. 100 grams
5. une bouteille   e. a pound

ANSWERS

Matching   1. e   2. d   3. a   4. c   5. b

Vous avez besoin de savoir les verbes *savoir* et *connaître*

(sa-vwar)   *(ko-nehtr)*

to know   to know

SAVOIR implies acquired knowledge; to know how to do something; to know a fact.

Je sais le français.   I know French.

Je sais où se trouve Paris.   I know where Paris is.

Je sais nager.   I know how to swim.

(meh)
Mais
But

CONNAÎTRE—to know, to be acquainted with, a person, place, or thing.

Je connais Paris.   I know Paris (because I was there).

Je connais Robert.   I know Robert (I have met him).

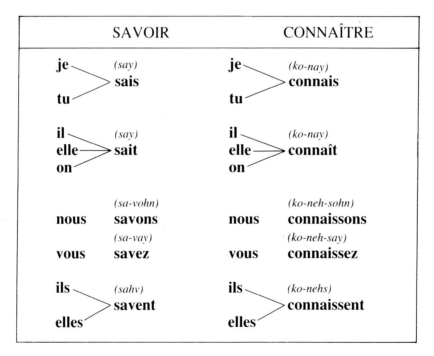

SAVOIR	CONNAÎTRE
je, tu — **sais** *(say)*	je, tu — **connais** *(ko-nay)*
il, elle, on — **sait** *(say)*	il, elle, on — **connaît** *(ko-nay)*
nous **savons** *(sa-vohn)*	nous **connaissons** *(ko-neh-sohn)*
vous **savez** *(sa-vay)*	vous **connaissez** *(ko-neh-say)*
ils, elles — **savent** *(sahv)*	ils, elles — **connaissent** *(ko-nehs)*

To practice the new verbs, fill in the blanks:

1. Je _____ Londres.
   know

2. Tu _____ qui est le
   know
   Président de la République française.

3. Il _____ Brigitte Bardot.
   knows

4. Nous _____ parler français.
   know (how)

ANSWERS

New Verbs   1. connais   2. sais   3. connaît   4. savons

(ko-mahn)   *(dee)*   *(tohn)*

Comment dit-on

How do you say

In English, you say: I am hot, you are hungry, she is cold, he is afraid, we are thirsty, they are sleepy. In French, the tendency is to say I have heat, you have hunger, and so forth.

Ils ont chaud.
They are hot.

(frwah)
Nous avons froid.
We are cold.

(pūhr)
Les garçons ont peur.
The boys are afraid.

(fan)
Le chien a faim.
The dog is hungry.

(ohnt)
Le garçon a honte.
The boy is ashamed.

(so-meh-y)
L'homme a sommeil.
The man is sleepy.

Can you match up the pictures and sentences below?

1. Ils ont froid.
2. La dame a chaud.

3. Il a sommeil
4. Les enfants ont peur.

5. Le garçon a faim.
6. La fille a honte.

a.   b.   c.   d.   e.   f.

ANSWERS

Match up sentences   1. d   2. a   3. f   4. e   5. b   6. c

105

Très bien! (Very good!) Now practice your irregular verbs, some old, some new, and adjective agreement.

1. Je suis ici.

   Tu _____ ici.

   Elle _____ ici.

   On _____ ici.

   Nous _____ ici.

   Vous _____ ici.

   Ils _____ ici.

2. Je ne sais pas.

   Ils ne _____ pas.

   Nous ne _____ pas.

   Vous ne _____ pas.

   On ne _____ pas.

   Il ne _____ pas.

   Tu ne _____ pas.

3. Nous pouvons aller à Paris.

   Je _____ aller à Paris.

   On _____ aller à Paris.

   Vous _____ aller à Paris.

   Elles _____ aller à Paris.

   Il _____ aller à Paris.

4. Vous avez faim.

   J'_____ faim.

   Il _____ faim.

   On _____ faim.

   Nous _____ faim.

   Ils _____ faim.

ANSWERS

Irregular Verbs

1. Tu es
   Elle est
   On est
   Nous sommes
   Vous êtes
   Ils sont

2. Ils ne savent pas
   Nous ne savons pas
   Vous ne savez pas
   On ne sait pas
   Il ne sait pas
   Tu ne sais pas

3. Je peux
   On peut
   Vous pouvez
   Elles peuvent
   Il peut

4. J'ai
   Il a
   On a
   Nous avons
   Ils ont

10

(tahn)   *(seh-zohn)*
Le temps, les saisons,
The Weather,   The Seasons
(mwah)   *(zhoor)*
les mois, et les jours
Months   and   Days

(lee-vehr)
C'EST L'HIVER.
winter

(nehzh)
Il neige.
snows

(vahn)
Il fait du vent.
windy

(frwah)
Il fait froid.
cold

(pran-tahn)
C'EST LE PRINTEMPS.
spring

(freh)
Il fait frais.
cool

(boh)
Il fait beau.
beautiful

(so-leh-y)
Il fait du soleil.
sunny

(ay-tay)
C'EST L'ÉTÉ.
summer

(shoh)
Il fait chaud.
warm

Il fait très chaud.
very hot

(a-vehrs)
Il fait des averses.
showers

(oh-ton)
C'EST L'AUTOMNE.
autumn

(broo-yar)
Il fait du brouillard.
fog

(plüh)
Il pleut.
rains

(zhel)
Il gèle.
freezes

107

(kehl) *(tahn)* *(fay)* *(teel)*

QUEL TEMPS FAIT-IL?

How Is the Weather?

As you noticed, the French don't say "It IS cold." They say "It MAKES cold," *"Il fait froid."*

Il fait

(sew-pehrb)   *(o-reebl)*

. . . **beau**   . . . **un temps superbe**   . . . **chaud**   . . . **un temps horrible**

    (window)

(mehr-veh-yūh)   *(frwah)*   *(a-frūh)*

. . . **un temps merveilleux**   . . . **froid**   . . . **un temps affreux**

marvelous   cold   awful

(ew-meed) *(loor)*

Il fait humide, lourd,   It is humid, heavy,   Note these exceptions:

(o-ra-zhūh)

orageux.   stormy.   **Il neige.**   It is snowing.

(vahn)

Il fait du vent.   It is windy.   **Il pleut.**   It is raining.

(vers)

Il pleut à verse.   It is pouring.

Can you describe the weather in the pictures below?

 1. Il fait _____   2. _____

 3. _____   4. _____

ANSWERS

Weather   1. un temps merveilleux   2. Il fait chaud.   3. Il neige.   4. Il fait un temps horrible.

108

Il fait clair.
light

(klehr)

(ma-tan)
C'est le matin.
morning

Il fait jour.
day

(sohnbr)
Il fait un peu sombre.

(a-preh-mee-dee)
C'est l'après-midi.
afternoon

Il fait sombre.

(swar)
C'est le soir.
evening

(nwee)
Il fait nuit.
dark

C'est la nuit.
night

ANNE   **Quelle heure est-il?**   What time is it?

SUZANNE   **Sept heures et demie.**   7:30.

ANNE   **Déjà? Quel**   Already? What's

   temps fait-il?   the weather like?

(ma-nee-feek)   *(luh-vay)*
SUZANNE   **Magnifique! Quel lever du**   Magnificent! What a sunrise!
(may-tay-oh) *(a-nohns)*
   soleil! La météo annonce: The weather forecast is:
     weather   report

(doo)
   "Cet après-midi, temps beau et doux.   "Beautiful, mild weather this afternoon.
       mild

109

Température entre quinze et dix-huit
(ahntr)
between

Temperature between 15 and 18°C.

degrés centigrades. Ce soir, nuageux
(duh-gray)   *(new-a-zhūh)*
cloudy

This evening, cloudy

à couvert avec baisse de température.
(behs)   *(tahn-pay-ra-tewr)*
lowering

and overcast with temperatures dropping.

Mercredi, partiellement couvert.
(par-syehl-mahn)
partially

Wednesday, partly cloudy.

Température entre dix-sept

Temperatures between 17

et vingt degrés centigrades.''

and 20°C.''

ANNE   **Levons-nous! J'ai faim!**

Let's get up! I am hungry!

Choose the correct answer:

1. Cet après-midi, il va faire
   A. très chaud   B. très froid
   C. mauvais   D. beau

2. C'est la météo pour un jour
   A. d'août   B. de janvier
   C. de février   D. d'avril

Temperature conversions

Centigrade   Degrés   Fahrenheit

Thermomètre

To change Fahrenheit to Centigrade: Subtract 32 and multiply by $\frac{5}{9}$.

To change Centigrade to Fahrenheit: Multiply by $\frac{9}{5}$ and add 32.

ANSWERS

Multiple choice   1. D   2. D

110

(ka-lahn-dree-yay)

LE CALENDRIER

The Calendar

(mwah)

THE MONTHS OF THE YEAR–LES MOIS DE L'ANNEE

(zhahn-vyay)	*(ah-vreel)*	*(zhwee-yeh)*	*(ok-tobr)*
janvier	**avril**	**juillet**	**octobre**
January	April	July	October
(fay-vree-yay)	*(may)*	*(oot)*	*(no-vahnbr)*
février	**mai**	**août**	**novembre**
February	May	August	November
(mars)	*(zhwan)*	*(sehp-tahnbr)*	*(day-sahnbr)*
mars	**juin**	**septembre**	**décembre**
March	June	September	December

(suh-men)

THE DAYS OF THE WEEK–LES JOURS DE LA SEMAINE

(dee-mahnsh)	*(luhn-dee)*	*(mar-dee)*	*(mehr-kruh-dee)*	*(zhuh-dee)*	*(vahn-druh-dee)*	*(sam-dee)*
dimanche	**lundi**	**mardi**	**mercredi**	**jeudi**	**vendredi**	**samedi**
Sunday	Monday	Tuesday	Wednesday	Thursday	Friday	Saturday

Si c'est mardi, je dois

(vee-zeet)
rendre visite à ma mère, parce que

pay a visit
le Mardi, je vais toujours visiter ma

mère.

If it's Tuesday, I must

pay a visit to my mother, because

I always go to visit my mother

on Tuesdays.

Use LE with days of the week when describing a habit, but if you want to say, "On Tuesday,

(this particular Tuesday) I am going to visit my mother," it is **Mardi, je vais rendre visite
à mère.**

(ehk-spree-may) *(dat)*

Comment exprimer la date

How to express the date

To express the date in French use:

LE + number + month + year

C'est le six avril mille neuf cent quatre-vingt-cinq (1985)
It is

Use this formula to express all dates, except for the first of the month:

C'est le premier mai.

first

111

La fête nationale *(feht)*
américaine est
le 4 juillet.

La fête nationale
française est
le 14 juillet.

(noh-ehl)
Noël est
le 25 décembre.

Pâques est
en avril.

La Saint-Sylvestre
est le trente-et-un
décembre.

La fête nationale suisse est le premier août.   **La fête nationale belge est le 21 juillet.**

Comment exprimer les mois
How to express the months

Use EN with months to express "in":

En janvier, je fais du ski.   In January, I ski.

With seasons, use AU before a consonant. Use EN before a vowel to express "in the":

au printemps, en été, en automne, en hiver.

Complete the following sentences, using the correct form:

(oh-zhoor-dwee)
1. Quel jour est-ce aujourd'hui?
   today

   C'est _____

2. Quelle est la date?

   C'est _____

(a-nee-vehr-sehr)
3. Quelle est la date de votre anniversaire?

   C'est _____

4. Quand est la fête nationale française?

   C'est _____

5. Quand est la fête nationale américaine?

   C'est _____

ANSWERS

Date   **1.** C'est aujourd'hui lundi. (example)   **2.** C'est aujourd'hui le onze juillet. (example)   **3.** C'est le douze janvier. (example)   **4.** C'est le quatorze juillet.   **5.** C'est le quatre juillet.

(ad-zhehk-teef)
Les adjectifs
Adjectives

Throughout your trip you will notice many wonderful things that you will want to describe.
In order to do this, you will have to know how to use French adjectives.
Adjectives agree in gender (masculine or feminine) and number (singular or plural) with the nouns they modify.

In most instances, add ⬛ **–E** to the masculine form of the adjective to obtain the

corresponding feminine form:

<table>
<tr><td>un garçon intelligent</td><td>une fille intelligente</td></tr>
<tr><td>un dîner parfait</td><td>une maison parfaite</td></tr>
</table>

<table>
<tr><td>LE DÎNER EST . . .</td><td>(noo-ree-tewr)
LA NOURRITURE EST . . .
food</td></tr>
<tr><td>Masculine</td><td>Feminine</td></tr>
</table>

Masculine	Feminine
(preh) **prêt** ready	*(preht)* **prête**

| *(loor)* **lourd** heavy | *(loord)* **lourde** |

| *(par-feh)* **parfait** perfect | *(par-feht)* **parfaite** |

If the masculine form of the adjective already ends in $-E$, add nothing to obtain the feminine form.

More examples.

MON HÔTEL EST . . .
My Hotel Is . . .

(shahnbr)
MA CHAMBRE EST . . .
My Room Is . . .

Masculine   **Feminine**

(brwee-yahn)   *(brwee-yahnt)*
bruyant   **bruyante**
noisy

(klehr)   *(klehr)*
clair   **claire**
bright

(grahn)   *(grahnd)*
grand   **grande**
big

(puh-tee)   *(puh-teet)*
petit   **petite**
small

BUT

(sahl)   *(sahl)*
sale   **sale**
dirty

(pūh) (kohn-for-tahbl)   *(pūh) (kohn-for-tahbl)*
peu confortable   **peu confortable**
not very comfortable

When a masculine adjective ends in $-É$, the adjective is considered regular. The feminine form, therefore, is simply obtained by adding another $-E$: *(ahn-shan-tay)* **enchanté, enchantée.**
delighted

JE SUIS
I am . . .

Masculine		Feminine

(sa-tees-fay)
satisfait
satisfied

(sa-tees-feht)
satisfaite

(kohn-tahn)
content
pleased, glad

(kohn-tahnt)
contente

(puh-tee)
petit
small

(puh-teet)
petite

(zho-lee)
joli
pretty,
handsome

(zho-lee)
jolie
pretty

AND

(fa-tee-gay)
fatigué
tired

fatiguée

(fa-shay)
fâché
angry

fâchée

Masculine		Feminine

Masculine   **Feminine**

(a-zhay)
âgé   **âgée**
old

(ee-ree-tay)
irrité   **irritée**
annoyed

(poor) (shahn-zhay)(oh) (plew-ryehl)
Pour changer au pluriel
To change to the plural

Add −**S** to the masculine or feminine singular form of the adjective to obtain the corresponding plural forms of most adjectives. Add nothing to form the plural of an adjective that ends in −**S** or −**X**. The −**AL** ending of a masculine singular adjective becomes −**AUX** in the plural;

des garçons intelligents	des filles intelligentes
des dîners parfaits	des maisons parfaites
des garçons surpris	des filles surprises
des problèmes nationaux	des fêtes nationales
	holidays

Fill in the correct form of the adjective in parentheses:

1. (content) Les garçons _____ .

2. (parfait) La voiture _____ .

3. (satisfait) La mère _____ .

ANSWERS

Adjectives   1. contents,   2. parfaite,   3. satisfaite.

4. (prêt) L'homme _____ .

5. (lourd) Les livres _____ .

6. (intelligent) Les filles _____ .

7. (général) Les problèmes (m.) _____ .

8. (surpris) Les pères _____ .

(oo) (lay)(mehtr)
Où les mettre
Where to put them

    Adjectives are usually placed after the nouns they modify except when they are short, common, and express <u>B</u>eauty, <u>A</u>ge, <u>G</u>oodness and <u>S</u>ize (**BAGS**): **beau, joli, jeune, vieux,**
young   old
nouveau, bon, petit, grand
new   good   big

        le garçon intelligent
        les femmes importantes

               but

        le petit garçon
        les jolies femmes

ANSWERS
4. prêt, 5. lourds, 6. intelligentes, 7. généraux, 8. surpris

11	*(vwa-yahzh)* **Voyages en avion** Plane Trips *(a-vyohn)*

(kew-ryoh-zee-tay)
Visites des curiosités
Sightseeing

A plane trip within a country is often an easy and enjoyable way to travel. Note that in
(la-ay-ro-por) (sharl) **(gohl)** *(boor-zheh)*
France, **l'Aéroport Charles de Gaulle** is for international flights; Le Bourget is mostly for
(or-lee)
domestic flights; Orly is for medium-length domestic and international flights. Study the
following vocabulary and then follow the tourist as he goes to one of France's most popular
resorts, Cannes.

Pouvez-vous trouver . . .

(kohn-pa-nyee) (a-ay-ryehn)
la compagnie aérienne
airline

(kohn-twar) *(bee-yay)*
le comptoir des billets
ticket counter

(or-lozh)
l'horloge
clock

(ehs-ka-lyay) (roo-lahn)
l'escalier roulant
escalator

(tro-twar)
le trottoir roulant
moving sidewalk

(dwah-nyeh) *(dwah-nyehr)*
le douanier, la douanière
customs officer

(kohn-trohl) *(pas-por)*
le contrôle des passeports

(ans-pehk-tuhr)
l'inspecteur
inspector

(sor-tee)
la sortie
gate, exit

(ba-gahzh)
les bagages
luggage

(pee-lot) *(koh-pee-lot)*
le pilote, le co-pilote

(oh-tehs) *(ehr)*
l'hôtesse de l'air
stewardess

(toor)
la tour de contrôle
control tower

(ka-myohn)
le camion
truck

118

L'HÔTESSE **Votre carte d'embarquement,** *(ahn-bar-kuh-mahn)* **s'il vous plaît.**	Your boarding pass, please.
LE TOURISTE **Oui . . . Je l'ai . . . Mais où est-elle?**	Yes ... I have it ... but where is it?
L'HÔTESSE *(day-pay-shay)* **Dépêchez-vous, s'il vous plaît.**	Hurry up, please.
(lohng) *(kuh)* **Il y a une longue queue derrière vous.**	There is a long line behind you.
LE TOURISTE *(foo-y)* **(Il fouille dans toutes ses poches.)**	(He searches through all his pockets.)
L'HÔTESSE **Monsieur, l'avion part dans** *(mee-newt)* **quelques minutes.**	Sir, the plane is leaving in a few minutes.
LE TOURISTE **Ça y est! La voilà enfin!**	There we are! Here it is at last!

L'AVION
The Plane

(day-ko-lazh)
le décollage
The takeoff

(ay-kee-pahzh)
L'équipage
crew

(ewr-zhahns)
la sortie d'urgence

(ew-bloh)
le hublot
porthole

(ka-been)
la cabine
cabin

(pla-toh)
le plateau
tray

(fewz-lahzh)
le fuselage

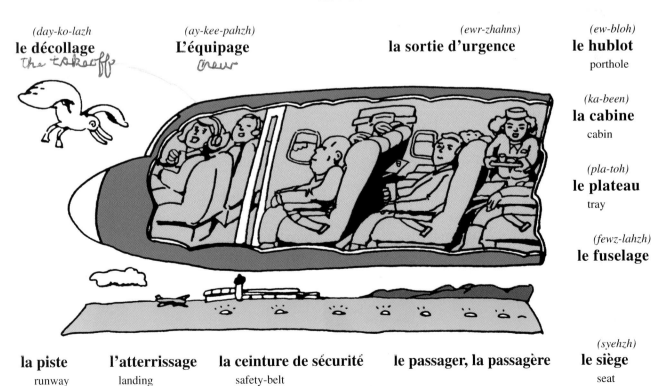

la piste
runway

l'atterrissage
landing

la ceinture de sécurité
safety-belt

le passager, la passagère

(syehzh)
le siège
seat

119

LE PILOTE *(day-ko-lay)* **Nous allons décoller dans**	We are going to take off in
(vuh-yay) **quelques minutes. Veuillez attacher**	a few minutes. Please fasten
vos ceintures de sécurité et redresser	your seat belts and straighten
le dossier de votre siège.	the back of your seat.

(Later)

LE PILOTE **Nous allons atterrir à Cannes à**	We are going to land in Cannes at
quatorze heures trente. Nous volons à	2:30 P.M. We are flying at
(al-tee-tewd) **une altitude de dix mille mètres. Le**	an altitude of 10,000 meters. The
temps à Cannes est nuageux et	weather in Cannes is cloudy and
(plew-vyūh) **pluvieux et la température est trente-**	rainy. And the temperature is 31
(sahn-tee-grad) **et-un degrés Centigrade.**	degrees Celsius.
PREMIER PASSAGER **Mademoiselle, est-ce**	Miss, do
(day-zhūh-nay) **que vous servez un déjeuner?** lunch	you serve lunch?
L'HOTESSE *(a-port)* **Je vous l'apporte dans un**	I'll bring it to you in a
instant.	moment.
DEUXIÈME PASSAGER *(sheek)* **Chic! J'adore**	Good! I love
(pah-say) **manger en avion. Ça fait passer le**	eating on the plane. It makes the
temps.	time pass quickly.
PREMIER PASSAGER **Mademoiselle!**	Miss!
(bwa-sohn) **Je voudrais une boisson,**	I would like a drink,
s'il vous plaît.	please.
L'HÔTESSE *(toot)* *(sweet)* **Tout de suite.**	Right away.

(Later)

PREMIER PASSAGER   **J'ai sommeil.**   I'm sleepy.

   Mademoiselle, pourriez-vous me   Miss, can you give me

          (koo-vehr-tewr)(sew-play-mahn-tehr)
   donner une couverture supplémentaire?   an extra blanket?

    (day-rahnzh)   *(ay-tan)*   *(lew-myehr)*
   Ça vous dérange si j'éteins la lumière?   Does it bother you if I turn off the light?

                   (rohnfl)
DEUXIÈME PASSAGER   **Mon Dieu! Il ronfle**   My God! He is already snoring!

   déjà! Et moi qui ne peux jamais   And I can never

   dormir en avion!   sleep on planes!

Can you give the French equivalent for these expressions?

1. Your boarding pass, please.
2. I have it.
3. Hurry up.
4. Right away.
5. I'm sleepy.

Encore des verbes
More verbs

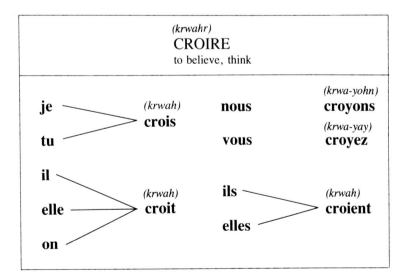

(krwahr) **CROIRE** to believe, think		
je *(krwah)* **crois** tu	nous	*(krwa-yohn)* **croyons**
il	vous	*(krwa-yay)* **croyez**
elle *(krwah)* **croit** on	ils *(krwah)* **croient** elles	

ANSWERS

Équivalents   **1.** Votre carte d'embarquement, s'il vous plaît.   **2.** Je l'ai.   **3.** Dépêchez-vous.   **4.** Tout de suite.   **5.** J'ai sommeil.

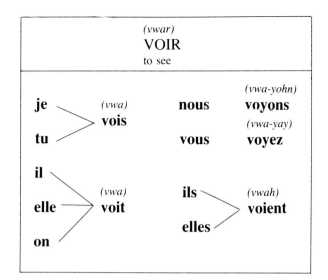

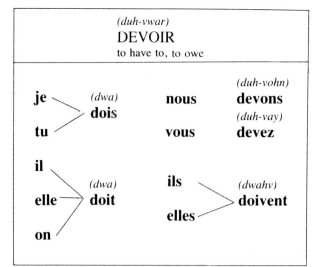

How about practicing these verbs in sentences:

1. Je _____ qu'il va faire beau temps demain.
   believe

2. _____ -vous ce beau lever du soleil?
   see

3. Nous _____ le garçon.
   believe

4. Marc _____ qu'il y a un terrain de camping près d'ici.
   believes

5. En France, on _____ la Tour Eiffel.
   sees

(gra-mehr)
Un peu de grammaire
Some grammar

The direct object pronouns are:

*me, m'	me	**nous**	us
te, t' (before a vowel)	you (fam.)	**vous**	you (polite, plural)
le, l' (before a vowel)	it, him	**les**	them
la, l' (before a vowel)	it, her		

***Me** becomes **moi** in affirmative commands.

ANSWERS

Verbs (fill ins)
1. crois 2. Voyez 3. croyons 4. croit 5. voit

They are placed before the verb:

Paul me voit.	Paul sees me.
Paul m'aime.	Paul loves me.
Paul te voit.	Paul sees you.
Paul t'aime.	Paul loves you.
Paul le (la) voit.	Paul sees him (her).

Direct object pronouns <u>replace</u> direct object nouns:

Je regarde le **film.**	I watch the film.
Je le **regarde.**	I watch it.
Il cherche Anne **.**	He looks for Anne.
Il la **cherche.**	He looks for her.

Direct object pronouns are placed <u>before</u> the verb except in an affirmative command:

Vous me **regardez.**	You look at me.
Vous le **prenez.**	You take it.
Regardez- moi **.**	Look at me.
Prenez- le **.**	Take it.

In negative sentences, the word order is:

Je ne le **regarde pas.**	I don't watch it.
Il ne la **cherche pas.**	He does not look for it.

In negative commands, the word order is:

Ne me **regardez pas.**	Don't look at me.
Ne le **prenez pas.**	Don't take it.

Replace the noun by a pronoun as in the example which follows:

Je prends le livre.

Nous regardons la télévision.

J'aime les films.

Je le prends.

1. **Nous** _____ **regardons.**

2. **Je** _____ _____ **aime.**

ANSWERS

Pronouns 1. la **2.** les

J'apporte le dîner.

Tu connais Jacques Chirac?

Il n'aime pas ce film.

Je ne comprends pas les exercices.

Regardez les garçons!

(foh-toh)
Prenez la photo!

(ad-mee-ray) *(mohn-ta-nyuh)*
Admirez les montagnes!

3. Je _____ apporte.

4. Tu _____?

5. Il ne _____ aime pas.

6. Je ne _____ comprends pas.

7. Regardez-_____!

8. Prenez-_____!

9. Admirez-_____!

(veel)

En ville

In the city

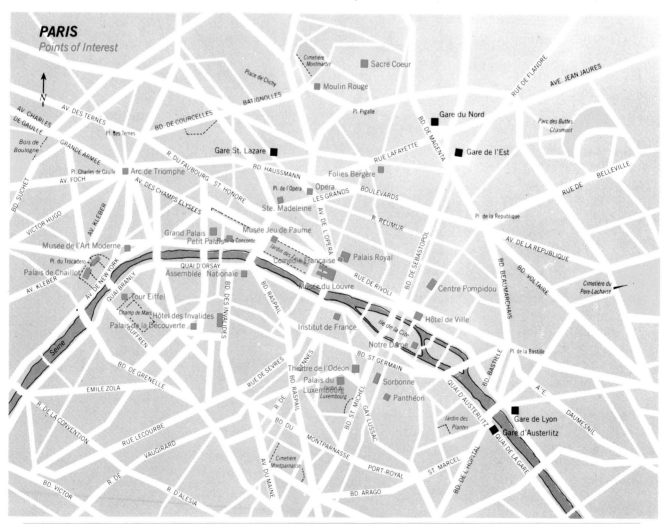

PARIS
Points of Interest

ANSWERS

Pronouns 3. l' 4. le 5. l' 6. les 7. les 8. la 9. les

Back in Paris, our tourist decides to do some sightseeing.

LE TOURISTE	**Pardon, Monsieur.**
	Excuse me, Sir.

Pouvez-vous me dire où se trouve le
(zhew) *(pom)* is found
"Jus de Pomme"?

Can you tell me where the
"Apple Juice" is?

(pa-ree-zyan) *(kwa)*
LE PARISIEN **Le quoi?**

The what?

(say-lehbr)
LE TOURISTE **Mais oui! Le célèbre**
(mew-zay) *(ta-bloh)*
musée qui a tous les tableaux
(an-preh-syo-neest)
impressionnistes.

But yes! The famous
museum which has all
the Impressionist paintings.

(mew-zay)
LE PARISIEN **Vous voulez dire le Musée**
(dor-say) *(zhews-tuh-mahn)*
d'Orsay? Je vais justement   dans cette
(dee-rehk-syohn) *(mohn-tray)*
direction. Je vais vous montrer.

You mean the Musée
d'Orsay? I happen to be going in that
direction. I'll show you.

(eh-mahbl)
LE TOURISTE **Vous êtes très aimable.**

You are very kind.

(dohtr)
LE PARISIEN **Avez-vous visité d'autres**
(mo-new-mahn)
monuments?

Have you visited other
monuments?

LE TOURISTE **Oui. La magnifique**

Yes. The magnificent

Cathédrale de Notre-Dame et la Sainte

Notre Dame and Sainte

Chapelle. Demain matin je vais faire
(oh-toh-kar)
le tour de la ville en autocar et

Chapelle. Tomorrow morning I'll tour
the city by bus and

demain après-midi je vais prendre un
(ba-toh) *(moosh)* *(sehn)*
bateau-mouche sur la Seine. Je
(kohnt)
compte aussi aller au Louvre,

tomorrow afternoon I'll take a
bateau-mouche on the Seine. I
sightseeing barge
also intend to go to the Louvre,

naturellement.

of course.

LE PARISIEN **Avez-vous vu des**
(plahzh)
plages et des montagnes?

Have you seen any
beaches and mountains?

125

LE TOURISTE **Je suis allé à Cannes et à Nice.**	I have been to Cannes and Nice.
(ruh-vuh-neer) **J'espère revenir une autre fois pour**	I hope to come back another time to
voyager dans les Alpes. Je voudrais	travel in the Alps. I would like
(tay-lay-fay-reek) **prendre le téléphérique de**	to take the Aiguille du Midi cable car.
(ay-gwee-y) *(mee-dee)* **l'Aiguille du Midi.**	

LE PARISIEN **Voilà le Musée d'Orsay.**	Here is the Musée d'Orsay!
(say-zhoor) **Au revoir et bon séjour!**	Good-bye, have a pleasant stay!

LE TOURISTE *(à lui-même)* **Que les**	How friendly the
Parisiens sont aimables!	Parisians are!

Can you match the questions in the left column with the answers in the right column?

1. Avez-vous visité d'autres monuments?
2. Avez-vous vu des plages?
3. Comment aller au Musée d'Orsay?
4. Qu'est-ce que vous allez faire demain matin?
5. Quel musée a des tableaux impressionistes?

A. Je suis allé à Cannes et à Nice.
B. Le Musée d'Orsay a des tableaux impressionistes.
C. Oui, la Cathédrale de Notre-Dame et la Sainte Chapelle.
D. Demain matin je vais faire le tour de la ville en autocar.
E. Je vais justement dans cette direction.

ANSWERS

Matching   1. C   2. A   3. E   4. D   5. B

ENTERTAINMENT

(dees-trak-syohn)
Les Distractions

12	**Le théâtre** *(tay-ahtr)*	**le cinéma** *(see-nay-ma)*	**les jours de fête** *(feht)*
	Theater	Movies	Holidays

Jack and Suzanne are a middle-aged couple
from Portland, Maine, who for the first time
take a trip to France. They like the theater.
It is their second day in Paris. Being of
French descent, they both speak French quite
well. ''Not one word of English during our
vacation,'' they decide.

LE THÉÂTRE
Theater

À L'HÔTEL

JACQUES **Qu'est-ce que tu as envie de faire** *(ahn-vee)*

ce soir?

What do you feel like doing

tonight?

SUZANNE **On pourrait aller au théâtre? Il**

paraît qu'il y a plus de 55 salles à

Paris.

We could go to the theater. It

seems there are more than 55 theaters in

Paris.

JACQUES **On donne *Phèdre* de Racine à la** *(fehdr)* *(ra-seen)*
Comédie Française. Mais c'est samedi *(ko-may-dee)*

et il ne reste probablement que des

places au poulailler. *(plas)* *(poo-la-yay)*

They are giving *Phèdre* by Racine is playing at the

Comédie-Française. But it's Saturday

and the only seats left are probably in the

chicken coop.

SUZANNE	Qu'est-ce que c'est que ça?	What's that?

JACQUES **Le quatrième balcon, tout en haut.** *(bal-kohn) (ahn) (oh)*

The 4th balcony, way up.

Est-ce que tu veux aller aux Folies-Bergère? *(fo-lee) (ber-zhehr)*

Do you want to go to the Folies-

Bergère?

SUZANNE **Ah non! C'est pour les touristes.**

No no! That's for tourists.

On pourrait aller voir un chansonnier *(shahn-so-nyay)*

We could go and see a stand-up comic

à Pigalle?

at Pigalle.

JACQUES **Mais, mon chou, ces gens-là parlent** *(shoo)*

But, my darling, those people speak

à toute vitesse! *(vee-tehs)*

horribly fast!

SUZANNE **Dans ce cas, peut-être un bon**

In that case, maybe a good

film français. . . . *(feelm)*

French film. . . .

JACQUES **Bonne idée!** *(ee-day)*

Good idea!

Promenons-nous sur les Champs-Elysées. *(prom-nohn)*

Let's walk on the

Champs-Elysees.

Et s'il n'y a pas de bon film,

And if there is no good film, we'll simply

nous allons simplement *(san-pluh-mahn)*

prendre un verre dans un café. *(vehr)*

have a drink in a cafe.

Answer these questions based on the dialogue:

1. Qu'est-ce que Marie a envie de faire ce soir? _____
2. Qu'est-ce qu'on donne? _____
3. Qu'est-ce que c'est que ''le poulailler''? _____
4. Pourquoi Marc, n'a-t-il pas envie d'aller voir un chansonnier? _____
5. Quelle est la bonne idée de Marie? _____

ANSWERS

Dialogue 1. Marie a envie d'aller au théâtre. 2. On donne Phèdre de Racine. 3. C'est le quatrième balcon, tout en haut. 4. Ces gens-là parlent à toute vitesse. 5. La bonne idée est de voir un bon film.

128

See how similar these words are:

le théâtre  theater **le balcon**  balcony

la comédie  comedy *(ee-day)* **l'idée**  idea

l'hôtel  hotel **le, la touriste**  tourist

If you go to the theater or the movies in France (and other European countries), be prepared to give a
(poor-bwar) *(oo-vrŭhz)*
small **pourboire** to the **ouvreuse** after she has led you to your seat. At the movies, there is usually an
woman usher

(ahn) (trakt)
entr'acte during which advertisements are projected on the screen.
intermission

(pŭh) *(tew)* *(muh)* *(do-nay)* *(uhn)* *(pŭh)* *(dahr-zhan)*
Peux-tu me donner un peu d'argent?
Can you give a little money . . . to me?

Indirect Object Pronouns			
* **me, m'**	to me	**nous**	to us
te, t'	to you (fam.)	**vous**	to you (polite, plur.)
lui	to him, to her	**leur**	to them
se, s'	to himself, to herself	**se**	to themselves

***Me** becomes **moi** in an affirmative command.

129

The chart below will show you how the direct and indirect pronouns are placed in sentences:

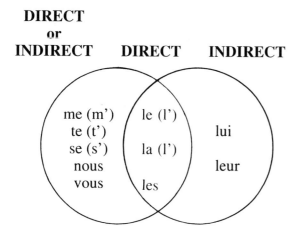

DIRECT or INDIRECT   **DIRECT**   **INDIRECT**

me (m')
te (t')
se (s')
nous
vous

le (l')
la (l')
les

lui

leur

Indirect object nouns are preceded by a form of à (TO): (à, à la, à l', au, aux). Indirect object pronouns may replace indirect object nouns:

Je parle | à Anne |.

I speak to Anne.

Je | lui | **parle.**

I speak to her.

Il parle | au garçon |.

He speaks to the boy.

Il | lui | **parle.**

He speaks to him.

Vous parlez | aux hommes |.

You speak to the men.

Vous | leur | **parlez.**

You speak to them.

Indirect object pronouns are placed before the verb except in an affirmative command:

Vous | lui | **parlez.**

You speak to him.

Vous | me | **parlez.**

You speak to me.

Vous ne | lui | **parlez pas.**

You don't speak to him.

Vous ne | me | **parlez pas.**

You don't speak to me.

Ne | lui | **parlez pas!**

Don't speak to him!

Ne | me | **parlez pas!**

Don't speak to me!

BUT

Parlez- | lui |!

Speak to him!

Parlez- | moi |!

Speak to me!

130

Replace the indirect object noun with the correct pronoun and then write the sentence.

1. Je parle *à Georges.* _____

2. Il n' écrit pas *au garçon.* _____
   writes

3. Ne lisez pas *aux enfants.* _____
   reads

4. Elle parle *à Henri et à Michel.* _____

5. Parlez *au docteur.* _____

Since ME, TE, NOUS, VOUS may be direct object pronouns, indirect object pronouns or reflexive pronouns, their use is relatively easy. For the other pronouns just remember:

le—him, it	lui—to him, to her	se—(to) himself
la—her, it	leur—to them	herself
les—them		itself
		themselves

LES JOURS DE FÊTE
Holidays

JACQUES **C'est intéressant** *(an-tay-reh-sahn)* — It's interesting to compare the French

de comparer les *(kohn-pa-ray)* — holidays with the

fêtes françaises — American ones.

avec les fêtes américaines. — Six days after New

Six jours après le — Year's Day, the

Nouvel An, les *(noo-vehl) (ahn)* — French celebrate

Français célèbrent — the Epiphany,

l'Épiphanie, la fête *(ay-pee-fa-nee)* — the feast of the

des rois mages. *(rwah) (mahzh)* — three kings.

SUZANNE **Peut-être qu'ils ont besoin d'un** — Maybe they need a holiday

jour de congé quelques jours après le *(kohn-zhay)* — a few days after the

réveillon . . . *(ray-veh-yohn)* — holiday meal . . .

ANSWERS

Indirect Object Pronouns **1.** Je lui parle. **2.** Il ne lui écrit pas. **3.** Ne leur lisez pas. **4.** Elle leur parle **5.** Parlez-lui.

131

JACQUES   *(pahk)*
Et à Pâques, ils ont congé le Jeudi Saint, le Vendredi Saint et le Lundi de *(pohn)* Pâques. Ils font le pont et ont presque une semaine de vacances! Ensuite il y *(a-sahn-syohn)* *(pahnt-koht)* a l'Ascension puis la Pentecôte . . .

And at Easter time, they have days off on Good Thursday, Good Friday and Easter Monday. They take a long weekend and have almost a week's vacation! Then there is Ascension Day, then Pentecost Day . . .

SUZANNE   *(prehsk)* . . . et c'est presque l'été et les grandes vacances.

. . . and it's almost summer and the big vacation.

JACQUES   Exactement. Au mois d'août.

Exactly. In August.

SUZANNE   Est-ce qu'on célèbre la Journée du *(tra-vah-y)* Travail?

Do they celebrate Labor Day?

JACQUES   Oui, le premier mai.

Yes, on May 1st.

SUZANNE   Et en automne?

And in the fall?

JACQUES   *(ahr-mees-tees)* Il y a la fête de l'Armistice le 11 *(too-san)* novembre et la Toussaint le premier *(pro-poh)* novembre. À propos, sais-tu pourquoi nous ne devons pas apporter de *(kry-zahn-tehm)* chrysanthèmes à ta tante Sophie demain?

There is Armistice Day on November 11 and All Saints Day on November 1. By the way, do you know why we mustn't bring mums to your Aunt Sophie tomorrow?

SUZANNE   Pourquoi?

Why?

JACQUES   Parce que la Toussaint est une *(so-la-nehl)* *(mor)* journée solennelle pour les morts et les gens apportent des chrysanthèmes *(seem-tyehr)* au cimetière.

Because All Saints Day is a solemn day for the dead and people bring mums to the cemetery.

SUZANNE   *(vreh-mahn)* Vraiment?

Really?

JACQUES   *(toot)* *(ma-nyehr)* De toute manière, peu après la *(no-ehl)* Toussaint, il y a Noël, et un autre réveillon!

Anyway, shortly after All Saints Day there is Christmas, and another big feast!

Fill in the correct French word:

1. À Paris, il y a plus de _____
55

théâtres.

2. C'est _____ de comparer les fêtes
interesting
françaises avec les fêtes américaines.

3. Jacques et Suzanne vont voir un film _____ .
French

4. Qui est-ce que Jacques et Suzanne vont voir demain?

Ils vont voir _____ .
Aunt Sophie

(shay)
5. Si vous êtes invités à dîner chez une famille
at the home of

française, il ne faut pas apporter de _____ .
Chrysanthemums

6. La fête de l'Armistice est _____ .
November 11

7. La Toussaint est une _____
day

solennelle.

8. Les Français ont beaucoup de jours de _____ .
off

9. Jacques et Suzanne _____ le théâtre.
like

10. Noël_____ .
is December 25

ANSWERS

Fill in blanks 1. cinquante-cinq **2.** intéressant **3.** français **4.** l'ante Sophie **5.** chrysanthèmes **6.** le onze novembre **7.** journée **8.** congé **9.** aiment **10.** est le vingt-cinq décembre.

133

LA MARCHE ET LE JOGGING
(marsh)   *(zho-geen)*

Hiking and Jogging

(ruh-por-tehr) *(luh-for)*		
UN REPORTER	**Monsieur Lefort?**	Mr. Lefort?
LEFORT	**Oui, c'est moi.**	Yes, that's me.
	(sharl) *(la-plewm)*	
LE REPORTER	**Je suis Charles Laplume.**	I am Charles Laplume.
(ay-kree) *(zhoor-nal)*		
	J'écris pour le journal *France-Amérique*.	I write for the paper *France-Amerique*.
	(ahn-shahn-tay)	
LEFORT	**Enchanté!**	Delighted!
	(mwa) *(mehm)*	
LE REPORTER	**Moi de même.**	Me too.
	(an-tehr-vyoo)	
LEFORT	**Vous voulez une interview?**	You want an interview?
LE REPORTER	**Exactement.**	Exactly.
	(sew-zheh)	
LEFORT	**À quel sujet?**	About what?
	(pray-zee-dahn)	
LE REPORTER	**Comme président de la**	As president of the
(leeg) *(a-ma-tuhr)*		
	Ligue Française des amateurs de	French Amateur Sport League,
	(sehr-tehn-mahn)	
	sport, vous êtes certainement très	you are certainly very

134

(koo-rahn) *(kohn-sehrn)*
au courant de tout ce qui concerne le well informed about everything concerning

(see-kleesm)
jogging, la marche, le cyclisme et la jogging, hiking, cycling and

(na-ta-syohn)
natation. swimming.

(fla-tay)
LEFORT **Vous me flattez.** You flatter me.

LE REPORTER **Je voudrais écrire un article** I would like to write an article

(lad-sew)
là-dessus. about that.

(a-lay) (zee) *(swee-vay)*
LEFORT **Allez-y! Et suivez-moi!** Go ahead! And follow me!

LE REPORTER **D'abord, le jogging.** First, jogging.

(po-pew-lehr)
LEFORT **Oui, c'est très populaire ici.** Yes, it's very popular here.

Comme beaucoup d'autres choses, ça Like many other things, it

vient naturellement d'Amérique et comes from America, and

(mant-nahn)
maintenant les Européens en sont now the Europeans are

(foo)
fous. crazy about it.

(an-por-tohn) *(moh)*
Nous importons même le mot. On ne We even import the word.

(koor)
court plus, on fait du jogging. One doesn't run any more, one jogs.

LE REPORTER **Vous aussi, Monsieur?** You too, Sir?

LEFORT **Et comment! Le jogging est un** And how! Jogging is a

(san) *(mar-shay)* *(suhl)*
sport sain et bon marché. Les seuls healthy and inexpensive sport. The only

(an-vehs-tees-mahn) *(sweht-shūhrt)*
investissements sont un sweatshirt investments are a sweat shirt

et une paire de and a pair of

(shoh-sewr)
chaussures de comfortable jogging shoes.

jogging

confortables.

LE REPORTER **Et que pensez-vous de la** And what do you think about

marche? hiking?

135

LEFORT   **Un sport merveilleux, et très**
(ray-pahn-dew)
répandu ici en France. Tous nos
(sahn-tyay)   (mar-kay)
sentiers sont bien marqués.

Impossible de se perdre.

LE REPORTER   **De quoi a-t-on**

besoin pour ce sport?
(sa-ka-doh)
LEFORT   **D'un sac à dos et d'une paire de**
(zhahnb)
bonnes jambes avec de bonnes
(shoh-sewr)
chaussures de marche. Si vous êtes
(ahn-bee-syūh)
ambitieux, peut-être un sac de

couchage, des ustensiles de

cuisine et une gourde.

A marvelous sport, and very

widespread here in France. All our

footpaths are well marked.

Impossible to lose one's way.

What does one

need for this sport?

A backpack and a pair of

good legs with good

walking shoes. If you are

ambitious, maybe a sleeping bag,

cooking utensils

and a canteen.

1. Qu'est-ce que c'est (what is it):

C'est un _____

2. Qu'est-ce que c'est?

C'est un _____

3. Qu'est-ce que c'est?

C'est un _____

4. Qu'est-ce que c'est?

Ce sont des _____

5. Qu'est-ce que c'est?

C'est une _____

There are many American expressions used as French words, such as *jogging* for *courir*,
(frahn-glay)
interview for *entrevue*. This new language is called "franglais" and its usage is controversial.

ANSWERS

Qu'est-ce que c'est? 1. sweatshirt   2. sac de couchage   3. sac à dos   4. ustensiles de cuisine   5. gourde

Retenez
Remember

Que pensez-vous de la marche? | **QUE, QU' (before a vowel)**
What | What do you think about hiking?

refers to a thing, but is not
preceded by a preposition.

De quoi a-t-on besoin? | **QUOI**
What | What does one need? (*lit:* of
what does one have need?)

refers to a thing and is
preceded by a preposition
(de, à, avec, sur).

Encore des verbes
More verbs

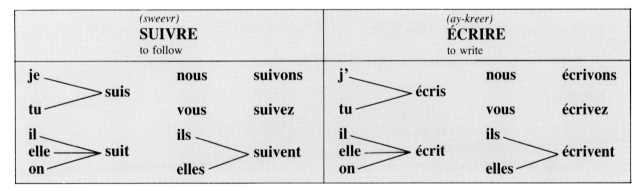

(sweevr) **SUIVRE** to follow			*(ay-kreer)* **ÉCRIRE** to write		
je		nous **suivons**	j'		nous **écrivons**
	suis			**écris**	
tu		vous **suivez**	tu		vous **écrivez**
il		ils	il		ils
elle	**suit**	**suivent**	elle	**écrit**	**écrivent**
on		elles	on		elles

Fill in the blanks with the appropriate form of the verb:

1. Le lundi, j'_____ toujours à ma mère.

write

2. _____ -moi, je vais vous montrer le Musée d'Orsay.

follow

3. Vous _____ bien en français.

write

4. Charles Laplume _____ pour France-Amérique.

writes

5. Est-ce que tu vas _____ à ton frère?

write

6. Nous _____ des cartes postales. *(kart) (pos-tahl)*

write

ANSWERS
Fill in blanks 1. écris 2. Suivez 3. écrivez 4. écrit 5. écrire 6. écrivons

137

LE CYCLISME ET LA NATATION

(see-kleesm) *(na-ta-syohn)*

Bicycling and Swimming

LE REPORTER **Que pensez-vous du** — What do you think of

cyclisme, Monsieur? — bicycle riding, Sir?

LEFORT **Un sport stupide, un moyen de** *(stew-peed)* *(mwa-yan)* — A stupid sport, unsatisfactory

transport insatisfaisant. C'est sans *(trahns-por)* *(an-sa-tees-fuh-zahn)* *(sahn)* — means of transportation. It's

intérêt. Pas de vitesse, rien. Et à la *(zan-tay-reh)* — without interest. No speed, nothing.

montée, il faut pousser le machin. Et *(ma-shan)* — And up hill you have to push the thing.

les règlements sont tellement stricts! *(reh-gluh-mahn)* *(tehl-mahn)* *(streekt)* — And the rules are so strict!

Est-ce qu'en Amérique vous devez — In America, do you have

avoir des phares devant et derrière? *(far)* — to have lights in front and in the rear?

LE REPORTER **Non. Que pensez-vous de la** — No. What do you think of swimming?

natation?

LEFORT **Ah! La natation! Là, je suis** — Ah! Swimming! There, I am

enthousiaste. Mon docteur me dit que *(ahn-too-zyast)* *(dok-tuhr)* *(dee)* — enthusiastic. My doctor tells me

c'est le meilleur et le plus sain des — it's the best and the healthiest of

sports. Et c'est un autre sport bon — sports. And it's another inexpensive sport:

marché: un maillot de bain, c'est tout *(ma-yoh)* *(ban)* — a bathing suit, that's all

ce qu'il faut. — you need.

LE REPORTER **Éventuellement un bikini.** *(ay-vahn-tew-ehl-mahn)* *(bee-kee-nee)* — Perhaps a bikini.

LEFORT **C'est tout . . . Peut-être des** — That's all . . . Maybe

lunettes de plongée. *(lew-neht)* *(plohn-zhay)* — diving goggles.

LE REPORTER **Comment un débutant** *(day-bew-tahn)* — How does a beginner

commence-t-il ici? — start here?

LEFORT **Avec la brasse. Ensuite viennent** *(bras)* — With the breast stroke. Then come

le crawl et la nage sur le dos.	the crawl and the backstroke.
(ay-prūhv)	
LE REPORTER **Vous avez des épreuves**	Do you have tests
(ray-gew-lyehr-mahn)	
régulièrement?	regularly?
LEFORT **Absolument. Si on passe l'épreuve**	Absolutely. If someone passes the free-swimming
(fyehr-mahn)	
de nage libre, on peut fièrement	test, one can proudly
(por-tay) *(an-seen-y)*	
porter un petit insigne sur son maillot	wear a little badge on one's bathing suit.
de bain.	
LE REPORTER **Monsieur, je vous remercie**	Sir, I thank you
pour l'interview.	for the interview.

Now let's see if you can remember the adjectives that describe M. Lefort's opinion about these sports:

Selon M. Lefort, le cyclisme est:
according to

1. _____

2. _____

3. _____

4. _____

Selon M. Lefort, la natation est:

5. _____

6. _____

Retenez
Remember

Éventuellement. Watch this word, and how you use it. In French it means *possibly* or *perhaps*.
Actuellement is another traitor: it means *now*, *at the present time*, not *in fact* or *actually*.

ANSWERS

Opinion   **1.** un sport stupide.   **2.** un moyen de transport insatisfaisant.   **3.** sans intérêt.   **4.** sans vitesse.   **5.** le meilleur et le plus sain des sports.   **6.** un autre sport bon marché.

Il faut, an expression you have encountered a few times before, is very common and very useful. It means: *It is necessary*, *one must*, *you have to*, *one needs to*, and may be followed by an infinitive:

C'est tout ce qu'il faut.   That's all that's required.

Il faut pousser le machin.   It's necessary to push the thing.

In the negative, put NE and PAS around FAUT:

Il ne faut pas partir.   It's not necessary to leave.
You don't need to leave.

Encore des verbes
More verbs

	(koo-reer) COURIR to run			*(deer)* DIRE to say	
je tu	*(koor)* cours	nous vous	*(koo-rohn)* courons *(koo-ray)* courez	je tu	*(dee)* dis	nous vous	*(dee-zohn)* disons *(deet)* dites
il elle on	*(koor)* court	ils elles	*(koor)* courent	il elle on	*(dee)* dit	ils elles	*(deez)* disent

Give the correct form of the verb.

COURIR

1. Nous _____ à l'école.

2. Il _____ vite.

3. _____ -tu au cinéma?

4. Vous ne _____ pas au marché.

DIRE

1. Que _____ -vous?

2. Je _____ la vérité.

3. Elles _____ ''Non''.

4. Paul ne _____ pas ''Bonjour''.

ANSWERS

Verbs **COURIR:** 1. courons 2. court 3. Cours 4. courez
DIRE: 1. dites 2. dis 3. disent 4. dit

140

ORDERING FOOD

(ko-mahn)   *(ko-mahn-day)*   *(ruh-pah)*

Comment commander un repas

14	*(noo-ree-tewr)* ## Les repas / la nourriture
	Meals Food

J'aime manger
I like to eat

You're going to want to taste some French specialties on your trip, whether it's **Pâté de foie gras,** or **coq au vin de Bourgogne,** or **framboises.** So be sure to learn how to request what you'd like. Note below, that you can request some items by saying you'd like *the* or *some* of it, just like in English.

<u>**THE**</u>

(sohs)

J'aime | la | sauce.

<u>**SOME**</u>

Je mange | de la | sauce.

(loh)   *(vee-shee)*

J'aime | l' | eau de Vichy.
Vichy water

Après le déjeuner, je

vais boire | de l' | eau de Vichy.

141

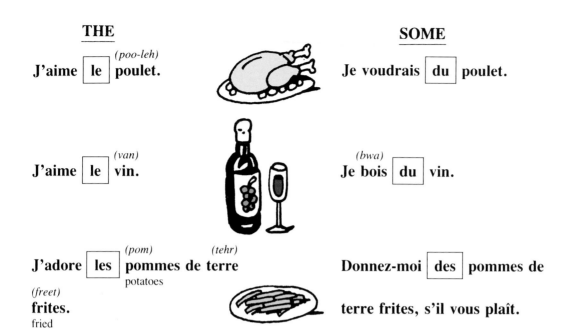

THE

J'aime | le | poulet.
(poo-leh)

J'aime | le | vin.
(van)

J'adore | les | pommes de terre
(pom) *(tehr)*
potatoes

(freet)
frites.
fried

SOME

Je voudrais | du | poulet.

Je bois | du | vin.
(bwa)

Donnez-moi | des | pommes de

terre frites, s'il vous plaît.

SOME, ANY

Sometimes you just can't eat the whole thing, but you can eat a part of it. Refer to the following chart to choose the form of "SOME" or "ANY" that you use before the noun.

	Singular	**Plural**
masculine noun (starting with a consonant)	DU	DES
feminine noun (starting with a consonant)	DE LA	DES
masculine or feminine noun (starting with a vowel)	DE L'	DES

Je mange le gâteau.

Je mange du gâteau.

When talking of something you like or dislike in general, use LE, LA, L' or LES.

J'aime | la | glace.

I like ice cream.

When talking of something you would like a part of, use DE LA, DU or DE L', DES.

Je mange | de la | **glace.**

I eat some ice cream.

When the item is countable (potatoes, string beans, strawberries, and so forth—in English, you use the plural), use LES or DES, and UN or UNE if you want one item.

Je n'aime pas | les | **légumes.**

I don't like vegetables.

In the negative, simply use DE or D', and no article. (DE means any in a negative sentence.)

Je ne veux pas | de | **légumes.**

I don't want any vegetables.

Try to remember that whenever SOME or ANY is implied, you must use DE LA, DU, DE L' in affirmative sentences, and DE (D') in negative sentences and after expressions of quantity.

Try this:

(mew-zeek)

1. Je fais _____ sport. 2. J'adore _____ musique (fem.)

(ay-pee-nar) *(a-nee-moh)*

3. Je déteste _____ épinards. 4. Les chiens sont _____ animaux.
spinach animals

A little practice? See the pictures of food items and the French words for them.
Then decide whether to use LE, LA, L', DU, DE LA, DES, or DE (D' before a vowel).

1. **fromage** (masc.)

(gah-toh) *(sho-ko-lah)*

2. **gâteau au chocolat** (masc.)

J'adore ____ **fromage**.

J'aime ____ **gâteau au chocolat**.

3. **vin rouge** (masc.)

(pwa-sohn)

4. **poisson** (masc.)

Je voudrais ____ **vin rouge**.

____ **poisson**, s'il vous plaît!

ANSWERS

Food 1. le 2. le 3. du 4. Du
Some, Any 1. du 2. la 3. les 4. des

143

5. **salade** *(sa-lad)* (fem.)

6. **eau** (fem.)

J'aimerais _____ **salade**.

J'ai soif! Donnez-moi _____ **eau**, s'il vous plaît.

Les adverbes de quantité
(lay) (zad-vehrb) (kahn-tee-tay)

Adverbs of quantity

Je bois beaucoup | de | **vin.**
a lot of

Il boit trop | de | **whisky.**
(troh)
too much

J'ai assez | de | **fromage.**
(fro-mahzh)
enough   cheese

Je voudrais un peu | de | **saucisson.**
(soh-see-sohn)
a little   salami

J'aimerais un tout petit peu | d' | **eau.**
(em-reh) (an) (toop) (tee) (pūh)
would like a tiny little bit

After expressions of quantity, use DE or D' (before a vowel).

Fill in the blanks:

1. Je mange _____ poulet.
a lot of

2. Il boit _____ vin.
enough

3. Je voudrais _____ eau.
a little

4. Elle a _____ gâteau.
too much

5. Aimerais-tu _____ sauce?
a tiny little bit of

ANSWERS

Food **5.** de la **6.** de l'

Fill in the blanks **1.** beaucoup de **2.** assez de **3.** un peu d' **4.** trop de **5.** un tout petit peu de

Un nouveau verbe

A new verb

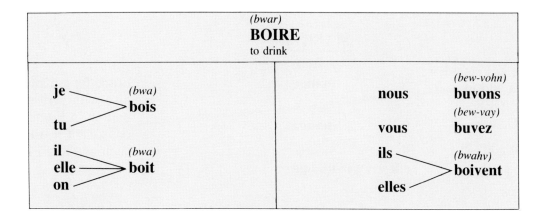

(bwar) **BOIRE** to drink	
je tu *(bwa)* **bois**	nous *(bew-vohn)* **buvons**
il elle on *(bwa)* **boit**	vous *(bew-vay)* **buvez** ils elles *(bwahv)* **boivent**

AMÉRIQUE    FRANCE

Fill in the blanks with the correct form: DE, DU, DE LA, DE L', DES.

1. Les Américains boivent _____ jus

   d'orange (masc.), _____ café

   (leh)
   (masc.) avec _____ lait (masc.)
   milk

   froid.

2. Les Français boivent _____ café

   avec beaucoup _____ lait chaud.

3. Les Américains boivent _____ lait,

   _____ Coca-Cola ou _____

   café.

4. Les Français boivent _____ vin

   (peh-ryay)
   et _____ Perrier (masc.)

ANSWERS

Fill in the blanks 1. du du du 2. du de 3. du du du 4. du du

Verbes avec des changements orthographiques
Verbs with spelling changes

To keep the ZH sound in verbs that end in -GER (MANGER, CHANGER), it is necessary to add ⬚E⬚ between A, O, or U that follows it.

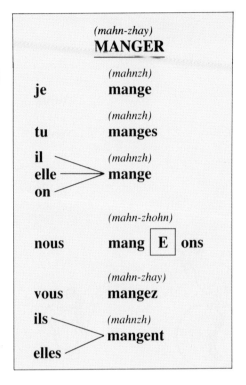

(mahn-zhay)
MANGER

	(mahnzh)
je	**mange**
tu	**manges** *(mahnzh)*
il **elle** → **mange** *(mahnzh)* **on**	
nous	**mang** ⬚E⬚ **ons** *(mahn-zhohn)*
vous	**mangez** *(mahn-zhay)*
ils **elles** → **mangent** *(mahnzh)*	

Something happens also with verbs ending in É or E + consonant + ER, such as PRÉFÉRER:

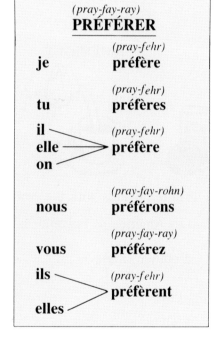

(pray-fay-ray)
PRÉFÉRER

	(pray-fehr)
je	**préfère**
tu	**préfères** *(pray-fehr)*
il **elle** → **préfère** *(pray-fehr)* **on**	
nous	**préférons** *(pray-fay-rohn)*
vous	**préférez** *(pray-fay-ray)*
ils **elles** → **préfèrent** *(pray-fehr)*	

To keep the S sound in verbs that end in -CER (COMMENCER), it is necessary to add a ⬚Ç⬚ before A, O, or U:

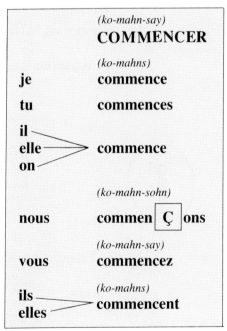

(ko-mahn-say)
COMMENCER

	(ko-mahns)
je	**commence**
tu	**commences**
il **elle** → **commence** **on**	
nous	**commen** ⬚Ç⬚ **ons** *(ko-mahn-sohn)*
vous	**commencez** *(ko-mahn-say)*
ils **elles** → **commencent** *(ko-mahns)*	

Note: ⬚'⬚ is called **accent aigu** *(ak-sahn) (tay-gew)*; ⬚`⬚ is called **accent grave** *(grahv)*. Now, let's practice some of the phrases you're going to use as you dine.

1. Les Américains _____
   eat

   (vyahnd)
   de la viande.
   meat

2. Les Français _____
   prefer

   des omelettes.

(day-zhūh-nay)
In France **le déjeuner** is still the most important meal in most places. In large cities, however,
lunch   *(poos)*
many people **mangent sur le pouce** (literally, on the thumb) that is, lightly and quickly, at a

(puh-tee)
McDonald's or other fast food place. Breakfast (**le petit déjeuner**) consists simply of bread,
small

(dee-nay)
croissants, or rolls, butter and jam and **café au lait**, and supper (**le dîner**) is more like lunch in
the U.S. But there are many exceptions to the rule.

LE PETIT DÉJEUNER
Breakfast

(tas)
une tasse de
(leh)
café au lait
a cup of coffee
with milk

SIMON **À quelle heure aimes-tu manger ton**

petit déjeuner?

LUCIE **À huit heures.**

SIMON **Je préfère le manger à huit heures**

moins le quart.

(poh)
un pot
(kohn-fee-tewr)
de confiture
a jar of jam

ANSWERS
Fill in blanks 1. mangent 2. préfèrent

147

un sachet *(sa-sheh)*
de thé *(tay)*
a tea bag

une tasse *(tas)*
a cup

de thé
of tea

du pain *(pan)*
grillé *(gree-yay)*
toast

les brioches *(bree-yuhsh)*
breakfast rolls

LUCIE **Est-ce que tu prends du café au lait**

ou du café noir?
black

SIMON Je n'aime pas le café. Je préfère le
(tay)
thé. **Ma mère sert toujours du thé.**
tea   serves always

LUCIE **Est-ce que tu aimes le pain grillé**

avec du beurre et de la confiture?

SIMON **Quelle idée! Dans ma famille, nous**
What an idea
mangeons des croissants.

LUCIE Aimes-tu le jus d'orange?

SIMON **Oui, mais je ne bois jamais de jus**
never
de fruit le matin.

LUCIE **Mon Dieu! Comment allons-nous**

voyager ensemble?
together

le beurre *(būhr)*
butter

un verre de jus *(vehr)* *(zhew)*
d'orange *(o-rahnzh)*
a glass of orange juice

le jus de tomate *(toh-maht)*
tomato juice

Imagining that you are in France, how would you answer these questions from the dialogue?

1. À quelle heure aimez-vous manger le petit déjeuner?
2. Est-ce que vous prenez du café au lait ou du café noir?
3. Est-ce que vous aimez le pain grillé avec du beurre et de la confiture?
4. Aimez-vous le jus d'orange?

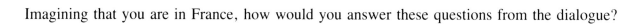

ANSWERS

Dialogue   **1.** J'aime manger le petit déjeuner à huit heures.   **2.** Je n'aime pas le café. Je prends du thé.   **3.** J'aime le pain grillé avec du beurre.   **4.** Je n'aime pas le jus d'orange.

148

(tah-bl)

LA TABLE

The Table

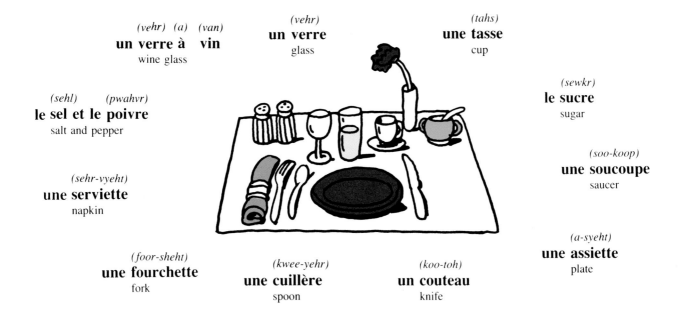

(vehr) (a) (van)
un verre à vin
wine glass

(vehr)
un verre
glass

(tahs)
une tasse
cup

(sewkr)
le sucre
sugar

(sehl)   (pwahvr)
le sel et le poivre
salt and pepper

(soo-koop)
une soucoupe
saucer

(sehr-vyeht)
une serviette
napkin

(a-syeht)
une assiette
plate

(foor-sheht)
une fourchette
fork

(kwee-yehr)
une cuillère
spoon

(koo-toh)
un couteau
knife

(vo-ka-bew-lehr)

Encore du vocabulaire

More vocabulary

(bwa-sohn)
une boisson — a beverage

(see-trohn) (preh-say)
un citron pressé — a lemonade

(byehr)
une bière — a beer

(ka-raf)   (freh'sh)
une carafe d'eau fraîche — a carafe of water

(soop)
une soupe — a soup

(day) (or)   (dŭhvr)
des hors-d'oeuvre — appetizers

(ar-tee-shoh)
des artichauts — artichokes

(as-pehrzh)
des asperges — asparagus

(shahn-pee-nyohn)
des champignons — mushrooms

(ehs-kar-goh)
des escargots — snails

(pah-tay)
du pâté — pate

(ra-dee)
des radis (masc.) — radishes

(soh-see-sohn)
du saucisson — sausage

de la viande — meat

(zhahn-bohn)
du jambon — ham

(la-pan)
du lapin — rabbit

(pwa-sohn)
du poisson fish

(poo-leh)
du poulet chicken

(ros-beef)
du rosbif roast beef

(voh)
du veau veal

des légumes vegetables

(ka-rot)
des carottes carrots

(shoo) (fluhr)
du chou-fleur cauliflower

(kohn-kohnbr)
du concombre cucumber

des épinards spinach

(day) (a-ree-koh) (vehr)
des haricots verts string beans

(o-nyohn)
des oignons onions

(ptee) (pwah)
des petits pois peas

(ree)
du riz rice

(to-mat)
des tomates tomatoes

(a-bree-koh)
des abricots apricots

(ba-nan)
des bananes bananas

(suh-reez)
des cerises cherries

(frehz)
des fraises strawberries

(frahn-bwahz)
des framboises raspberries

(muh-lohn)
du melon melon

(o-rahnzh)
des oranges oranges

(pahn-pluh-moos)
des pamplemousses grapefruit

(pehsh)
des pêches peaches

(pwar)
des poires pears

(pom)
des pommes apples

(reh-zan)
des raisins grapes

(sek)
des raisins secs raisins
dry

(dee-zhes-teef)
un digestif an after-dinner drink

(lee-kuhr)
une liqueur a sweet after-
dinner drink
(Grand Marnier, etc.)

(ehks-prehs)
un express an espresso

(sho-ko-la)
du chocolat hot chocolate

(say-ray-ahl)
des céréales cereal

(ya-oort)
du yaourt yogurt

LE REPAS PRINCIPAL (LE DÉJEUNER)

(ruh-pah) *(pran-see-pal)*

The Main Meal

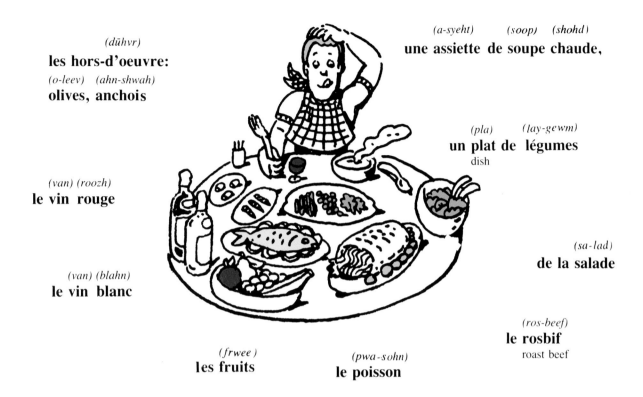

(dūhvr)
les hors-d'oeuvre:
(o-leev) *(ahn-shwah)*
olives, anchois

(a-syeht) *(soop)* *(shohd)*
une assiette de soupe chaude,

(pla) *(lay-gewm)*
un plat de légumes
dish

(van) *(roozh)*
le vin rouge

(van) *(blahn)*
le vin blanc

(sa-lad)
de la salade

(ros-beef)
le rosbif
roast beef

(frwee)
les fruits

(pwa-sohn)
le poisson

Note that cheese is not served as an appetizer and green salad is not served as a first course.

UN REPAS FRANÇAIS
A French Meal

1. **les hors-d'oeuvre**

2. **la soupe**

   (ahn-tray)
3. **l'entrée (viande ou poisson avec légumes)**

4. **la salade**

5. **le fromage**

   (deh-sehr)
6. **le dessert**

   (lee-kuhr)
7. **le café et la liqueur ou le digestif.**

Following are pictures of the courses of a French meal, but they are out of order, and the patron doesn't know where to start. Help him by writing numbers above each to show the right order. Of course, he can start the wine when he likes.

Now can you say the courses aloud, in order and from memory?

ANSWERS

Courses 1. hors-d'oeuvre 2. soupe 3. viande/poisson/légumes 4. salade 5. fromage 6. dessert 7. café

"A LA CUISSE   DE GRENOUILLE"

42 RUE DES GOURMETS
Paris 6e

CUISINE RAFFINÉE
P. Lebon, Propriétaire

| **MENU TOURISTIQUE— € 24** | **CARTE** |

HORS-D'OEUVRE

(va-ryay)
Hors-d'oeuvre variés
      assorted

(ko-kee-y)   *(frwee)*   *(mehr)*
Coquille de fruits de mer
shell   fruit   sea

(teh-reen)   *(shehf)*
Terrine du Chef

(kwees)   *(gruh-noo-y)*
Cuisses de grenouille
legs   frog

Soupe du jour

Hors-d'oeuvre variés   € 4

(shar-kew-tree)
Assiette de charcuterie   € 5
      cold cuts

(ko-kee-y)   *(san)*   *(zhahk)*
Coquille St. Jacques   € 5, 50
Terrine Maison   € 6

(grah)   *(trew-fay)*
Pâté de foie gras truffé   € 12
goose liver with truffles

(cok-tehl)   *(kruh-veht)*
Cocktail de crevettes   € 7
      shrimps

Soupe du jour   € 3

PLATS DU JOUR

Steak, frites
    French fried potatoes

(ro-nyohn)   *(voh)*   *(ma-dehr)* *(ree)*
Rognons de veau, sauce madère, riz
kidneys   veal   madeira

(kok)   *(rees-leen)*   *(va-puhr)*
Coq au Ricsling, pommes vapeur
capon   potatoes   steamed

(boor-gon-y)
Coq au vin de Bourgogne   € 11
      Burgundy

Coq au Riesling   € 11

(foh)   *(fee-leh)*
Faux-filet pommes rissolées   € 13
Sirloin   potatoes

(toor-nuh-doh)   *(bay-ar-nehz)*
Tournedos sauce béarnaise   € 17

(ro-tee)   *(ree-so-lay)*
Poulet rôti, pommes rissolées
roasted   sauteed

Salade verte

(fee-leh)   *(sol)*   *(mūh-nyehr)*
Filet de sole meunière   € 10
(vehrt)
Salade verte   € 3
green

DESSERTS

Au choix:
choice of

(pla-toh)
Plateau de fromages
tray   cheese

(krehm)   *(ka-ra-mehl)*
Crème caramel
flan

(tart)   *(ta-tan)*
Tarte Tatin maison
tart

(trahnsh)   *(na-po-lee-tehn)*
Tranche napolitaine
slice

(pla-toh)
Plateau de fromages   € 4
(pro-fee-trol)
Profiterolles   € 5, 50
(par-feh)   *(mees-tehr)*
Parfait-Mystère   € 4, 25
(soo-flay)   *(grahn)*   *(mar-nyay)*
Soufflé au Grand Marnier (2 pers.) € 12

(oh)   *(mee-nay-rahl)*   *(ay-vyahn)*
BOISSONS—Eaux minérales (Vichy, Évian)

(roh-zay) *(blahn)*
Vins (rouge, rosé, blanc):

(ka-ra-fohn)
carafon (4 dl)   € 4
(ka-raf)
carafe (8 dl)   € 7, 50

(mews-ka-deh)   *(lee)*
Muscadet sur lie   € 8, 50
lees

(bor-doh)   *(blahn)*
Bordeaux blanc   € 8, 50

(boh-zho-leh)
Beaujolais   € 7, 75
(shah-toh-nuhf)   *(pap)*
Châteauneuf du Pape   € 16
pope

Service 15% en sus—Boissons non comprises

Note: **SERVICE COMPRIS** on the menu means that the service is included. If service is **EN SUS**, pay a **pourboire** of 15%.

François et Pierre go to a fine restaurant in Paris, one rated with three forks and two stars. (Five forks indicate extremely expensive and posh places, three stars indicate the highest possible quality according to the *Guide Michelin*). The waiter arrives and brings them the menu. They order the dishes they are going to have.

(or) *(dūhvr)*
les hors-d'oeuvre
appetizers

(soop)
la soupe
soup

(poo-leh)
le poulet
chicken

(pom) *(freet)*
les pommes frites
french fried potatoes

(pan)
le pain
bread

(reh-zan)
les raisins
grapes

(ka-fay)
le café
coffee

(gar-sohn) *(meh-syūh)* *(kart)*
LE GARÇON **Messieurs, voici la carte.**
menu

Nos spécialités sont les cuisses de
(spay-sya-lee-tay)
legs

grenouille et le coq au Riesling.
frog capon

FRANÇOIS **Apportez-nous des hors-d'oeuvre et une**

assiette de charcuterie.

PIERRE **Ensuite je vais prendre un coq au Riesling**

avec des pommes rissolées.

FRANÇOIS **Pour moi, du poisson: un filet de sole**
(fee-leh) *(sol)*
meunière.
(mūh-nyehr)

LE GARÇON **De la salade?**

PIERRE **Oui, deux salades vertes. Ensuite, apportez-**
Then bring
nous le plateau de fromages.

LE GARÇON **Et comme boisson?**

FRANÇOIS **Du vin de la maison—un carafon**
(meh-zohn)

de blanc, un de rouge.

LE GARÇON **Vous prendrez un dessert?**
(prahn-dray)
will take

PIERRE **Un soufflé au Grand Marnier pour deux**
personnes. Et ensuite deux express et deux
(pehr-son)
cognacs. Et l'addition, s'il vous plaît.
(ko-nyak) *(a-dee-syohn)*
check

FRANÇOIS **(À Pierre) N'oublions pas le pourboire!**
Let's not forget tip
(poor-bwar)

(shar-kew-tree)
la charcuterie
cold cuts

(sa-lad)
la salade
salad

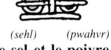

(sehl) *(pwahvr)*
le sel et le poivre
salt and pepper

(pwa-sohn)
le poisson
fish

(fro-mahzh)
le fromage
cheese

(ko-nyak)
le cognac
brandy

Using the menu, the pictures and the conversation, try filling in the blanks:

(klee-yahn)

1. _____ (The waiter) apporte le menu aux clients.
   customers

2. La _____ (specialty) de la maison est

   les _____ ____ _____ (frog's legs).

3. François demande des _____ (appetizers).

4. Le garçon _____ (brings) des haricots verts.
   (ko-mahnd)

5. Pierre commande _____ ____ _____ (some salad).
   orders

   (boo-teh-y)

6. Ils vont boire une bouteille de _____ (red wine).
   bottle

ANSWERS

Menu 1. Le garçon 2. spécialité, cuisses de grenouilles 3. hors-d'oeuvre 4. apporte 5. de la salade 6. vin rouge

HOW'RE WE DOING?

(ko-mahn)   (sa) (va)
Comment ça va?

This section is designed to help you see where you are at this point. We have covered a lot of ground so far. The following activities and games may help you define your strengths and weaknesses.

Can you match the questions on the left with the answers on the right?

1. Comment vous appelez-vous?
2. Quelle heure est-il?
3. Pouvez-vous nous donner une chambre pour une semaine?
4. Combien coûte un billet aller et retour?
5. À quelle heure aimes-tu prendre ton petit
   at what

   déjeuner?
6. Qu'est-ce que vous allez prendre?
7. Quel temps fait-il?
8. Qu'est-ce qui se passe?
9. Comment allez-vous?
10. Pouvez-vous nous dire où se trouve le musée?

A. Je vais très bien merci, et vous?
B. Il fait un temps superbe.
C. Continuez tout droit jusqu'à la rue Molière.
D. Je m'appelle Mark Smith.
E. Il est midi.
F. Impossible, il n'y a plus de chambres.
G. Quatre-vingt-dix euros.
H. Je vais prendre un coq au Riesling.
I. À huit heures.
J. Cet idiot a tamponné ma voiture.

Would you use **TU** or **VOUS** when speaking to the following people?

1. votre mari _____

2. votre soeur _____

3. un agent de police _____

4. vos parents _____

5. un pompiste _____

ANSWERS

Match questions-answers   1. D 2. E 3. F 4. G 5. I 6. H 7. B 8. J 9. A 10. C

TU or VOUS   1. tu 2. tu 3. vous 4. vous 5. vous

157

Can you fill in the correct French word below?

1. _____ mère
   His

2. _____ parents
   Her

3. _____ automobile
   My

4. _____ hôtel
   Their

5. _____ dîner
   Your (polite)

Can you make five questions from the five following statements using EST-CE QUE? Two examples:

Il aime les épinards. _____ Est-ce qu'il aime les épinards _____?

Vous aimez manger (quand). _____ Quand est-ce que vous aimez manger _____?

1. François et Pierre

   vont manger (quand). _____?

2. Vous allez en France (pourquoi?). _____?

3. Il y a un terrain de

   camping près d'ici (où). _____?

4. Tu aimes manger ton petit

   déjeuner (à quelle heure?). _____?

5. Ils voyagent à Paris (comment). _____?

Magnifique! See how it's all making sense? Now form questions using inversion, for instance:

Vous parlez français (quand?). _____ Quand parlez-vous français _____?

Vous allez à Paris (pourquoi?). _____ Pourquoi allez-vous à Paris _____?

1. Vous aimez voyager (quand?). _____?

2. Vous allez (comment?). _____?

ANSWERS

Inverted questions   1. Quand aimez-vous voyager?   2. Comment allez-vous?

Make five questions   1. Quand est-ce que François et Pierre vont manger?   2. Pourquoi est-ce que vous allez en France?   3. Où est-ce qu'il y a un terrain de camping près d'ici?   4. À quelle heure est-ce que tu aimes manger ton petit déjeuner?   5. Comment est-ce qu'ils voyagent à Paris?

Fill in   1. sa   2. ses   3. mon   4. leur   5. votre

Amusez-vous as you continue your review.

(Moh)   *(krwah-zay)*

Mots croisés
Crossword puzzle

ACROSS

1. Boy, waiter
5. Plate
6. Ticket
8. To see
9. Spinach
11. Museum
13. Mountain
14. Too much
15. To be

DOWN

2. Naturally
3. Summer
4. The (pl.)
7. Eight
8. Car
10. Salt
12. Pie

ANSWERS

DOWN **2.** naturellement **3.** été **4.** les **7.** huit **8.** voiture **10.** sel **12.** tarte

13. montagne **14.** trop **15.** être

Crossword puzzle ACROSS **1.** garçon **5.** assiette **6.** billet **8.** voir **9.** épinards **11.** musée

Can you make the following sentences negative?

Example: Je prends du poisson. ___Je ne prends pas de poisson.___

1. Je suis très fatigué. _____

2. Vous avez soif. _____

3. Je me sens très bien. _____

4. J'aime les haricots verts. _____

5. La banque est loin d'ici. _____

Describe the pictures in simple sentences.
Example:

Le chat est sous la table.

1. Le garçon _____

2. M. Smith _____

3. Le chien _____

4. La souris _____

ANSWERS

Négative sentences   **1.** Je ne suis pas très fatigué.   **2.** Vous n'avez pas soif.   **3.** Je ne me sens pas très bien.   **4.** Je n'aime pas les haricots verts.   **5.** La banque n'est pas loin d'ici.
Describe pictures   **1.** Le garçon est à côté de la porte.   **2.** M. Smith est dans la cuisine.   **3.** Le chien est devant le garage.   **4.** La souris est derrière la porte.

Can you order your **déjeuner** at the TROIS CANARDS?

(ka-nar)
AUX TROIS CANARDS
ducks

Plat du Jour:
Menu à 20 euros

Lapin au vin blanc
ou
Steak/pommes frites

Salade verte

Desserts—
Crème caramel
(moos)
Mousse au chocolat
Parfait
(sa-ba-yohn)
Sabayon (€ 3 supplément)

Boissons—eaux minérales (Évian, Vichy)
vins de la maison (rouge, blanc, rosé)
café, thé
(Boissons non comprises)

Plat du Jour:
Menu à € 22

(ehs-ka-lop)
Escalopes de veau au madère
ou
(kan-tohn)
Caneton rôti

Salade verte

4 RUE LECOQ
MONBOUDIN

JEAN LAPOULE,
PROPRIÉTAIRE

You don't know what **caneton** and **sabayon** mean, so you ask the waiter.

1. _____?

You find this meal delicious, so you tell the waiter:

2. _____!

At the end of the meal, you ask if the service is included.

3. _____?

Check please!

4. _____!

ANSWERS

Conversation with waiter (sample answers)
1. Qu'est-ce que c'est que ça? 2. C'est délicieux! 3. Est-ce-que le service est compris? 4. L'addition, s'il vous plaît!

AT THE STORE
(ma-ga-zan)
Au Magasin

16	*(ma-ga-zan)* *(kohn-fek-syohn)* ## Les magasins de confection Clothing Stores *(ta-y)* *(muh-zewr)* *(koo-luhr)* *(pran-see-pal)* ## Tailles et mesures/Couleurs principales Sizes and Measurements Basic Colors

(veht-mahn)
Vous essayez des vêtements
Trying on clothes

METTRE	**ESSAYER**	**S'HABILLER**	**ENLEVER**
To put (on)	To try, to try on	To get dressed	To take off

IL ME FAUT
I need

(por-tay)   *(preht)*
PORTER   **PRÊT-À-PORTER**
to wear, to carry   ready-to-wear

Here are some verbs that will come in very handy if you want to purchase any of the lovely French fashions.

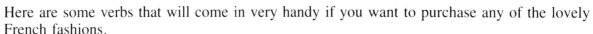

(ahnl-vay) **ENLEVER**			*(ash-tay)* **ACHETER** to buy		
j'	*(ahn-lehv)* **enlève**	nous	*(ahnl-vohn)* **enlevons**	j'	*(a-sheht)* **achète**	nous	*(ash-tohn)* **achetons**

(ahnl-vay) **ENLEVER**				*(ash-tay)* **ACHETER** to buy			
j' *(ahn-lehv)* **enlève**	nous *(ahnl-vohn)* **enlevons**			j' *(a-sheht)* **achète**	nous *(ash-tohn)* **achetons**		
tu *(ahn-lehv)* **enlèves**	vous *(ahnl-vay)* **enlevez**			tu *(a-sheht)* **achètes**	vous *(ash-tay)* **achetez**		
il elle on → *(ahn-lehv)* **enlève**	ils elles → *(ahn-lehv)* **enlèvent**			il elle on → *(a-sheht)* **achète**	ils elles → *(a-sheht)* **achètent**		

> NOTE: **Enlever** and **Acheter** undergo spelling changes, like **Préférer**.
> to buy

The verbs **enlever** and **acheter** (as well as other French verbs whose infinitives end in E + CONSONANT + ER) take an accent grave over the E that precedes a silent E in the **je, tu, il, elle, on, ils, elles** forms.

	(mehtr) **METTRE** to put, to put on		(sa-bee-yay) **S'HABILLER**	

		(meh-tohn)			(ma-bee-y)		(a-bee-yohn)
je		**nous**	**mettons**	je	**m'habille**	nous	**nous habillons**
	(meh)		(meh-tay)		(ta-bee-y)		(a-bee-yay)
	mets			tu	**t'habilles**	vous	**vous habillez**
tu		**vous**	**mettez**				
il		ils		il		ils	
	(meh)		(meht)		(sa-bee-y)		(sa-bee-y)
elle	**met**		**mettent**	elle	**s'habille**		**s'habillent**
		elles				elles	
on				on			

S'HABILLER is a reflexive verb (remember SE LAVER and S'AMUSER in Chapter 6):

Give the correct form of the verb for the persons listed.

	JE, J'	NOUS	ILS
1. **enlever**			
2. **acheter**			
3. **mettre**			
4. **s'habiller**			

Il me faut is another idiomatic way of saying I need (you have encountered **J'ai besoin de**). It means, literally, it is necessary to me (to you, to him, etc.). You use the personal pronoun-indirect object and place it between **il** and **faut**:

Il me faut	I need
Il te faut	You (fam.) need
Il lui faut	He/she needs
Il nous faut	We need
Il vous faut	You (pol., plur.) need
Il leur faut	They need

When **aller** is preceded by these indirect object pronouns, its meaning changes to **fit**:

Cette chemise vous va bien!   This shirt fits you well (or looks nice on you).

ANSWERS

Verbs 1. enlève, enlevons, enlèvent 2. achète, achetons, achètent 3. mets, mettons, mettent 4. m'habille, nous habillons, s'habillent

163

VÊTEMENTS D'HOMME

Men's Clothes

CLIENT **Ces pantalons sont trop petits.** *(pahn-ta-lohn)*

Pouvez-vous me montrer la taille
au-dessus? *(oh) (duh-sew)*

These trousers are too small. Can you show me the next larger size?

VENDEUR **(apportant des pantalons** *(zhohn) (see-trohn)*
jaunes citron): Voilà. Nous n'avons lemon
pas votre taille en bleu. *(blūh)*

(Bringing bright yellow trousers):

Here you are. We don't have your size in blue.

CLIENT **Quelle horreur!** *(oh-ruhr)*

How horrible!

VENDEUR **C'est la grande mode en**
France. Essayez-les! Ils vous vont
bien! Super chic! *(sew-pehr)*

It's the fashion in France. Try them on! They look nice on you!

Very chic!

CLIENT **Non, vraiment, je ne peux pas**
porter ça. *(por-tay)*

No, really, I can't wear that.

VENDEUR **(revient avec des pantalons** *(ruh-vyan)*
bleus beaucoup trop grands):
Excusez-moi! Essayez cette paire de *(pehr)*
pantalons bleus exactement de votre taille. *(ehg-zak-tuh-mahn)*

(comes back with blue trousers that are much too big):

Excuse me! Try this pair of blue trousers which are exactly your size.

CLIENT **(l'air épuisé):** *(ehr)*
the air
Ça y est. Qu'est-ce que vous pensez?

(looking exhausted):

There . . . what do you think?

VENDEUR **Ils vous vont parfaitement!** *(par-feht-mahn)*
Comme un gant . . . *(gahn)*

They fit you perfectly! Like a glove . . .

164

Match the French phrases with their English equivalents.

1. Ces pantalons sont trop petits.
2. Pouvez-vous me montrer la taille au-dessus?
3. Nous n'avons pas votre taille.
4. C'est la grande mode en France.
5. Ils vous vont bien.

a. Can you show me the next size?
b. It's the fashion in France.
c. These trousers are too small.
d. They look nice on you.
e. We don't have your size.

(shoh-seht)
des chaussettes
socks

Un villageois va à un magasin de confection
villager

pour hommes dans la grande ville.

(par-duh-sew)
un pardessus
coat

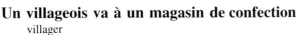

LE VENDEUR   **Vous désirez?**

(shuh-meez)
une chemise
shirt

(ma-ree)
LE VILLAGEOIS   **Je me marie ce week-end**
I'm getting married
(nuhf)
et il me faut des vêtements neufs. Il me
new
(soo) (veht-mahn)
faut des sous-vêtements et aussi une
underwear
(shuh-meez) (blahnsh)   (kra-vat)   (nwar)
chemise blanche et une cravate noire.

(po-sheht)
une pochette
(moo-shwar)
un mouchoir
handkerchief

(kra-vat)
une cravate
tie

LE VENDEUR   **Est-ce qu'il vous faut un**
(kohn-pleh)
complet?
suit

LE VILLAGEOIS   **Oui. Pourriez-vous me**

montrer un complet noir? Je porte du

quarante-quatre.

(kal-sohn)
un caleçon
undershorts

(pahn-ta-lohn)
des pantalons
trousers

LE VENDEUR   **Nous n'avons rien dans cette**
nothing
(vehs-tohn)
taille. Puis-je vous montrer un veston et
sport jacket

pantalon de sport?

(pew-lo-vehr)
un pullover
sweater

(ma-yoh)   (kor)
un maillot de corps
undershirt

(sha-poh)
un chapeau
hat

LE VILLAGEOIS   **D'accord. Puis-je les**
Can I
essayer? (Il les essaie.)

(kas-ket)
une casquette
cap

ANSWERS

Matching   1. c   2. a   3. e   4. b   5. d

(pa-ra-plwee)
un parapluie
umbrella

(an-per-may-ahbl)
un imperméable
raincoat

(kohn-ple)
un complet
suit

(gahn)
des gants
gloves

(ves-tohn)   *(spor)*
un veston de sport
sport jacket

LE VENDEUR   **Ils vous vont à merveille.**
(mer-ve-y)
marvelously

Maintenant je crois qu'il vous faut une
(san-tewr)
nouvelle ceinture!

Voilà la facture. Vous payez à la caisse,
(fak-tewr)   *(kes)*
bill   cash register

s'il vous plaît.

(san-tewr)
une ceinture
belt

(bot)
des bottes
boots

FACTURE	
(eh-gwee-y) **3, rue de l'Aiguille du Midi** needle **Chamonix, Haute Savoie**	
VESTON	€ 84
PANTALON	€ 44, 50
CHEMISE	€ 23
CRAVATE	€ 13
CEINTURE	€ 19, 50
SOUS-VÊTEMENTS	€ 11
TOTAL	€ 198

(e-ruhr)
LE VILLAGEOIS   **Monsieur, Il y a une erreur dans votre facture.**

(reh-zohn)
LE VENDEUR   **Ah! Vous avez raison. Cent quatre-vingt-quinze.**
You are right.

   Au revoir Monsieur.
   good bye

Le client a raison.

The customer is right.

Le vendeur a tort.

The clerk is wrong.

Can you tell me if the following statements are correct? Write **vous avez raison** or **vous avez tort**:

                                                    you are right   you are wrong

1. Le villageois a besoin de vêtements neufs. _____

2. Il ne lui faut pas de sous-vêtements. _____

3. Le villageois porte du 54. _____

4. Il essaie les pantalons. _____

5. Les pantalons sont trop petits pour lui. _____

Tailles
Sizes

VÊTEMENTS D'HOMME							
Men's Clothes							
CHEMISES (SHIRTS)							
Taille Américaine	14	14½	15	15½	16	16½	17	17½
Taille Européenne	36	37	38	39	40	41	42	43
AUTRES VÊTEMENTS (OTHER CLOTHING)							
Taille Américaine	34	36	38	40	42	44	46	48
Taille Européenne	44	46	48	50	52	54	56	58

If you are a man, what size shirt do you wear? (Je porte du _____.) What size pants,

suit and jacket do you wear? (Je porte du _____.)

If you are a female, look for the sizes of a male friend or relative: (Il porte du _____

pour les chemises et du _____ pour les pantalons, les vestons et les complets).

ANSWERS

True or False 1. vous avez raison 2. vous avez tort 3. vous avez tort 4. vous avez raison 5. vous avez tort

Fill in the blanks with the words depicted:

1. Quand il fait froid, je porte un _____

2. Quand il fait frais, j'enlève mon pardessus et je mets un _____

3. Quand il neige, je mets mes _____

4. Quand il pleut, j'enlève mon pardessus et je mets mon _____

5. Quand il pleut, je porte aussi mon _____

(fam)
VÊTEMENTS DE FEMME
Women's Clothes

(koo-luhr)   *(pran-see-pal)*
Les couleurs principales
Basic Colors

(blooz) (vehrt) (shuh-mee-zyay)
la blouse verte chemisier
green blouse

(sleep)(zhohn)
le slip jaune
yellow panties

(zhew-pohn) (blahn)
le jupon   blanc
white slip

(soo-tyahn)(gorzh)(zhohn)
le soutien-gorge jaune
yellow bra

(zhewp) (roozh)
la jupe rouge
red skirt

(rob)   (blūh)
la robe bleue
blue dress

(sak)   (mahn)
le sac à main noir
black purse

(foo-lar)   (zhohn)
le foulard jaune et noir
yellow and black scarf

Remembering the rules about adjective agreement—final letter E for feminine, ES for feminine plural; no change with an adjective like **rose** and **rouge** in the feminine because the masculine form ends with E; irregular feminine of **blanc: blanche**—can you answer these questions about the pictures? Example: De quelle couleur est la jupe? La jupe est rouge.

1. De quelle couleur est le foulard? _____

2. De quelle couleur est la blouse? _____

Can you continue asking yourself questions and answering them about the remaining pictures above?

Tailles
Sizes

VÊTEMENTS DE FEMME
Women's Clothing

LES BLOUSES OU CHEMISIERS (BLOUSES)

Taille Américaine	32	34	36	38	40	42	44
Taille Européenne	40	42	44	46	48	50	52

AUTRES VÊTEMENTS (OTHER CLOTHING)

Taille Américaine	8	10	12	14	16	18
Taille Européenne	36	38	40	42	44	46

Et moi, je porte du 48.
And I wear size 48.

(shoh-sewr)
CHAUSSURES POUR HOMMES ET FEMMES
Shoes for Men and Women

Elles sont trop
(ay-trwat)
étroites pour moi.
(sehr)
Elles me serrent.
They are too narrow for me. They pinch me.

Elles sont trop
(larzh)
larges pour moi.
They are too wide for me.

ANSWERS

De quelle couleur . . . . (sample answers)

1. Le foulard est jaune et noir.

2. La blouse est verte.

Tailles
Sizes

What size shoes do you wear? (Consult the two charts below.)

(shohs)

Je chausse du _____.

CHAUSSURES POUR HOMMES (CHAUSSURES DE VILLE, BOTTES, SANDALES) *(veel)* *(sahn-dahl)*									
Men's Shoes (city shoes, boots, sandals)									
TAILLE AMÉRICAINE 7	7½	8	8½	9	9½	10	10½	11	11½
TAILLE EUROPÉENNE 39	40	41	42	43	43	44	44	45	45
CHAUSSURES POUR FEMMES									
Women's Shoes									
TAILLE AMÉRICAINE 5	5½	6	6½	7	7½	8	8½	9	
TAILLE EUROPÉENNE 35	35	36	37	38	38	38	39	40	

We don't suppose you are the least bit fussy. But if you were very particular, here are some words and expressions just made to impress the clerk:

(kel-kuh) *(shohz)*

Je voudrais quelque chose en:

something

(nee-lohn)

nylon _____ **nylon**

(dan)

suede _____ **daim**

(twahl) *(dzheen)*

denim _____ **toile à jean**

(kweer)

leather _____ **cuir**

(ko-tohn)

cotton _____ **coton**

(swah)

silk _____ **soie**

Pourriez-vous prendre mes mesures? Could you take my measurements?

(meh-yuhr)

Je voudrais quelque chose de meilleure I would like something of better quality.

(ka-lee-tay)

qualité.

(a) (la) (man)

Est-ce fait à la main? Is it handmade?

(sahnbl) *(lohn)* *(koor)*

Ça me semble un peu long (grand, court, petit). It looks a little long (big, short, small) on me.

(ruh-toosh)

Pouvez-vous faire une retouche? Can you do alterations?

Je n'aime pas cette couleur; je préfère le bleu. I don't like this color; I prefer blue.

Note that, when used as nouns, colors are masculine.

Les magasins d'alimentation
(a-lee-mahn-ta-syohn)
Food Stores

Poids et mesures
(pwah)
Weights and Measures

(leh-tree) (krehn-ree)
la laiterie-crémerie
dairy

(boosh-ree)
la boucherie
butcher shop

(ay-pees-ree)
l'épicerie (fem.)
grocery

(boo-lahnzh-ree)
la boulangerie
bakery

(leh)
le lait
milk

(vyahnd)
la viande
meat

(frwee) *(lay-gewm)*
les fruits, les légumes
fruit   vegetables

(pan)
le pain
bread

(pwa-son-ree)
la poissonnerie
fish store

(kohn-feez-ree)
la confiserie
candy store

(pah-tees-ree)
la pâtisserie
pastry shop

(shar-kew-tree)
la charcuterie
delicatessen

(van) (spee-ree-tew-ūh)
les vins-spiritueux
liquor store

(pwah-sohn)
le poisson
fish

(bohn-bohn)
les bonbons (m.)
candy

(gah-toh)
les gâteaux (m.)
cakes

(soh-see-sohn)
le saucisson
sausage

(van)
le vin
wine

Trop de questions?

(troh) *(duh)* *(kehs-tyohn)*

Too many questions?

(kew-ryūh)
LE CURIEUX (THE INQUISITIVE ONE) **Excusez-moi, je voudrais vous poser une question. Où**

puis-je acheter du lait?

L'AGENT **On vend du lait à la laiterie du coin.**
on the corner

LE CURIEUX **Et si j'ai besoin de légumes et de viande, où est-ce que je vais?**

L'AGENT **À l'épicerie et à la boucherie, bien sûr.**
of course

LE CURIEUX **Et si je veux des fruits et du pain, où est-ce que je peux les acheter?**

L'AGENT **À l'épicerie et à la boulangerie.**

LE CURIEUX **Et s'il me faut du poisson et des bonbons, où puis-je les trouver?**

L'AGENT **Vous pouvez aller à la poissonnerie et à la confiserie.**

LE CURIEUX **Et si je veux des gâteaux?**

L'AGENT **Vous allez à la pâtisserie.**

(glas)
LE CURIEUX **Et pour la glace et le vin?**
ice cream

(shay) *(ehg-zas-pay-ray)*
L'AGENT **Allez à la pâtisserie et chez le négociant en vin. (exaspéré) Et si vous me posez encore**
wine merchant   exasperated

(kree-yay)
une question, je vais crier.
shout

Draw a line through the items which you could *not* find in each store:

(rohs-beef)

1. crémerie—beurre, fromage, vin rosé

2. boucherie—rosbif, oranges, veau

(sew-kray) *(leh-tew)*
3. épicerie—petits pains sucrés, raisins, laitue
sweet rolls   lettuce

4. charcuterie—raisins, pain, salami

5. boulangerie—jambon, crevettes, croissants

ANSWERS

Items that you could not find
1. vin rosé   2. oranges   3. petits pains sucrés   4. raisins, pain   5. jambon, crevettes

172

6. poissonnerie—bonbons, sole, eau ... e, asperges, truite *(trweet)* / trout

8. pâtisserie—riz, lait, petits fours ... poulet, bouteilles, épinards
(ree) rice *(foor)* small cakes

Notice that many of the store names are formed by adding ... he end of the product they sell. To name the person who sells the product, we often start the name of his/her store and substitute the ending -ER/-ÈRE Example:

lait	**laiterie**	**laitier**	**laitière**
milk	dairy	milkman	milkwoman

And if we want to say "I am going to the butcher's" instead of "I am going to the butcher shop," we use the preposition CHEZ: *(shay)*

Je vais à la boucherie. — I am going to the butcher shop.

Je vais chez le boucher. — I am going to the butcher's.

Je vais chez la bouchère. — I am going to the butcher's (fem.).

(pwah) *(muh-zewr)*

POIDS ET MESURES
Weights and Measures

(puh-zay)
PESER
To Weigh

_____

LE POIDS
The Weight

_____

ANSWERS

Items that you could not find
6. bonbons, eau minérale 7. asperges, truite 8. riz, lait 9. poulet, épinards

Although it has not yet caught on in the U.S., the metric system is the standard means for measuring in many other countries. Here are some common weights and measures:

(gram)
100 grammes = 3.5 ounces (a little less than ¼ pound)

1.000 grammes *(kee-loh)* **un kilo** $\Big\}$ = 2.205 pounds

500 grammes *(leevr)* **une livre** $\Big\}$ = 17.5 ounces (1 pound + 1.5 ounces)

Note that "one thousand" is 1.000, not 1,000, and that "three point five" is 3,5, not 3.5. *Just the opposite of the American system.*

(mee-lee-leetr)
1 millilitre = 0.034 liquid ounces

(sahn-tee-leetr)
1 centilitre = 0.33 liquid ounces

(day-see-leetr)
1 décilitre = 3.3 liquid ounces

(duh-mee)
1 demi-litre ½ = 0.53 quarts

1 litre = 1.06 quarts

Here are some useful expressions to use when buying food. Try writing them out:

(doo-zen)
une douzaine de (d')   a dozen of _____
une demi-douzaine de (d')   a half dozen of _____
un kilo de (d')   a kilo of _____
une livre de (d')   a half kilo of _____
deux cent cinquante grammes de (d')   a quarter kilo of _____
un litre de (d')   a liter of _____
Ça pèse combien?   How much does it weigh? _____
C'est trop.   It's too much. _____
C'est combien la douzaine?   How much are they per dozen? _____
C'est combien?   How much does it cost? _____
Ils/elles sont à combien?   How much do they cost? _____
C'est trop cher.   It's too expensive. _____

A L'ÉPICERIE

(roo-loh) *(pa-pyay)*
un rouleau de papier
(ee-zhyay-neek)
hygiénique
a roll of toilet paper

(boh-kal)
un bocal de café
(ans-tahn-ta-nay)
instantané
a jar of instant coffee

Ask the clerk for the items in the pictures. Use the names of the containers they come in or the measurement. Try asking some questions like HOW MUCH DOES IT (DO THEY) COST? HOW MUCH ARE THEY PER DOZEN, PER BOX, and so forth?

(suh-reez)
des cerises pesées
cherries being weighed
(ba-lahns)
sur une balance
on a scale

(leevr)
une livre de cerises
a pound of cherries

(bwaht) *(bees-kwee)*
une boîte de biscuits
box of cookies

(doo-zehn) *(dūh)*
une douzaine d'oeufs
a dozen eggs

(sa-vo-net)
une savonnette
cake of soap

(kee-loh) *(sewkr)*
un kilo de sucre
1 kilo of sugar

1. Je voudrais _____.

   Combien coûte _____?

(leetr) *(leh)*
un litre de lait
a liter of milk

2. J'ai besoin d'_____.

   Combien coûte _____?

(duh-mee) *(doo-zehn)* *(see-trohn)*
une demi-douzaine de citrons
½ dozen lemons

3. Je voudrais _____.

   Combien coûte _____?

(lay-gewm) *(kohn-sehrv)*
une boîte de légumes en conserve
can of vegetables

ANSWERS

Fill in blanks (À l'épicerie) **1.** un litre de lait **2.** une demi-douzaine de citrons **3.** une boîte de légumes en conserve

Nowadays, it is not always necessary to go to different stores to buy groceries. Many countries have North American style supermarkets where we can buy them in one place: bakery items, meat, eggs, a box of cookies, a roll of toilet paper, a liter of milk, a half-dozen oranges, a kilo of sugar, a package of candy. Of course, it is still interesting to go to the

(mar-shay) (ahn) (pleh) (nehr)   *(vo-la-y)*
open-air markets (**les marchés en plein air**) to see the great variety of **volaille, fruits,**
                                                            poultry

(fehr-myay)
légumes, and other products which the **fermiers**
                                    farmers

sell each day. It is a good way to observe the

foods typical of the country or the region.

Indicate the correctness of the statements by writing
vous avez raison or **vous avez tort**.

(dee-fay-rahn)
1. De nos jours, il est nécessaire d'aller dans beaucoup de magasins différents pour acheter
Nowadays

(a-lee-mahn-tehr)
    des produits alimentaires. _____
          food

(sew-per-mar-shay)
2. Il n'y a pas de supermarchés dans les autres pays.

_____

3. On ne peut pas acheter de papier hygiénique dans les supermarchés français.

_____

4. Dans les marchés en plein air, on peut acheter beaucoup de produits différents.

_____

5. Pour trouver les produits typiques de la région, il faut aller dans les supermarchés.

_____

ANSWERS

True or false

1. Vous avez tort.
2. Vous avez tort.
3. Vous avez tort.
4. Vous avez raison.
5. Vous avez tort.

176

The **pharmacies** and the **drogueries** are often combined **(Pharmacie-Droguerie)**. Otherwise, one buys prescriptions, drugs, things like tissues, sanitary napkins and some cosmetics in the **pharmacie**. Drugstores sell no prescriptions. But they carry over-the-counter drugs, all kinds of cosmetics and beauty products and also teas and some health foods, as well as cleaning products for the house. What you do not find in either place are ice cream, coffee or sandwiches. Lunch counters are nonexistent in drugstores and pharmacies, unless you go to the now famous *Le Drugstore des Champs-Élysées*, a big and fancy imitation of an American drugstore.

À LA DROGUERIE
At the Drugstore

(ay-pangl)
les épingles à
(shuh-vūh)
cheveux
bobby pins

la crème
(day-ma-kee-yahnt)
démaquillante
cleansing cream

(dee-sol-vahn)
le dissolvant
nail polish remover

(vehr-nee)
le vernis à
(ohngl)
ongles
nail polish

(fahr)
le fard
rouge

(mee rwar)
un miroir
mirror

(paht)
la pâte
(dahn-tee-frees)
dentifrice
toothpaste

(peh-ny)
un peigne
comb

(mas-ka-ra)
le mascara
mascara

(lak)
la laque
hairspray

(bros)
la brosse
(dahn)
à dents
toothbrush

(roo-zh)
le rouge
(lehvr)
à lèvres
lipstick

(moo-shwar)
les mouchoirs
(pa-pyay)
en papier
tissues

177

Monique and Pascale enter the drugstore and go to the cosmetics section. Monique looks at herself in the mirror.

MONIQUE **Je dois acheter** des épingles à cheveux, un pot de crème démaquillante
(poh)
jar

et des mouchoirs en papier.

PASCALE Je n'utilise jamais de crème démaquillante; **c'est trop cher.** Tu achètes
(ew-tee-leez)
toujours ton maquillage ici? C'est un magasin pour les riches, pas pour les
(ma-kee-yahzh)   *(reesh)*
pauvres comme nous.
(pohvr)
poor   like

MONIQUE **Tu as raison,** mais je ne peux jamais trouver de bons

produits dans mon quartier.
(kar-tyay)
neighborhood

PASCALE Je vais te dire quelque chose. Je ne vais rien acheter ici. C'est trop cher.
something

LA VENDEUSE **Bonjour Mesdames. Vous désirez?**
(may-dam)

MONIQUE **J'ai besoin** d'un peigne, d'une brosse à cheveux et d'un flacon de laque.
(fla-kohn)
bottle
Il me faut aussi une brosse à dents et de la pâte dentifrice. Ça coûte combien?

LA VENDEUSE La brosse à dents coûte 1 euro 60 et la pâte dentifrice 1 euro 20.

PASCALE Tu vois? Tu vas dépenser beaucoup d'argent!
(day-pahn-say)
to spend

MONIQUE Maintenant **je voudrais voir** vos produits de maquillage—le fard,
make-up
le rouge à lèvres, le mascara, s'il vous plaît. Ah! et

aussi le vernis à ongles et le dissolvant.

PASCALE **Mais tu dépenses trop.**

MONIQUE **Ça ne fait rien.** Ce n'est pas
it doesn't matter
pour moi, c'est pour mon mari.

PASCALE **(l'air étonné): Qu'est-ce que tu**
(ay-to-nay)
astonished
dis?

178

True or false?

1. Je peux acheter des mouchoirs en papier   T
   à la droguerie.   F

2. On trouve des produits de maquillage **au**
   (ray-ohn)   T
   rayon des cosmétiques.   F
   department

(pree)

3. Les prix sont chers à la droguerie.   T
   prices   F

4. Pascale ne veut rien dépenser
   à la droguerie.   T
                                     F

Ce qu'il faut dire quand vous *devez* faire quelque chose

What you must say when you *have* to do something

DEVOIR + INFINITIVE
must, to have to do something

Je dois acheter quelque chose.
I have to buy something.

IL FAUT + INFINITIVE
it is necessary to do something

Il faut aller à la laiterie pour acheter du lait.
It is necessary to go to the dairy to buy milk.

(duh-vwar) DEVOIR — must, to have to, to owe		
je	*(dwa)* dois	nous *(duh-vohn)* **devons**
tu		vous *(duh-vay)* **devez**
il elle on	*(dwa)* doit	ils elles *(dwahv)* **doivent**

Il faut is a generalization (It is necessary, one must . . .). To make it more specific, you can use the construction **il me faut** (+ infinitive), **il te faut**, and so on, which you learned in lesson 16.

Let's practice **devoir** + infinitive first. Try starting each sentence with the subjects suggested in parentheses. Say the sentences aloud:

1. **Je dois acheter quelque chose.** (Nous, Tu, Ils, Elle, Vous, Il)
2. **Il ne doit rien manger.** (Je, Nous, Tu, Vous, Ils, Elle)
3. **Elle ne doit pas trop dépenser.** (Vous, Nous, Ils, Je, Elles, Tu)

Can you answer these questions with il faut + INFINITIVE?

1. Est-ce qu'il faut manger pour vivre? _____

2. Où faut-il aller pour acheter de la viande? _____

3. Qu'est-ce qu'il faut utiliser pour enlever le vernis à ongles?

_____

4. Où faut-il aller pour acheter du maquillage? _____

ANSWERS

True or false 1. T 2. T 3. T 4. T

Answer questions 1. Oui, il faut manger pour vivre. 2. Il faut aller à la boucherie pour acheter la viande. 3. Il faut utiliser du dissolvant. 4. Il faut aller à la droguerie.

Let's hope you will never have the problems that this unfortunate traveler has.

HENRI **Est-ce que vous avez des bonbons?**

VENDEUR **Non, nous n'avons pas de bonbons. Pour**

acheter des bonbons, il faut aller à la confiserie.

HENRI **Et où trouve-t-on des cigarettes et des**

briquets?

VENDEUR **Pour acheter des cigarettes, vous devez**
(bew-roh)   *(ta-ba)*
aller au bureau de tabac.

(day-o-do-rahn)
HENRI **Merci. Je voudrais un flacon de déodorant,**
(lahm)
un rasoir et des lames de rasoir. Mon rasoir
(marsh)
électrique ne marche pas dans ce pays.
function

VENDEUR **Il vous faut aller dans un autre**
(trahns-for-ma-tuhr)
magasin pour acheter un transformateur.
voltage converter

HENRI **Mon Dieu! Que de problèmes!**
What
(so-lew-syohn)
VENDEUR **J'ai la solution. Laissez-vous pousser la**
Let   grow
barbe et la moustache comme moi. Les femmes
beard
m'adorent.

1. Name two things you find at the tobacco shop:

———————— , ————————

2. What things does a man use to shave with?

———————— , ————————

(bree-keh)
un briquet
lighter

(see-ga-reht)
des cigarettes
cigarettes

(fla-kohn)   *(day-o-do-rahn)*
un flacon de déodorant
bottle of deodorant

(rah-zwar) *(ay-lehk-treek)*
un rasoir   électrique
electric razor

(lahm)
les lames de rasoir
razor blades

(rah-zwar)
un rasoir
razor

ANSWERS
Tobacco shop (sample answers)   1. un briquet, des cigarettes   2. un rasoir, des lames de rasoir

À LA PHARMACIE

At the Pharmacy

You can identify the pharmacy by the green cross displayed outside its door. Pharmacies will not only fill a prescription

(or-do-nahns)

(une ordonnance), some will also treat *minor* emergencies.

Practice writing the new words.

Anne va à la pharmacie pour faire des
(a-shah)
achats. Elle demande des sparadraps,
purchases
de l'alcool, et un thermomètre. Elle
(far-ma-syan)   *(mal)*
dit au pharmacien qu'elle a mal à la
                                 ache
(teht)
tête, et il lui donne de l'aspirine.
head
Elle dit également qu'elle grossit,
                              grows fat
(noh-zay)
se sent mal le matin et a des nausées.
                       nausea

Le pharmacien dit: "Je crois qu'il

vous faut du talc, des épingles de

sûreté et des couches!"

(as-pee-reen)
un flacon d'aspirine
bottle of aspirin
_____

(pee-lewl)
les pilules (f.)
pills
_____

(spa-ra-dra)
le sparadrap
adhesive tape
_____

(tehr-mo-mehtr)
un thermomètre
thermometer
_____

(ay-pangl)   *(sewr-tay)*
les épingles de sûreté
safety pins
_____

(talk)
le talc
talcum powder
_____

(koosh)
les couches
diapers

_____

Here are some useful phrases for your *minor* complaints and hygienic needs:

(an-dee-zhehs-tyohn)(rewm)   *(kohns-tee-pa-syohn)*   *(gorzh)*
Il me faut quelque chose pour l'indigestion, le rhume, la constipation, le mal de gorge.
                                   cold   sore throat

181

J'ai . . . *(dya-ray)* **la diarrhée**

(mee-grehn) **une migraine**
migraine

(fyehvr) **de la fièvre**

(krahnp) **des crampes**
cramps

(greep) **la grippe**
flu

(dahn) **mal aux dents**
a toothache

(koo) *(so-leh-y)* **un coup de soleil**
sunburn

(toos) **Je tousse**
I cough

(koo-pay) **Je me suis coupé (e)**
I cut myself

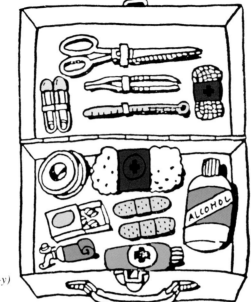

Je voudrais . . . *(a-see-dee-tay)* **un produit contre l'acidité**
acidity

(day-zan-fehk-tahn) **un désinfectant**
antiseptic

(yod) **de l'iode**
iodine

(pahns-mahn) **des pansements**
bandages

(ko-tohn) *(wat)* **du coton (de l'ouate)**
absorbent cotton

(see-zoh) **des ciseaux**
scissors

Je dois acheter . . . *(lak-sa-teef)* **un laxatif**
laxative

(sehr-vyeht) *(ee-zhyay-neek)* **des serviettes hygiéniques**
sanitary napkins

(see-roh) *(too)* **du sirop pour la toux**
cough syrup

Match the ailment in column 1 with the thing you would most likely ask for at the pharmacy in column 2. Sometimes more than one answer may be possible.

Column 1	Column 2
_____ 1. constipation	A. des sparadraps
_____ 2. une coupure	B. de l'insuline
_____ 3. de la fièvre	C. un laxatif
_____ 4. une migraine	D. un produit contre l'acidité
_____ 5. des crampes	E. de l'aspirine
_____ 6. diabète *(dya-beht)*	F. un désinfectant
_____ 7. la toux	G. des couches
_____ 8. mal à l'estomac *(es-to-ma)*	H. un thermomètre
	I. du sirop pour la toux
	J. des pansements

ANSWERS

Match 1. (C) 2. (A)(F)(J) 3. (H) 4. (E) 5. (E) 6. (B) 7. (I) 8. (D)

Laundromats are not as common in France as in the United States. Laundries are very good but fairly slow (3–4 days) and many are closed Saturdays and Monday morning. For your dry cleaning needs, you can find 24-hour service in most cities. August is vacation month, and many shops are closed at that time. In general, the easiest method is to ask your hotel to take care of your dry cleaning and laundry. Even easier—and cheaper—is to take as many permanent press clothes with you as possible.

Avoir l'air
To seem, to look

This is another very common and idiomatic construction with **avoir** (remember **avoir chaud**, **avoir froid**, **avoir envie**, **avoir besoin**, and so forth). It means, literally: to have the air. . . . **Vous avez l'air fatigué aujourd'hui.** You look tired today. **L'agent de police a l'air exaspéré.** The policeman looks exasperated. **Pascale a l'air étonné.** Pascale looks (seems) astonished. **Ça n'a**

(ew-mūhr)

pas l'air suffisant. It doesn't look sufficient. **Il a l'air de mauvaise humeur.** He seems to be in a bad mood. **Il a l'air de bonne humeur.** He seems to be in a good mood.

(la-vree) *(oh-to-ma-teek)* LA LAVERIE AUTOMATIQUE
The Laundromat

Susan, a foreign exchange student, goes to wash her clothes for the first time at the laundromat. Fortunately for her, a woman who has several children with her is also doing her wash.

(pa-keh)
le paquet
(le-seev)
de lessive
box of soap powder

SUSAN **S'il vous plaît, pouvez-vous**

m'aider? Combien de lessive est-ce
soap powder

(ma-sheen)
que je dois mettre dans la machine à
(la-vay) *(lanzh)*
laver pour laver mon linge?
laundry

(plahnsh)
la planche
(ruh-pah-say)
à repasser
ironing board

(say-shwar)
le séchoir
dryer

LA DAME **Jamais plus d'une demi-tasse** *(duh-mee)(tas)*
½ cup

pour si peu de vêtements.

(fehr)
**le fer à
repasser**
iron

SUSAN **(à elle-même) Ça n'a pas l'air**

(sew-fee-zahn)
suffisant. (Elle met deux tasses de
sufficient

lessive dans la machine qui commence

(pans)
**les pinces à
linge (fem.)**
clothespins

(kord)
**la corde à
linge**
clothesline

(day-bor-day)
à déborder.)
overflow

LA DAME **Jamais plus d'une tasse.**

Probablement moins . . .

(kor-beh-y)
la corbeille
(lanzh)
à linge
laundry basket

Susan is ready to dry her clothes. Another young woman, a student, is nearby.

SUSAN **Pouvez-vous me dire combien de pièces de monnaie il faut mettre dans la fente du** *(pyehs)* *(mo-neh)* *(fahnt)*
pièces · change · slot

(a) (proh-poh)
séchoir? Et, à propos, où est la fente? (Le séchoir ne marche pas.)
on the subject

L'ÉTUDIANTE **Il faut appuyer sur ce bouton. Comme ça, la machine marche et sèche** *(a-pwee-yay)* *(boo-tohn)* *(kom)* *(sa)*
press · button · This way

(a-bee)
vos habits.
clothes

SUSAN **C'est la première fois que je lave mes habits depuis que je suis étudiante ici.** *(duh-pwee)*
since

L'ÉTUDIANTE **Tu es une nouvelle étudiante? C'est ma troisième année.**

SUSAN **Tu es étudiante aussi? J'aimerais bien te revoir. J'ai tant de questions à te poser!** *(ehm-reh)* *(ruh-vwar)* *(tahn)*
would like · see again · so many

1. If you are going to the laundromat, what should you take along?

_____ , _____

ANSWERS

Going to the laundromat 1. un paquet de lessive, une corbeille à linge

184

2. In the laundromat, with what machines do you have to deal?

_____ , _____

SERVICES DE BLANCHISSAGE ET DE
(blahn-shee-sahzh)

NETTOYAGE À SEC DANS LES HÔTELS
(neh-twa-yahzh) *(a)* *(sehk)*

Hotel Laundry Services and Dry Cleaning

If you decide to use the laundry services of the hotel where you are staying, these expressions might get you by:

Est-ce que vous avez un service de blanchissage?　　Do you have a laundry service?

J'ai du linge à faire laver.　　I have some clothes to be washed.

Pouvez-vous coudre un bouton sur ma chemise?　　Can you sew a button on my shirt?

(ruh-koodr) *(mahnsh)*

Pouvez-vous recoudre la manche de cette blouse?　　Can you mend the sleeve of this blouse?

(na-mee-do-nay)

N'amidonnez pas mes caleçons.　　Don't use starch on my undershorts.

Pourriez-vous repasser cette chemise encore une fois?　　Could you iron this shirt again?

(neh-twa-yay)

Pourriez-vous faire nettoyer à sec ce complet?　　Could you have this suit dry cleaned?

(tash)

Pouvez-vous enlever cette tache?　　Can you take out this spot?

Try filling in the blanks with the key words from the sentences above. Then read the sentences aloud:

1. Pouvez-vous enlever cette _____?

2. Pouvez-vous _____ un bouton sur ma chemise?

3. Est-ce que vous avez un service de _____?

ANSWERS

Fill in blanks 1. tache? 2. coudre 3. blanchissage?

Going to the laundromat 2. une machine à laver, un séchoir

185

4. Pouvez-vous faire _____ ce complet?

5. Pouvez-vous _____ la _____ de cette blouse?

(ahn-vwah)
Jean envoie toujours son linge à la blanchisserie de l'hôtel. Mais cette fois, il y a des
sends   time

(par-tee)   *(ra-port)*   *(a-par-tyehn)*   *(kel-kuhn)*
problèmes. Une grande partie des vêtements qu'on lui rapporte appartiennent à quelqu'un
                part   brings back belong   somebody else

(dohtr)   *(plandr)*   *(zhay-rahn)*   *(soo-tyan)* *(gorzh)*
d'autre. Il va se plaindre au gérant. D'abord, il ne porte jamais de soutien-gorge ou de
             complain   manager First of all   never   bra   or

(ko-lahn)   *(a-mee-do-nay)*   *(fee-shew)*   *(brew-lay)*
collants. Ensuite, ses chemises sont trop amidonnées et une d'elles est fichue; elle est brûlée.
pantyhose Next   starched   ruined   scorched

(ahn) *(plews)*   *(mahnk)*
En plus, il lui manque deux chaussettes, une rouge et une verte. Le complet qu'il reçoit
In   addition   he's missing   receives

(tash)
de la teinturerie a une tache sur la manche. Il a raison de se plaindre, vous ne trouvez pas?
                           spot   complain

How would you complain about such things? You might want to use some of the following phrases:

I have to complain.	**Je dois me plaindre.**
There is a mistake.	**Il y a une erreur.**
These clothes are somebody else's.	**Ce linge est à quelqu'un d'autre.**
This shirt has too much starch.	**Cette chemise est trop amidonnée.**
My clothes are ruined.	**Mes habits sont fichus.**
This shirt is scorched.	**Cette chemise est brûlée.**
There's a button missing.	**Il manque un bouton.**
There's a spot on these trousers.	**Il y a une tache sur ces pantalons.**
I'm missing a pair of socks.	**Il me manque une paire de chaussettes.**

ANSWERS

Fill in blanks   4. nettoyer à sec   5. recoudre   manche

20

(sa-lohn) *(boh-tay)* *(kwah-fuhr)*
Le salon de beauté Le coiffeur pour
The Beauty Shop   The Hairdresser

(dam) *(om)*
dames Le coiffeur pour hommes
The Barber Shop

AU SALON DE BEAUTÉ
At the Beauty Shop

Mon Dieu! Je suis blonde!

Henriette goes to the beauty shop for her weekly visit.

(shuh-vūh)
**on lave les cheveux
de la jeune femme**
young woman's hair
being washed

(shahn-pwan)
le shampooing
shampoo

(per-ma-nahnt)
la permanente
permanent

LA COIFFEUSE **Qu'est-ce que vous désirez**

cette semaine, Madame?

(mee) (zahn) (plee)
HENRIETTE **Un shampooing– mise en plis,**
set
(ruh-toosh)
s'il vous plaît. Et une retouche.
touch up

Pouvez-vous aussi me faire un

massage facial et une manucure?

(brew-neht)
LA COIFFEUSE **Vous êtes brunette maintenant.**

(ran-sahzh) *(tant)*
Vous voulez un rinçage de quelle teinte?
rinse   color
(fohn-say)
De la même couleur ou plus foncé?
darker
(kler)
HENRIETTE **Un peu plus clair, s'il vous plaît.**
lighter
(bookl)
Je voudrais aussi des boucles sur le côté et
curls

(bee-goo-dee)
les bigoudis
curlers

(ma-new-kewr)
la manucure
manicure

(ma-sahzh) (fa-syal)
le massage facial
facial massage

187

(ohn-dew-la-syohn)

des ondulations sur la tête. Pourriez-vous
waves

(ra-koor-seer)

raccourcir un peu mes cheveux sur
shorten

(bro-say)

brosser
to brush

(newk)

la nuque? Je n'aime pas avoir les cheveux
back of neck

**une brosse
à cheveux**
hairbrush

(lohn)   **(koor)**

longs, je préfère les avoir courts.
long   short

(Une heure plus tard, la coiffeuse
brosse les cheveux d'Henriette, et
Henriette se regarde dans le miroir.)

se regarder

(say-shwar)

le séchoir
hair dryer

(blohnd)

HENRIETTE   **Je suis blonde!**
blond

(meer-wahr)

dans le miroir
to look at oneself in the mirror

FOR WOMEN ONLY: You are going to the "salon de beauté." What would you say to
the "coiffeuse"?

Je désire   1. _____

2. _____

3. _____

Here are some useful expressions a woman might want to know before she goes to the beauty shop.
Try writing them out:

I'd like to make an appointment for
tomorrow.

(rahn-day) (voo)

**Je voudrais prendre rendez-vous pour
demain.**

_____

Could you give me a rinse?

(ran-sahzh)

Pourriez-vous me faire un rinçage?

_____

Could you cut my hair?

(koo-pay)

Pourriez-vous me couper les cheveux?

_____

ANSWERS

FOR WOMEN ONLY   1. un shampooing–mise en plis.   **2.** une retouche.   **3.** une manucure.

Don't use any hairspray.	**Ne mettez pas de laque.**

I would like my hair cut in bangs.	*(frahnzh)* **Je voudrais une frange.**

CHEZ LE COIFFEUR
At the Hairdresser

Unisex hairdressers are just beginning to appear but are not widespread. Here are a few more useful expressions you may need at **LE COIFFEUR POUR DAMES, LE COIFFEUR POUR**

(ew-nee-sehks)

HOMMES (or **MESSIEURS**) or **LE COIFFEUR UNISEXE**.

	(bra-sheeng)
Could you blow dry my hair?	**Pourriez-vous me faire un brushing?**
I would like a light trim.	*(ay-ga-lee-zay)* **Je voudrais me faire égaliser les cheveux.**
Can you give me a light tint?	*(tan-tay)* *(lay-zhehr-mahn)* **Pouvez-vous me teinter légèrement les cheveux?**
I would like an Afro.	*(kwah-fewr)(a-froh)* **Je voudrais une coiffure afro.** *hairdo*
I would like my hair frosted.	*(day-ko-lo-ra-syohn)* **Je voudrais une légère décoloration des** *(mehsh)* **mèches.** *locks*
Can you tease my hair just a little?	*(kreh-pay)* **Pouvez-vous me crêper les cheveux un tout petit peu?**

After practicing these expressions aloud, try to fill in the blanks in the sentence below, using the words which follow.

1. Pourriez-vous me faire un _____ ?

2. Je voudrais me faire _____ les cheveux.

3. Je voudrais une _____ afro.

égaliser

un brushing

coiffure

ANSWERS
Fill in blanks   1. un brushing   2. égaliser   3. coiffure

4. Pouvez-vous me _____ les cheveux un tout petit peu?

5. Je voudrais une légère _____ .

décoloration des mèches

crêper

CHEZ LE COIFFEUR POUR HOMMES
At the Barber Shop

Mon Dieu! Je suis chauve!

(rah-zay)
raser
to shave

(moos-tash)
une moustache
(barb)
une barbe
beard

(peh-nyay)
peigner
to comb

se raser
to shave oneself

(pat)
des pattes
sideburns

se peigner
to comb one's hair

(ay-bar-buhr)
un ébarbeur—
(tohn-dūhz)
(une tondeuse)
clippers

la crème à raser
shaving cream

le rasoir

(koop)
une coupe de cheveux
haircut

(shohv)
un homme chauve
bald

(see-zoh)
les ciseaux

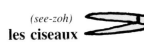

ANSWERS

Fill in blanks 4. crêper 5. décoloration des mèches

Philippe va chez le coiffeur parce qu'il a besoin d'une coupe de cheveux. D'abord, le

(ra-freh-shee)

coiffeur le rase et lui rafraîchit la barbe. Puis il lui fait un shampooing et lui coupe les

             trims   then

cheveux. Comme Philippe aime avoir les cheveux très courts, le coiffeur coupe beaucoup

                                                      (sahn-dor)   *(foh-tuh-y)*

sur la tête et sur la nuque. Philippe est très fatigué, et il s'endort dans son fauteuil. Le

                                                falls asleep   armchair

(plew)(zahn)(plew)

coiffeur coupe de plus en   plus. Finalement il déclare: "Voilà, Monsieur." Philippe se

                 more and more

regarde dans le miroir et voit qu'il est chauve. "Combien est-ce que je vous dois?"

demande-t-il. Le coiffeur répond: "Vous pouvez me payer pour six mois. Je ne crois pas

(byan-toh) (ruhv-neer)

que vous allez bientôt revenir.

      soon   come back

Try writing out these expressions, which could come in handy. Then read the sentences aloud:

Where is there a good barber shop?   **Où y a-t-il un bon coiffeur pour hommes?**

Do I have to wait long?   *(lohn-tahn)*
                                          Faut-il attendre longtemps?

Whose turn is it?   **C'est à qui le tour?**

I would like a shave.   **Je voudrais me faire raser.**

I would like a haircut.   **Je voudrais une coupe de cheveux.**

Long in back, short in front.   **Longs derrière, courts devant.**

Cut a little bit more here.   *(plews)*
                                      Coupez un peu plus ici.

AU KIOSQUE

le magazine *(ma-ga-zeen)*
magazine

le journal *(zhoor-nal)*
newspaper

(kart) *(pos-tahl)*
les cartes postales
postcards

les timbres (avion) *(tanbr)*
postage stamps (air mail)

(see-ga-reht)
les cigarettes

LE JEUNE HOMME **Pardon. Avez-vous des** *(zhoor-noh)* **journaux en anglais?**

Excuse me. Do you have newspapers in English?

(pro-pry-ay-tehr)
LE PROPRIÉTAIRE DU KIOSQUE **Oui, nous**
owner
avons un bon choix de journaux *(shwah)*
selection
anglais et américains.

Yes, we have a good selection of English and

American newspapers.

LE JEUNE HOMME **Je voudrais aussi des cartes postales de Paris.**

I would also like some postcards of Paris.

LE PROPRIÉTAIRE **Voilà des vues** *(vew)*
intéressantes de la capitale. *(ka-pee-tahl)*

Here are some interesting views of the capital.

LE JEUNE HOMME **Avez-vous des**
timbres-poste?

Do you have postage stamps?

LE PROPRIÉTAIRE **Non, mais vous pouvez**
en trouver au bureau de tabac.

No, but you can find some at the tobacco shop.

LE JEUNE HOMME **Et du tabac? Je voudrais** *(ta-ba)*
un paquet de cigarettes américaines.

And tobacco? I would like a package of American cigarettes.

LE PROPRIÉTAIRE **Vous voyez l'enseigne** *(ahn-sehn-y)*
devant le bureau de tabac là-bas? Ça
veut dire qu'on vend des cigarettes.

You see the sign with a plug of tobacco on it in front of the tobacco shop down there? That means they sell cigarettes.

LE JEUNE HOMME **Merci. Et est-ce que vous**
avez des magazines avec des photos? *(foh-toh)*
Oui par exemple? Ce n'est pas pour
moi, c'est pour mon grand-père.

Thank you. And do you have picture magazines? *Oui*, for example? It's not for me; it's for my grandfather.

LE PROPRIÉTAIRE *(frohns)* *(soor-see)* **(il fronce les sourcils):**
frowns   eyebrows
Oui, naturellement.

Yes, of course.

LE JEUNE HOMME **Bon. Je prends le**
journal, les cartes postales et le
magazine. Je vous dois combien?

Good. I'll take the newspaper, the postcards, and the magazine. How much do I owe you?

NOTE: Au bureau de tabac, on peut aussi acheter des bonbons, du chocolat, des allumettes, *(a-lew-met)*
(letr) *(kehl-kuh-fwa)*   *(soo-vahn) (oo-vehr)*
du papier à lettres, quelquefois de la glace. Les bureaux de tabac sont souvent ouverts le
stationery sometimes   often   open
dimanche matin.

Try reading aloud several times the conversation between the youth and the owner of the kiosk. When you feel confident of its meaning, see if you can match the phrases on the next page.

Match these French words or phrases from the dialogue with their English equivalents:

1. les journaux
2. les cartes postales
3. les timbres-poste
4. le bureau de tabac
5. le paquet de cigarettes

a. postcards
b. tobacco store
c. newspapers
d. package of cigarettes
e. postage stamps

À LA PAPETERIE
At the Stationery Store

(stee-loh) (bee-y)
un stylo à bille
ballpoint pen

(ka-yay)
un cahier
notebook

(ahnv-lop)
une enveloppe
envelope

(blok)
un bloc
writing pad

(kreh-yohn)
un crayon
pencil

(skotsh)
du scotch
transparent tape

(fee-sehl)
de la ficelle
string

(lehtr)
du papier à lettres
stationery

Si j'ai besoin d'un stylo à bille ou d'un crayon, je vais à la papeterie. Si je veux écrire une lettre, j'utilise du papier à lettre, et je mets la lettre dans une enveloppe. On vend aussi des cahiers à la papeterie. Je peux écrire des notes dans un cahier ou dans un bloc. Si je
(ahnv-lo-pay)
veux envelopper un paquet, il me faut du scotch, de la ficelle, et du papier d'emballage.
wrap wrapping paper
(ahn-ba-lahzh)

Pour demander quelque chose, je dis: *Je voudrais . . .*

ANSWERS

Matching   1. c   2. a   3. e   4. b   5. d

Now, let's take a trial run.

1. What two objects can you write with? _____ , _____ .

2. If you write a letter, what do you write it on? _____ .

3. What two things do you use to wrap a package? _____ , _____ .

4. What two things can you write notes on? _____ , _____ .

   (a-vyohn)
5. Where can you buy des timbres-avion? _____ .
   airmail stamps

6. Can you find the following words below? Circle them as in the example. (You should be able to find six more): envelope, pencil, newspaper, cigarettes, stamp, paper

E	M	I	G	U	J	O	N	B	L	O	C
N	E	X	C	E	O	T	R	O	S	U	A
V	I	C	E	S	U	S	D	U	R	E	T
E	C	I	G	A	R	E	T	T	E	S	I
L	S	R	E	C	N	L	E	E	E	H	M
O	A	M	A	L	A	P	A	I	E	R	B
P	U	T	I	Y	L	P	A	P	I	E	R
P	T	E	D	E	O	R	E	L	A	T	E
E	B	L	I	M	S	N	E	E	A	Q	U

ANSWERS

Fill in the blanks

1. un stylo, un crayon 2. du papier à lettres 3. de la ficelle, du scotch 4. un bloc, un cahier 5. au kiosque 6. enveloppe, crayon, journal, cigarettes, timbre, papier

Practice writing the new words on the lines provided under the pictures.

À LA BIJOUTERIE
At the Jeweler's

(a-noh)
un anneau
ring without stone

_____

(bag)
une bague
ring (with setting)

_____

(ko-lyay)
un collier
necklace

_____

LE BIJOUTIER   **Vous désirez, Monsieur?**

LE CLIENT   **Je voudrais acheter un cadeau pour ma**
(ka-doh)
present

femme.

LE BIJOUTIER   **Voulez-vous regarder ces bracelets et** _____

ces bagues en argent?
(ar-zhahn)
silver

LE CLIENT   **Je n'aime pas l'argent. Je préfère l'or.**
(or)
gold

LE BIJOUTIER   **Voudriez-vous voir une broche ou un**
(voo-dryay)
would you like

collier?

(bras-leh)
un bracelet
bracelet

_____

(brosh)
une broche
brooch

_____

196

(bookl)
les boucles (fem.)

(o-reh-y)
d'oreille
earrings

_____

_____

les boucles d'oreille
(pahn-dahn-teef)
à pendentif
pendant earrings

_____

_____

LE CLIENT   **Oui. Montrez-moi un bracelet,**
(pūh-tehtr)
un anneau en or, ou peut-être une paire
maybe

de boucles d'oreille, s'il vous plaît.

LE BIJOUTIER   **À pendentif?**

(mohn-tewr)
LE CLIENT   **Oui. Et une bague avec une monture de**
setting

(pyer)   *(pray-syūhz)*
pierres précieuses, et une chaînette en or.
stones   precious

(em-rohd)
LE BIJOUTIER   **Que pensez-vous de cette émeraude?**

(nes-pah)
Elle est superbe, n'est-ce pas?
isn't it true?

(fohn)
LE CLIENT   **Combien font les boucles d'oreille, la**
make

(ahn) (too)
bague et la chaînette en or en   tout?
altogether

LE BIJOUTIER   **8.400 euros.**

(oh-see)
LE CLIENT   **La Place Vendôme est aussi chère que**
as . .   as . .

la Cinquième Avenue à New York!
(me-tahn)   *(man)*
(Mettant sa main dans sa poche) haut les
putting   hand   pocket   hands up

mains, s'il vous plaît!

(sheh-neht)
une chaînette
chain

_____

1. Name two items of jewelry you might wear on your fingers.

   _____ , _____

2. What two sorts of jewelry do women wear on their ears?

   _____ , _____

ANSWERS

Jewelry
1. une bague, un anneau   **2.** des boucles d'oreille, des boucles d'oreille à pendentif

197

3. What two types of jewelry are worn around the neck?

_____ , _____

4. What is worn on the wrist? _____

5. What might a woman pin on her dress? _____

If you're a big spender and well-heeled, you might want to know the names of some valuable **pierres précieuses**. Try writing them out even if your wallet is not too thick.

(dya-mahn)
un diamant
diamond

_____

(peh'rl)
des perles
pearls

_____

(sa-feer)
un sapphir
sapphire

_____

(aym-rohd)
une émeraude
emerald

_____

(rew-bee)
un rubis
ruby

_____

(to-pahz)
une topaze
topaze

_____

(pla-teen)
le platine
platinum

_____

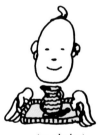
(ar-zhahn)
l'argent
silver

_____

(or)
l'or
gold

_____

ANSWERS

3. un collier, une chaînette 4. un bracelet 5. une broche

L'HORLOGERIE

The Watchmaker's Shop

(mohntr)
une montre-bracelet
wristwatch

(ray-veh-y) (ma-tan)
un réveille-matin
alarm clock

(or-lozh-ree)
l'horlogerie
watchmaker's shop

(or-lo-zhay)
l'horloger
watchmaker

Practice writing the new words by filling in the blanks under the pictures. Once you have done this, read aloud the sentences below which may help you when you visit the watchmaker's. After you have practiced them aloud, try writing them out in the spaces provided:

(ray-pa-ray)
Pouvez-vous réparer cette montre?   Can you fix this watch?

_____

Pouvez-vous nettoyer ma montre?   Can you clean my watch?

_____

(a-vahns)
Ma montre avance.   My watch is fast.

_____

Mon réveille-matin retarde.   My alarm clock is slow.

_____

(a-reh-tay)
Ma montre s'est arrêtée.   My watch has stopped.

_____

Elle ne marche pas bien.   It doesn't run well.

_____

199

Notice: In France, watches, clocks (as well as cars, washing machines and other machines) don't run; they're more leisurely; they walk (the verb *marcher* literally means to walk).

(ruh-mohn-tay)
Je ne peux pas la remonter.   I can't wind it.

(krees-tal)
Il me faut un cristal.   I need a crystal.

Quand est-ce qu'elle va être prête?   When will it be ready?

(ruh-sew)
Pouvez-vous me donner un reçu?   Can you give me a receipt?

Try reading this paragraph to see if you can understand it. You may need to refer to the previous sentences.

Ma montre ne marche pas bien. Un jour elle avance; un autre jour elle retarde. Aujourd'hui elle s'est arrêtée et je ne peux pas la remonter. Je vais l'apporter chez

(leh-say)

l'horloger et l'horloger va la réparer. Il va aussi la nettoyer. Si je dois laisser ma montre à

l'horlogerie, l'horloger va me donner un reçu.   leave

1. If you are always arriving late, what could be wrong with your watch?

   Ma montre ne _____ bien. Elle _____ .

2. When you always seem to be early for appointments, what might be the matter?

   Ma montre _____ .

ANSWERS

Fill in blanks
1. marche pas retarde.   2. avance.

200

23 Le magasin de souvenirs
(soov-neer)
Gift Shop

Le magasin de musique
(mew-seek)
Music Store

Le magasin de photographie
(fo-to-gra-fee)
Photography Shop

(ka-doh)
un cadeau
present

(foo-lar)
un foulard
scarf

(ruh-pro-dewk-syohn)
une reproduction
reproduction

(par-fuhn)
du parfum
perfume

(por-tuh-fuh-y)
un portefeuille
wallet

(por-tuh) (klay)
un porte-clés
key ring

(port) (bo-nūhr)
un porte-bonheur
charm

(bee-zhoo)
un bijou
jewel

(port) (mo-neh)
un porte-monnaie
change purse

(sa) (ka) (man)
un sac à main
handbag

(kweer)
du cuir
leather

(ar-zhahn-tree)
de l'argenterie
silverware

(boo-teek)
UNE BOUTIQUE
boutique

Here are a few adjectives which may be useful when shopping for gifts and souvenirs:

(boh) (bel) **beau, belle**	beautiful	(tee-peek) **typique**	typical
(zho-lee) **joli, jolie**	pretty	(fohn-say) **foncé, foncée**	dark
(ra-vee-sahn) (ra-vee-sahnt) **ravissant, ravissante**	lovely	(klehr) **clair, claire**	light
cher, chère	expensive	(bohn) (mar-shay) **bon marché**	inexpensive

AU MAGASIN DE SOUVENIRS

At the gift shop

LA VENDEUSE **Vous désirez?**	Can I help you?
LE TOURISTE **Je voudrais un cadeau typiquement français.**	I would like a typically French present.
LA VENDEUSE **Pour un monsieur ou pour une dame?**	For a man or for a woman?

LE TOURISTE **Pour une dame.**	For a woman.
LA VENDEUSE **Un foulard en soie peut-être? Un sac en cuir, du parfum? Nous avons aussi ces belles reproductions des tableaux du Louvre et du Musée d'Orsay.**	A silk scarf perhaps? A leather bag, some perfume? We also have these beautiful reproductions of paintings from the Louvre and from the Musée d'Orsay.
LE TOURISTE **Combien coûte ce foulard?**	How much does the scarf cost?
LA VENDEUSE **Quarante-huit euros. C'est un beau souvenir. Regardez: c'est une carte de la France avec tous** *(mo-new-mahn)* **les monuments.**	Forty-eight euros. It is a beautiful souvenir. Look: it is a map of France with all the monuments.

LE TOURISTE **Je le prends. Pouvez-vous faire un joli paquet?**	I'll take it, Can you gift-wrap it?

(While the clerk gift-wraps the package, the tourist takes out his wallet.)

LE TOURISTE	**Zut! Je n'ai pas assez d'argent. (À ce moment, sa femme entre dans le magasin.)**	Darn it! I don't have enough money. (At this moment, his wife enters the store.)
LA TOURISTE	**Mais qu'est-ce que tu fais ici?**	But what are you doing here?
LE TOURISTE	**Euh . . . . j'achète un** *(shay-ree)* **cadeau pour toi . . . . Chérie, peux-tu** *(pre-tay)* **me prêter vingt-cinq euros?** lend	Uh . . . . I bought you a present . . . . Darling, can you lend me 25 euros?

darling (under Chérie)

Answer these questions based on the dialogue in French.

1. Qu'est-ce que le touriste voudrait acheter?
2. Pour qui?
3. Qu'est-ce que la vendeuse suggère?
4. Combien coûte le foulard?
5. Quel est le problème du touriste?
6. Le touriste a besoin de combien de francs?

AU MAGASIN DE DISQUES
At the Record Store

NOTE: A **magasin de musique** sells records, cassettes, radios, musical scores and musical instruments. A **magasin de disques** sells records, cassettes and record players, as well as radios.

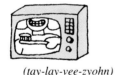

(tay-lay-vee-zyohn)
une télévision
television

(dee-ah-mahn)
un diamant
needle

(trahnt) (trwah) (toor)
un 33 tours
33 rpm

(ka-rahnt) (san) (toor)
un 45 tours
45 rpm

(ra-dyoh)
une radio
radio

(toorn) (deesk)
un tourne-disque
record player

(ma-nyay-to-fon)
un magnétophone
tape recorder

ANSWERS

Dialogue 1. Le touriste voudrait acheter un cadeau typiquement français. **2.** Pour une dame. **3.** La vendeuse suggère un foulard en soie, un sac en cuir, du parfum, et des belles reproductions. **4.** Le foulard coûte quarante huit euros. **5.** Il n'a pas assez d'argent. **6.** Il a besoin de vingt-cinq euros.

(kohn-pakt)
un disque compact
compact disk

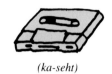

(ka-seht)
une cassette
cassette

(lehk-tūhr)
un lecteur de cassette portatif
portable cassette player

(bahnd)
une bande
tape

La musique française

French music

La musique américaine

American music

(kla-seek)
La musique classique

Classical music

(fol-klo-reek)
La musique folklorique

Folk music

La musique pop (pop)

Pop music

(groh) *(sewk-seh)*
Un (gros) succès

A hit

Monsieur Laflûte adore la musique classique, mais il n'a

pas beaucoup d'argent. Tous les samedis après-midi, il

prend l'autobus ou le métro pour aller dans un magasin

(kar-tyay) *(dee-fay-rahn)*
de disques, chaque fois dans un quartier différent de la
section   different

(sans-tal)
ville. Il prend trois ou quatre disques, s'installe dans une
settles

(kohn-poh-see-tūhr) *(pahn-dahn)*
cabine et écoute ses compositeurs préférés pendant deux
for

(mwan) *(ūh-rūh)* *(suh)* *(ray-zhoo-ee-sahn)* *(kohn-sehr)*
heures au moins. Puis il retourne chez lui, heureux, se réjouissant déjà du concert de la
at least   to his home happy   looking forward   concert

(pro-shehn)
semaine prochaine.
next

204

Can you answer the following questions?

1. Où va M. Laflûte le samedi? _____

2. Qu'est-ce que M. Laflûte aime? _____

3. Est-ce que M. Laflûte est riche? _____

4. Qu'est-ce que M. Laflûte écoute tous les samedis après-midi?
   (ay-koot)
   listens

_____

5. Pourquoi M. Laflûte est-il heureux quand il retourne chez lui? Parce qu'il se réjouit du

_____

AU MAGASIN DE MUSIQUE
At the Music Store

(pro-mehn)   *(pehr-dew)*
Madame Smith se promène, l'air un peu perdu, dans
    walks around   lost

un magasin de disques. Après un long moment,

(sa-prosh)
le vendeur s'approche d'elle.
    comes near

LE VENDEUR   **Qu'est-ce que je peux faire pour vous?**

MARIE SMITH   **Je cherche un disque pour un jeune Américain.**

LE VENDEUR   **Est-ce qu'il aime la musique classique? La**

        musique populaire? Les chansons?

(shan-sohn)   *(po-pew-lehr)*
Les chansons populaires
Folk songs

(nuh-vūh)
MARIE SMITH   **Je ne sais pas vraiment. C'est mon neyeu, je ne le connais pas très bien.**
                       nephew   know

(dehr-nyehr)   *(mak-seem)* *(fo-rehs-tyay)*
LE VENDEUR   **Peut-être les dernières chansons de Maxime Forestier?**
          latest

MARIE SMITH   **Maxime? Le restaurant?**

ANSWERS

Reading Paragraph 1. Il va au magasin de disques. **2.** Il aime la musique classique. **3.** Il n'a pas beaucoup d'argent. **4.** Il écoute des disques. **5.** concert de la semaine prochaine.

LE VENDEUR **N'y pensez plus.** *(nee)* **J'ai une idée: les Grateful Dead. Un gros succès ici.**
forget it

MARIE SMITH **C'est un groupe français?**

LE VENDEUR **Mais oui! Superbe!** *(sew-pehrb)*

MARIE SMITH **D'accord.**

(Un peu plus tard, à l'hôtel)

MARC **Alors, qu'est-ce que tu as trouvé pour Johnny?**
what did you find

MARIE **Les Grateful Dead. Ils sont superbes.**

MARC **Mais mon pauvre chou, les Grateful Dead sont américains. Tu vas retourner au** *(pohvr)* *(shoo)*
poor darling

magasin demain, ça va être un bon exercice de français pour toi.

True or false?

1. Madame Smith voudrait acheter de la musique de Claude Debussy.   T
   F

2. Il y a un restaurant à Paris qui s'appelle Chez Maxime.   T
   F

3. Les Grateful Dead sont un groupe français.   T
   F

4. Si Madame Smith retourne au magasin de disques demain, elle va faire un bon   T
   exercice de français.   F

AU MAGASIN DE PHOTOGRAPHIE
At the Photography Shop

une photo
print

(a-grahn-dees-mahn)
un agrandissement
enlargement

(ka-may-rah)
une caméra
movie camera

(dya-poh-zee-teev)
des diapositives (fem.)
slides

(a-pa-reh-y) (foh-toh-gra-feek)
un appareil photographique
camera

(roo-loh) *(feelm)*
un rouleau de film
roll of film

ANSWERS

True or False 1. F 2. T 3. F 4. T

MARC **Je voudrais faire développer ce film.** *(dayv-lo-pay)*

L'EMPLOYÉ **Vous voulez des diapos?** *(dya-poh)*

MARC **Non. Des photos sur papier**

mat, sept sur onze centimètres. *(mat)*
mat

L'EMPLOYÉ **Vos photos vont être prêtes dans trois** *(foh-toh)*

jours. Voilà votre reçu.

(Three days later)

MARC **Je viens chercher mes photos. Voilà mon reçu. Je voudrais aussi un rouleau de** *(shehr-shay)*
pick up

film en noir et blanc, trente-cinq millimètres, 20 photos.

(On the street, Mark opens the envelope.)

Mais qui est ce gros bonhomme? *(groh)* *(bo-nom)*
fat   fellow

(He goes back to the store.)

L'EMPLOYÉ **Mon Dieu! J'ai fait une erreur. Le gros monsieur vient de partir avec vos** *(fe)* *(eh-ruhr)* *(vyan)*
I made   mistake   just left

photos dans sa poche. Il a dit: "Je suis très pressé, je prends le train pour Marseille *(preh-say)*
he said   in a big hurry

dans vingt minutes."

1. Quand Marc arrive au magasin de photos, il dit: "Je voudrais faire _____ ce film."

2. L'employé demande: "Vous voulez des _____?"

3. Marc répond: "Non. Des _____, sur papier _____, sept sur _____ centimètres."

4. L'employé dit que les photos vont être _____ dans trois _____.

ANSWERS
Questions 1. développer 2. diapos 3. photos mat onze 4. prêtes jours

24

(ray-pa-ra-syohn)
Les réparations:
Repair Services

(kor-do-nyay)
Le cordonnier
The Shoemaker (cobbler)

(op-tee-syan)
L'opticien
The Optometrist

Pour vraiment bien voir une ville ou un village, il faut marcher. Vous faites partie de la
are part

(fool)   *(va-kahn)*   *(o-kew-pa-syohn)*   *(a-tahn-syohn)*
foule et la foule, vaquant à ses occupations, ne fait pas attention à vous. Vous pouvez
crowd   going about   chores   pays no attention

(ob-sehr-vay)   *(vee-zahzh)*   *(ehg-za-mee-nay)* *(ay-ta-lahzh)*   *(ahn)* *(plehn)*
observer les visages, entrer dans les magasins, examiner les étalages des marchés en plein
     faces   displays

(ehr) *(mar-shan-day)*   *(pews)* *(flah-nay)*   *(zhar-dan)* *(pew-bleek)*
air, marchander dans les marchés aux puces, flâner dans les jardins publics, lire les
   bargain   flea markets   stroll   public gardens

(ans-kreep-syohn)   *(sta-tew)*   *(suh-la)*   *(swa)* *(po-seh-day)*
inscriptions sur les statues. Pour tout cela, il vous faut soit posséder de bonnes chaussures
                            that   either own

(swee-vahnt)
de marche, soit connaître les mots et les expressions suivantes:
   or   following

Pardon, pourriez-vous me dire s'il y a un

cordonnier près d'ici?

Excuse me. Could you tell me if there is a

shoemaker near here?

CHEZ LE CORDONNIER
At the Shoemaker

(shoh-sewr)
des chaussures
shoes

(la-seh)
des lacets
shoelaces

(sahn-dahl)
des sandales
sandals

le cordonnier
shoemaker

(ta-lohn) *(kah-say)*
Mon talon est cassé.
heel   broken

My heel is broken.

(ray-pa-ray)
Est-il possible de réparer ma chaussure

Is it possible to fix my shoe while I wait?

(pahn-dahn) (kuh) (zha-tahn)
pendant que j'attends?

Pour quand pouvez-vous la réparer?
for when

When can you fix it?

Retenez . . .
Remember . . .

ouvert	open
jusqu'à	until
(suh-mel)	
la semelle	sole
(ew-zay)	
usé	worn
(ruh-suh-muh-lay)	
ressemeler	to resole
le plastique	plastic
temporaire	temporary
le talon	heel

CHEZ L'OPTICIEN
At the Optometrist's

l'opticien
optometrist

(lew-neht) *(kah-say)*
des lunettes cassées
broken glasses

LA TOURISTE **La monture et un verre de mes lunettes sont fendus. Je ne vois rien** *(fahn-dew)*
cracked

sans lunettes.

L'OPTICIEN **Avez-vous une paire de rechange?** *(pehr)* *(ruh-shahnzh)*
extra pair

LA TOURISTE **Malheureusement pas.** *(ma-lūh-rūhz-mahn)*

L'OPTICIEN **Vous êtes myope ou hypermétrope?** *(myop)* *(ee-pehr-may-trop)*
near-sighted far-sighted

la monture *(mohn-tewr)*
frame

un verre *(vehr)*
lens
(de contact)
(contact)

LA TOURISTE **Hypermétrope.**

L'OPTICIEN **Essayez cette paire . . . Qu'est-ce que vous voyez?** *(eh-say-ay)*
try on

LA TOURISTE **Elles me vont bien! Écoutez:**
fit me well   listen

(say)
C
(oh) *(ew)* *(vay)*
o   u   v

(doobl vay) *(day)* *(es)* *(er)* *(tay)* *(kah)* *(ee grek)*
w   d   s   r   t   k   y

L'OPTICIEN **Hum . . . Asseyez-vous là. Je vais essayer**
Sit there

de réparer vos lunettes tout de suite. . . .

(Quelques minutes plus tard). *(tar)*
later

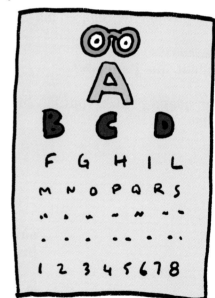

L'OPTICIEN **Voilà. Attention! Vos lunettes sont très fragiles. C'est une réparation temporaire.** *(fra-zheel)* *(tahn-po-rehr)*
fragile   temporary

LA TOURISTE **Merci mille fois, Monsieur. Je vous suis très reconnaissante.** *(ruh-ko-ne-sahnt)*
grateful

210

Retenez . . .

Remember . . .

réparer	to fix
(se-ray)	
serrer	to tighten
(so-leh-y)	
les lunettes de soleil	sunglasses
remplacer	to replace
(tood-sweet)	
tout de suite	right away
(fahn-dew)	
fendu	cracked
(ruh-shahnzh)	
une paire de rechange	a spare pair

After studying the optometrist and shoemaker vocabulary, try to draw lines between the French words and their English equivalent:

1. réparer	A. the cobbler
2. des lunettes	B. the shoelaces
3. des chaussures	C. to tighten
4. fendu	D. the heel
5. la monture	E. shoes
6. le talon	F. glasses
7. serrer	G. lens
8. les lacets	H. frame
9. les verres	I. to repair
10. le cordonnier	J. cracked

ANSWERS

Matching 1. I 2. F 3. E 4. J 5. H 6. D 7. C 8. B 9. G 10. A

ESSENTIAL SERVICES

(ser-vees) *(eh-sahn-syel)*

Services essentiels

25	*(bahnk)* **La banque** Bank

(bee-yeh) *(mo-neh)*

LES BILLETS ET LA MONNAIE
Bills and Coins

In 2002 the French franc passed into history and was replaced by the euro (*er-ro*). The new currency is identical throughout the European Union countries. The seven euro notes come in different colors and sizes, and the eight new French coins go from 1 cent to 2 euros.

French bank notes

5 euros	100 euros
10 euros	200 euros
20 euros	500 euros
50 euros	

French coins

1 cent	1 euro
2 cents	2 euros
5 cents	
10 cents	
20 cents	
50 cents	

To obtain the best exchange rate for your foreign currency, you will want to go to the nearest bank. Most French banks remain open from 9:30 A.M.–4:30 P.M. Some close for lunch, especially during the slower summer months. All banks close at noon on the day before a holiday.

Most large hotels will exchange your dollars if you are staying there. You can find
(bew-roh)
BUREAUX DE CHANGE in large banks, in airports and railroad stations, and at the border. **Attention!** If you are traveling during the weekend, don't forget to change your money promptly, as you may have difficulty finding a **bureau de change** open in small towns.

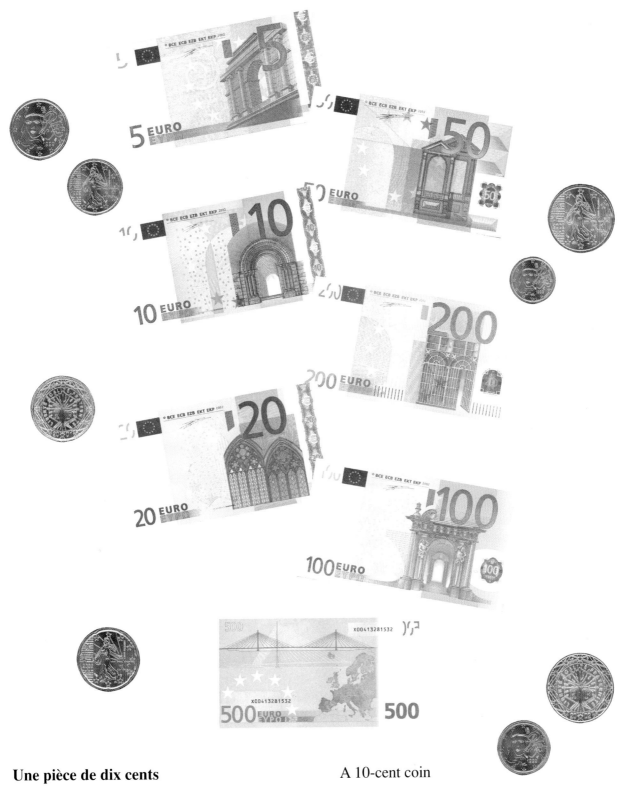

Une pièce de dix cents

A 10-cent coin

Un billet de cinquante euros

A 50-euro bill

The abbreviation for euro is €. Bear in mind that when using numbers, the French use commas where we use periods. € 5.000,50 is five thousand euros and fifty cents.

LES BANQUES, LE CHANGE,

(shahnzh)

LES CHÈQUES DE VOYAGE

(shehk) *(vwa-yahzh)*

Banks, Money Exchange, Traveler's Checks

Les gens et les choses

People and things

(ahn-plwah-yay)
l'employé de banque
bank employee

la banque
bank

(lee-keed)
l'argent liquide
cash

(ahn-pruhn)
l'emprunt (masc.)
loan (money you borrow)

(keh-syeh) *(keh-syehr)*
le caissier, la caissière
cashier (male and female)

l'argent
money

le billet de banque
banknote

(gee-sheh)
le guichet
teller's window

(bewl-tan) *(vehr-suh-mahn)*
le bulletin de versement
deposit slip

(kohnt)
le compte
account

(dee-rehk-tuhr)
le directeur
manager

(kar-neh)
le carnet de chèques
checkbook

(vwa-yahzh)
le chèque de voyage
traveler's check

(mo-neh)
la monnaie
small change

Read the following dialogue out loud several times. It contains expressions you will need to conduct business in a bank.

Mr. Smith and his wife enter a bank in Paris in order to exchange some American dollars and traveler's checks.

M. SMITH	**Bonjour Monsieur. Je voudrais changer ce chèque de voyage de** *traveler's checks* **100 dollars en euros.**	Good day sir. I would like to exchange this $100 American traveler's check for euros.
LE CAISSIER	**J'ai besoin de votre passeport.**	I need your passport.
M. SMITH	**Pourquoi?**	Why?
LE CAISSIER	**C'est comme ça. Il faut** *(ee-dahn-tee-tay)* **montrer une carte d'identité.**	That's the way it is. You have to show some identification.
M. SMITH	**Je l'ai oubliée à l'hôtel.**	I left it at the hotel.
MME SMITH	**J'ai mon passeport.**	I have my passport.
L'EMPLOYÉ	**Très bien, Madame.**	Very well, Madam.
MME SMITH	**Je voudrais aussi changer 500 dollars américains.**	I would also like to change 500 American dollars.
L'EMPLOYÉ	**Bon. Alors ça fait 600 dollars américains en tout?**	Okay. Then, it is 600 American dollars in all?
MME SMITH	**Oui.**	Yes.

L'EMPLOYÉ		That will be 730 euros. Take this slip
		to the cashier.
M. SMITH	**Mais vous parlez anglais?**	But you speak English?
	(stahzh)	
L'EMPLOYÉ	**Bien sûr. J'ai fait un stage**	Of course. I did a two-year internship at a
	de deux ans à une banque à New York.	bank in New York City.
	(sa-pehr-lee-po-pet) *(oh-ryay)*	
M. SMITH	**Saperlipopette! Vous auriez**	For heavens sake! You could
	(pew)	
	pu nous le dire plus tôt . . .	have told us earlier . . .
L'EMPLOYÉ (souriant)	**Au revoir . . . et**	(smiling) Good-bye . . . and
	bon séjour en France!	enjoy your stay in France!

(ko-mahn)
COMMENT. . .
How to . . .

(shahn-zhay)
changer
to exchange

(koor) *(shahnzh)*
le cours du change
exchange rate

(pay-yay)
payer
to pay

(day-poh-zay)
déposer
to deposit

(prayl-vay)
prélever
to withdraw

(oo-vreer) *(kohnt)*
ouvrir un compte
to open an account

(too-shay) *(shek)*
toucher un chèque
to cash a check

(see-nyay)
signer
to sign

Now see if you can remember these useful things. Match each expression or word to each picture by checking off the appropriate box:

1. l'argent ☐
   le caissier ☐

2. le carnet de chèques ☐
   l'argent liquide ☐

3. le directeur ☐
   le billet ☐

4. le guichet ☐
   le directeur ☐

(day-poh)
5. le dépôt ☐
   le chèque de voyage ☐

6. le bulletin de versement ☐
   le bulletin de prélèvement ☐

Now, try to complete the following:

1. Je voudrais _____ dix dollars américains.

   exchange

2. Je voudrais _____ soixante-quinze euros.

   withdraw

3. Je voudrais _____ un chèque.

   cash

4. Je voudrais _____ 75 euros.

   deposit

ANSWERS

Complete the following   1. changer 2. prélever 3. toucher 4. déposer

Match each expression   1. le caissier 2. le carnet de chèques 3. le billet 4. le guichet 5. le chèque de voyage 6. le bulletin de versement

Match up the French expressions at the left with the English terms on the right:

1. L'emprunt
2. Les chèques de voyage
3. La monnaie
4. L'echange
5. Le caissier
6. Le guichet
7. Le compte
8. Le carnet de chèques

A. Exchange rate
B. Cashier
C. Loan
D. Small change
E. Teller's window
F. Traveler's checks
G. Checkbook
H. Account

(bahnk)

Comment aller à la banque?

Which way to the bank?

Suppose someone stops you on the street and asks for directions to get to the bank. You are now at the shoemaker's shop. Can you give him or her proper instructions? Use the map below.

ANSWERS

Which way to the bank Tournez à gauche. Allez tout droit. Tournez à gauche. Tournez à droite.

Banking 1. C 2. F 3. D 4. A 5. B 6. E 7. H 8. G

26   *(sehr-vees)*   *(post)*
Le service de poste
Postal Service

(vyan)
Je viens de . . .
I just . . .

Remember the immediate future, simply formed with **aller** in the present tense followed by an infinitive? To express the immediate past, you simply use **venir** (to come) + **de** or **d'** before a vowel + infinitive. The English equivalent of this construction is: "I just went to the post office." (*Je viens d'aller à la poste.*)

(ahn-vwa-yay)

Je viens d'envoyer une lettre à ma mère.   I just sent a letter to my mother.

Tu viens d'arriver?   Did you (familiar) just arrive?

Il vient d'acheter une voiture.   He just bought a car.

Nous venons d'aller à Paris.   We just went to Paris.

Vous venez d'apprendre quelque chose   You just learned something new.

de nouveau.

Marc et Marie viennent de partir.   Marc and Marie just left.

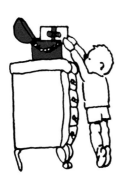  

It's lunch time. Jeannot, 5 years old, comes home, out of breath and looking happy.

(fak-tuhr)

JEANNOT   **Je viens de jouer au facteur,**   I just played mailman, mommy.

(ma-mahn)

   maman!

MAMAN   **Au facteur? Comment peut-on**   Mailman? How can one play mailman

   jouer au facteur sans lettres?   without letters?

JEANNOT **Mais j'ai des lettres.**	But I do have letters.
MAMAN **Quelles lettres?**	What letters?
(ko-mod) JEANNOT **Dans la commode de ta**	In the bureau of your room, you know . . .
chambre, tu sais bien . . . le paquet	the package of letters with a beautiful pink
(rew-bahn) **de lettres avec un beau ruban rose**	ribbon around . . .
(oh-toor) **autour . . .**	
MAMAN **Oui . . . eh bien?**	Yes . . . so?
JEANNOT **Eh bien! Je viens de mettre une**	So! I just put one letter under each door of
(shah-kewn) **lettre sous chacune des portes de**	our street.
notre rue.	

You may find it very useful, upon your arrival in France, to stop in a large post office and pick

up their brochures for foreigners. Under the heading **"Les P.T. sont heureux de vous**
(soo-eh-tay) *(byanv-new)*
souhaiter la bienvenue," (The French P.T. [Poste et Télécommunications] are glad to
to wish   welcome
welcome you), these publications will give you all sorts of information **(en français, en anglais, en allemand, en italien et en espagnol)** about their services, which are generally efficient. They even give tourists some key phrases such as: **Y a-t-il un bureau de poste ouvert le dimanche matin?** The answer to that is yes, but only in large railroad stations. Mail **(le courrier)** is distributed twice a day (three times in businesses). And now, of course, as in the United States, you can send a **fax.** There is even a new verb, **faxer,** conjugated like **parler.**

le facteur	**la boîte aux lettres**	*(ko-lee)* **le paquet/le colis**	*(rehs-tahnt)* **poste restante**
mailman	mailbox	package	general delivery

(gee-shay)
le guichet
window

la poste
post office

(koo-ryay)
le courrier
mail

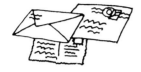

(a-frahn-sheer)
affranchir
to put stamps on a
letter or package

(fahx)
le fax
fax

faire suivre
to forward

Jean et Françoise vont à la poste.

(John has quite a few chores to do. His Parisian friend Françoise helps him out.)

JEAN **Combien de timbres faut-il que je mette sur cette lettre-avion pour Seattle?**	How many stamps should I put on this airmail letter to Seattle?
FRANÇOISE **Je ne sais pas. Allons la faire peser à la poste.**	I don't know. Let's go and have it weighed at the post office.
(kah) JEAN **Dans ce cas, je vais aussi envoyer ce colis à New York. D' où puis-je** *(pa-trohn)* **envoyer un fax à mon patron?**	In that case, I'll also mail this package to New York. From where can I send a fax to my boss?
FRANÇOISE **De la poste.**	From the post office.
(ko-mod) JEAN **C'est commode. Je dois aussi faire** *(an-teh-rewr-ban)* **un coup de téléphone interurbain**	That's handy. I must also make a long-distance telephone call. . . .
FRANÇOISE **À la poste.**	At the post office.
JEAN **Et il me faut payer la facture de mon dentiste . . .**	And I have to pay my dentist's bill. . . .
FRANÇOISE **À la poste.**	At the post office.

(ehks-tror-dee-nehr) JEAN **Extraordinaire!**	Extraordinary!
Est-ce que je peux aussi faire nettoyer	Can I also have my suit cleaned, rent a car,
mon complet, louer une voiture, faire	make my plane reservation and eat a
(ray-zehr-va-syohn) **ma réservation d'avion et manger de**	chocolate ice cream at the post office?
la glace au chocolat à la poste?	

À LA POSTE
At the Post Office

FRANÇOISE **Voilà le guichet-colis.**	Here is the parcel post window.
LE POSTIER (postal employee): **Pourriez-** *(for-mewl)* **vous remplir cette formule s'il vous** **plaît?**	Could you please fill out this form?
JEAN **D'accord. Avez-vous des timbres?**	Okay. Do you have stamps?
LE POSTIER **Allez au guichet-timbres** **là-bas.**	Go to the stamp window over there.
JEAN **Il y a aussi des cartes postales?**	Are there also postal cards?
LE POSTIER **Bien sûr.**	Of course.
JEAN **Mademoiselle, pourriez-vous peser** **cette lettre?**	Miss, could you weigh this letter?

| LA POSTIÈRE | **Cinquante cents.** | 50 cents. |

JEAN   **Et est-ce que vous avez de la glace**   And do you have any chocolate ice cream?

   au chocolat?

How about changing the immediate future into an immediate past as in the example below:

Je vais aller à la poste.   **Je viens d'aller à la poste.**

1. Jean va envoyer un colis.   Jean _____ envoyer un colis.

2. Jean va aussi acheter des timbres-poste.   Jean _____ acheter des

   timbres-poste.

3. Nous allons oublier notre   Nous _____ oublier notre

   passeport.   passeport.

4. Anne et Jean vont voyager en Europe.   Anne et Jean _____ voyager

   en Europe.

5. Qu'est-ce que vous allez faire?   Qu'est-ce que vous _____ faire?

Fill in blanks with French words:

Pour envoyer son _____, Jean va au guichet-colis.

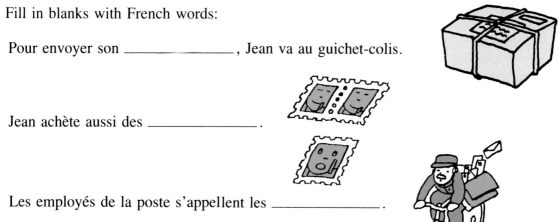

Jean achète aussi des _____.

Les employés de la poste s'appellent les _____.

ANSWERS

Fill in blanks   colis (paquet)   timbres-poste   facteurs

Immediate past   1. vient d'   2. vient d'   3. venons de   4. viennent d'   5. venez de

27 *(sehr-vees)* *(tay-lay-foh-neek)*
Le service téléphonique
Telephone Service

(a-loh) *(a-loh)*
ALLÔ? ALLÔ?
Hello? Hello?

(a-loh)
Allô? Allô?   Hello . . . Hello?

(kee) (eh) (ta) (la-pa-reh-y)
Qui est à l'appareil?   Who is it?

Je voudrais parler à . . .   I would like to speak to . . .

(me-sahzh)
Puis-je laisser un message?   May I leave a message?

Dites à . . . que Marc Smith   Tell . . . that Mark Smith will call back
(ra-play)   (tar)
va rappeler plus tard.   later.

Mademoiselle/Monsieur!   Operator! (Address an operator as

                                         "mademoiselle" or "monsieur.")

(ko-mew-nee-ka-syohn) (moh-vehz)
La communication est mauvaise.   This is a bad connection.
(ay-tay) (koo-pay)
Nous avons été coupés.   We have been cut off.

C'est une erreur.   This is the wrong number.

(pay-say-vay)
Je voudrais faire un appel en P.C.V. I would like to make a collect call.

(pray-a-vee)
Je voudrais faire un appel avec préavis. I would like to make a person-to-person call.

(kee-tay)
Ne quittez pas!   Don't hang up. (Wait a minute.)

(kohn-poh-say)
Composer un numéro   To dial a number

(day-kro-shay) (ray-sehp-tuhr)
Décrocher (le récepteur)   To pick up the receiver

(ra-kro-shay)
Raccrocher (le récepteur)   To hang up

(a-new-ehr)
L'annuaire   Telephone book

(zhuh-tohn)
Le jeton   Token

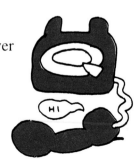

The easiest method for telephoning is to do it through the **réceptionniste** at the hotel. Another possibility is to go to the post office. Public pay phones often require a token (**un jeton**), which can be purchased at cafés, the post office, etc. You can also buy, at the post office, a telephone credit card valid throughout Europe. You insert it in a slot in public telephones, just as you insert your bank card in the United States. As you know, **les P. T. sont heureux de vous souhaiter la bienvenue.** But if you want to be challenged and to practice your **français**, you might follow the example of **Marc et Marie**, who wish to reach their friend **à Versailles**.

MARC (à un passant) **Pourriez-vous me dire où il y a une cabine téléphonique?**

(To a passerby) Could you tell me where there is a telephone booth?

LE PASSANT **Vous voyez l'écriteau avec un téléphone, devant ce café? Ça veut dire qu'il y a un téléphone public.**

You see the sign with a telephone on it, in front of that cafe? That means that there is a public telephone.

MARC **Merci, vous êtes très aimable. Viens, Marie.**

Thank you, you are very kind. Come on, Mary.

(ka-been) *(tay-lay-foh-neek)* À LA CABINE TÉLÉPHONIQUE

At the Telephone Booth

MARIE **Tu as un jeton?**

Have you got a token?

MARC **Oui. (À lui-même): Je décroche, je mets le jeton dans la fente. J'attends**
(to-na-lee-tay)
la tonalité. Bon, ça
dial tone   it's
sonne. Je compose
ringing
le numéro: 44-53-42.

Allô? Allô?

Alice? C'est Marc à l'appareil.
(vwah)

Yes. (To himself): I pick up the receiver, I put the token into the slot, I wait for the dial tone. Good, it's ringing. I'm dialing the number: 44-53-42.

Hello, hello?

Alice? This is Mark calling.

UNE VOIX **Quel numéro appelez-vous?**

What number are you calling?

MARC	Le quatre quatre cinq trois . . . Zut! On a été coupé. Opérateur?	Four four five three . . . Darn it! We've been cut off. Operator?
L'OPÉRATEUR	Allô, j'écoute.	Hello, I'm listening.
MARC	Pouvez-vous me donner la communication avec Mme Alice Dupont à Versailles	Can you connect me with Mrs. Alice Dupont in Versailles . . . .

L'OPÉRATEUR (très vite)	**D** Daniel, *(day)* **U** Ursule, *(ew)* **P** Pierre, *(pay)* **O** Oscar, *(oh)* **N** Nadine et **T** comme Théodore? *(tay)*	(Very fast): D Daniel, U Ursula P Peter O Oscar N Nadine and T as in Theodore?
MARC (pris de panique)	Mademoiselle, je ne comprends pas un mot de ce que vous dites.	(Suddenly panicky) Miss, I don't understand a word of what you're saying.
		(He hangs up and leaves the booth.)
MARC	Viens, Marie. Nous allons retourner à l'hôtel et demander au gentil *(zhahn-tee)* réceptionniste de nous aider.	Come on, Mary. We're going to return to the hotel and ask the nice receptionist to help us.

After studying the expressions at the beginning of this section and the dialogue, can you fill in the blanks in the sentences below?

1. Si je veux téléphoner, d'abord, je demande où il y a une _____ .

telephone booth

2. Ensuite, je _____ le récepteur.

pick up

3. Puis j'attends la _____ .

dial tone

4. Alors, je _____ .

dial the number

5. Si la personne à qui je voudrais parler n'est pas là, je dis: "Puis-je laisser un _____ ?"

message

ANSWERS

Fill in blanks 1. cabine téléphonique 2. décroche 3. tonalité 4. compose le numéro 5. message

(dok-tūhr) *(mayd-san)*

Les docteurs/Les médecins
Doctors

(dahn-teest) *(o-pee-toh)*

Les dentistes   Les hôpitaux
Dentists   Hospitals

(ray-pay-tee-syohn)   *(zhay-nay-rahl)*

UNE RÉPÉTITION GÉNÉRALE
A Once Over . . .

(Paul and Anne are at it again. This time they test each other on the parts of the human body.)

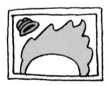   

PAUL	**Alors, qui commence, toi ou moi?**	Well, who starts, you or me?
ANNE	**Tu me demandes en premier.**	You ask me first.
PAUL	**Bon. Qu'est-ce que tu as là?**	Good. What do you have there?
	(shuh-vūh)	
ANNE	**Les cheveux.**	Hair.
	(yūh)	
PAUL	**Entre les cheveux et les yeux?**	Between the hair and the eyes?
	(frohn)	
ANNE	**Le front.**	The forehead.
	(oh) (duh-sew)	
PAUL	**Au-dessus des yeux?**	Over the eyes?
	(soor-see)	
ANNE	**Les sourcils.**	The eyebrows.

227

PAUL Et qu'est-ce qu'on ferme

quand on dort?

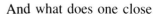

(poh-pyehr)

ANNE Les paupières.

And what does one close

when one sleeps?

The eyelids.

PAUL Et sur les paupières il y a . . .

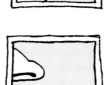

(seel)

ANNE les cils.

And on the eyelids there are . . .

lashes.

PAUL Et entre les yeux il y a . . .

(nay)

ANNE le nez.

And between the eyes there is

the nose.

PAUL Et entre le nez

(boosh)

et la bouche, beaucoup d'hommes ont

(moos-tash)

ANNE une moustache.

And between the nose

and the mouth, many men have

a moustache.

PAUL Tu as deux . . .

(o-reh-y)

ANNE oreilles

You have two . . .

ears

PAUL et deux . . .

(zhoo)

ANNE joues

and two . . .

cheeks

PAUL mais seulement un . . .

(vee-zahzh)

ANNE visage

but only one . . .

face

PAUL et seulement une . . .

(tet)

ANNE tête.

and only one . . .

head.

(ree)

PAUL Quand tu ris, on voit . . .

(dahn)

ANNE les dents

When you laugh, one sees . . .

the teeth

PAUL et quand tu vas chez le docteur,

tu lui montres la

and when you go to the doctor's,

you show him the

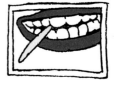

228

ANNE	*(lahng)* **langue, aaaaaaah . . .**	tongue, aaa. . .
PAUL	**Ça, c'est le . . .**	This is the . . .
ANNE	*(mahn-tohn)* **menton**	chin

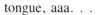

PAUL	**et ça, le . . .**	and this, the . . .
ANNE	*(koo)* **cou.**	neck.
PAUL	**Voilà deux . . .**	Here are two
ANNE	*(ay-pohl)* **épaules**	shoulders,
PAUL	**deux . . .**	two . . .
ANNE	*(brah)* **bras**	arms
PAUL	**et deux . . .**	and two . . .
ANNE	*(kood)* **coudes**	elbows
PAUL	**deux . . .**	two
ANNE	*(man)* **mains**	hands
PAUL	**et dix . . .**	and ten . . .
ANNE	*(dwa)* **doigts.**	fingers.
PAUL	**Mon tour maintenant.**	My turn now.
ANNE	**Ça, c'est le**	This is the . . .
PAUL	*(doh)* **dos**	back
ANNE	**et là-devant, la . . .**	and here in front, the . . .
PAUL	*(pwa-treen)* **poitrine.**	chest.
ANNE	**Quelque chose te fait mal quand tu**	Something hurts you when you
	manges trop de gâteau:	eat too much cake:

229

PAUL	*(es-to-ma)* **l'estomac.**	the stomach.
ANNE	**Et un peu plus bas il y a le...**	And a little lower is the
PAUL	*(vahntr)* **ventre.**	belly.
ANNE	**Et derrière il y a le...**	And behind there is the ...
PAUL	*(de-ryer)* **derrière**	behind
ANNE	**et d'ici jusque là tu as deux...**	and from here to there you have two ...
PAUL	*(kwees)* **cuisses**	thighs
ANNE	**et ensuite deux**	and then two ...
PAUL	*(zhuh-noo)* **genoux**	knees
ANNE	**et plus bas les deux...**	and farther down the two ...
PAUL	*(mo-le)* **mollets**	calves
ANNE	**jusqu'aux deux...**	down to the two ...
PAUL	*(shuh-vee-y)* **chevilles.**	ankles.
ANNE	**Et ce que tu te laves une fois par an, ce sont les...**	And what you wash once a year are the ...
PAUL	*(pyay)* **pieds**	feet
ANNE	**avec les dix...**	with the ten ...
PAUL	*(or-te-y)* **orteils.**	toes.

Draw lines between the matching words:

1. le front   A. tongue
2. les orteils   B. face
3. la bouche   C. eyelids
4. les chevilles   D. forehead
5. la langue   E. ankles
6. les paupières   F. toes
7. l'estomac   G. stomach
8. le visage   H. mouth
9. la moustache   I. teeth
10. les dents   J. moustache

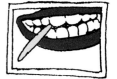

(sehn-teer)

Se sentir (bien, mal)

To feel

Do you remember the second group of **IR** verbs you studied in Chapter 5? When the verb **SENTIR** (to smell, to feel) is made reflexive, it is used to describe the state of one's health.

Toilettes (W.C.)

Dames   **Messieurs**

Je me sens bien.	I feel well.
Je me sens mal.	I feel sick.
Je ne me sens pas très bien.	I don't feel very well.

Parts of the body are usually preceded with the definite article ⬚LE⬚, ⬚LA⬚, ⬚L'⬚, ⬚LES⬚.

Je me lave ⬚les⬚ **mains.**   I wash my hands.

J'ai mal à ⬚la⬚ **tête.**   My head hurts, I have a headache.

Remembering that À + LE becomes ⬚AU⬚ and À + LES ⬚AUX⬚,

can you practice this construction with parts of the body?

Example: **J'ai mal à la tête.**
                  J'ai mal au dos.
                  J'ai mal aux oreilles.

ANSWERS

Match words 1. (D) 2. (F) 3. (H) 4. (E) 5. (A) 6. (C) 7. (G) 8. (B) 9. (J) 10. (I)

Draw lines between the expressions which match:

1. **J'ai mal aux dents.**
2. **J'ai mal au dos.**
3. **J'ai mal à la tête.**
4. **J'ai mal au pied.**
5. **J'ai mal aux oreilles.**
6. **J'ai mal aux yeux.**
7. **J'ai mal à l'estomac.**
8. **J'ai mal au genou gauche.**
9. **Je me suis fait mal.**
10. **Je me suis fait mal au doigt.**

A. I have a headache.
B. I have an earache.
C. My foot hurts.
D. I have a toothache.
E. I have a backache.
F. My left knee hurts.
G. My eyes hurt.
H. I hurt my finger.
I. I have a stomach-ache.
J. I hurt myself.

In case of a minor medical complaint which cannot be solved with **des aspirines,** you can always walk into a **pharmacie** and say:

Excusez-moi Monsieur/Madame.	Excuse me.
(kohn-se-y) **Pouvez-cous me donner un conseil? J'ai** **très mal _____.**	Can you give me some advice? My _____ hurts badly.

(far-ma-syan)   *(far-ma-syehn)*
If the **pharmacien** or **pharmacienne** cannot help you, he/she will give you the address of a doctor. So will the hotel's receptionist. Doctors usually have consultation hours for patients who do not have an appointment. You may have to wait a long time, so it's better, if possible, to make an appointment ahead of time. In case of an emergency in Paris, you can call

(prohn)   *(suh-koor)*
707.77.77, 336.03.86, the Police (17), or **Prompt Secours** (18), and even ask for an
prompt   assistance

English-speaking doctor. In the provinces, all the emergency numbers are on page one of the telephone book. A few pharmacies remain open all night and during the weekend. The local paper carries a list. In case of a toothache, the procedure is the same.

ANSWERS

Match words 1. (D) **2.** (E) **3.** (A) **4.** (C) **5.** (B) **6.** (G) **7.** (I) **8.** (F) **9.** (J) **10.** (H)

DITES AAAAAAAAH . . .

Say Aaaaaaaaah . . .

(gorzh)
Marie a mal à la gorge. (Mary has a sore throat.) She makes an appointment with

(zhay-nay-rah-leest)
Dr. Rebouteux, a general practitioner (**généraliste**).

LE DOCTEUR **Bonjour, Madame.**   Hello, madam.

(khes)   (keen)   (va) (pah)
Qu'est-ce qui ne va pas?   What's wrong?

(a) (pehn)
MARIE **Je peux à peine parler.**   I can hardly speak.

LE DOCTEUR **Ouvrez la bouche et dites**   Open your mouth and say

    "trente-trois."   "trente-trois."

MARIE **Pourquoi trente-trois?**   Why 33?

LE DOCTEUR **C'est comme ça. Oui, la**   That's the way it is. Yes, your

    gorge est un peu rouge. Comment throat is a little red. How

(oh-truh-mahn)
    vous sentez-vous autrement?   do you feel otherwise?

(boo-shay)
MARIE **Mal. J'ai le nez bouché et j'ai** Poorly. I have a stuffed nose and

    mal à la tête.   a headache.

LE DOCTEUR **Prenons votre température.** Let's take your temperature.

    (Mary opens her mouth).

LE DOCTEUR **La température est normale.** Your temperature is normal. It's a

(may-shahn) (rewm)
    C'est un méchant rhume avec un peu bad cold with a little angina . . . .

(ahn-zheen)
    d'angine . . . .

MARIE **Angine?**   Angina?

(an-fek-syohn)
LE DOCTEUR **Oui, une petite infection à la** Yes, a mild throat infection. I'll

    gorge. Je vais vous donner une   give you a prescription. Take one

(kohn-pree-may)
    ordonnance. Prenez un comprimé pill every four hours.

    toutes les quatre heures.

(oo-vray)   *(boosh)*

OUVREZ LA BOUCHE!
Open Wide!

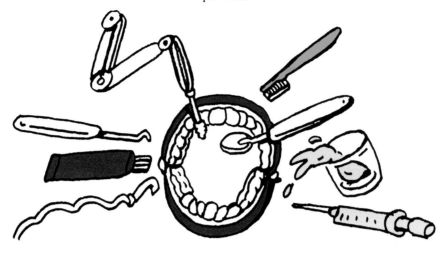

Mark has a toothache. A friend recommends a dentist with whom she is most satisfied. Mark's appointment is today at 2:00 P.M.

MARC (à la réceptionniste) **J'ai un rendez-vous.**   (To the receptionist) I have an appointment.

LA RÉCEPTIONNISTE **Avec le Docteur**   With Dr. Buisson?
(bwee-sohn)
Buisson?

MARC **Oui, pour deux heures.**   Yes, for 2 o'clock.

LA RÉCEPTIONNISTE **Votre nom, s'il vous**   Your name, please?

plaît?

MARC **Marc Smith.**   Mark Smith.

LA RÉCEPTIONNISTE (Elle examine le livre de   (She examines the appointment book.) That's
(eh-feh)
rendez-vous.) **En effet.**   correct.

(plas)
LA RÉCEPTIONNISTE **Prenez place. Il y a**   Take a seat. There are a lot of people today. Is

du monde aujourd'hui. C'est votre   this your first visit?

première visite?

MARC **Oui.**   Yes.

234

LA RÉCEPTIONNISTE **Pourriez-vous remplir cette carte s'il vous plaît?**	Could you fill out this card please?
(Une heure plus tard) *(a-sees-tahnt)* *(dahn-ter)* L'ASSISTANTE DENTAIRE **Monsieur Smith?**	(One hour later) Mr. Smith?
MARC **Oui?**	Yes?
L'ASSISTANTE **Prenez place dans ce** *(foh-tuh-y)* **fauteuil. Le docteur arrive.**	Sit in this armchair. The doctor will be here soon.
(Quinze minutes plus tard.)	(15 minutes later)
LE DENTISTE **Monsieur Smith? Où avez-vous mal? Ici? Voyons . . . Ça** *(brahnl)* **fait mal? Et ça? Oui—et ça branle un** *(plohn-bahzh)* **peu par ici. Le plombage est tombé.** *(a-nehs-tay-zee)* **Je vais vous faire une anesthésie** *(lo-kahl)* *(boo-shay)* **locale. Puis je vais boucher la dent** *(tahn-po-rehr)* **avec un amalgam temporaire. Ce** **bridge ici est mal placé et cette** *(koo-ron)* *(mwa-tyay)* *(fee-shew)* **couronne est à moitié fichue. Dans** **deux ou trois ans vous allez avoir** *(dahn-tyay)* **besoin d'un dentier.**	Mr. Smith? Where does it hurt? Here? Let's see . . . It hurts? And that? Yes—and it wobbles a bit around here. The filling has fallen out. I'm going to give you a local anesthesia. Then I'll fill the tooth with a temporary amalgam. This bridge here doesn't sit well and this crown is half-finished. In two to three years you're going to need a denture.
(ray-zwee) *(kuhr)* MARC **Cela me réjouit le coeur.**	That makes my heart rejoice.
LE DENTISTE **Au revoir Monsieur, et** *(bon)* *(va-kahns)* **bonnes vacances!**	Good-bye, and enjoy your vacation!

Can you match up the words in the left column with the definitions in the right column?

1. **généraliste**
2. **mal à la gorge**
3. **le nez bouché**
4. **rendez-vous**
5. **anesthésie locale**
6. **plombage**
7. **dentier**

A. stuffed nose
B. appointment
C. general practitioner
D. filling
E. sore throat
F. denture
G. local anesthesia

A L'HÔPITAL
At the Hospital

(André, Aunt Agnes's husband, has symptoms which look like a heart attack. The ambulance takes him to the hospital; Agnes and Suzanne stay in the waiting area.)

AGNÈS *(zhahn-te-y)* **Tu es vraiment gentille d'être venue avec moi. Je suis un peu** *(an-kyet)* **inquiète.**

You are really kind to have come with me. I am a little worried.

SUZANNE **Où est-il maintenant?**

Where is he now?

AGNÈS *(ewr-zhahns)* **Dans la salle des urgences.**

In the emergency room.

SUZANNE **Est-ce qu'il est souvent malade?**

Is he often sick?

AGNÈS *(kos-toh)* **Pas du tout. Il est costaud comme un cheval.**

Not at all. He's as strong as a horse.

SUZANNE *(an-feer-myehr)* **Voilà l'infirmière.**
nurse

Here is the nurse.

ANSWERS

Match up 1. C 2. E 3. A 4. B 5. G 6. D 7. F

AGNÈS **Comment va mon mari?**	How is my husband?
L'INFIRMIÈRE **Tout va bien! Le docteur** *(muh-zewr)* *(tahn-syohn)* *(ar-tay-ryehl)* **mesure sa tension artérielle.** **Suivez-moi.** (In the room)	Everything is fine! The doctor is taking his blood pressure. Follow me.
AGNÈS **Alors, mon trésor, comment te sens-tu?**	So, my treasure, how are you feeling?
ANDRÉ **Un peu fatigué, mais bien autrement.**	A little tired, but fine otherwise.
AGNÈS (au docteur): **Docteur, qu'est-ce qu'il a?**	Doctor, what's the matter with him?
(fa-teeg) LE DOCTEUR **Un peu de fatigue, c'est tout.**	A little fatigue, that's all.

AGNÈS (à André) **Tu vois, mon chou? Je te répète tout le temps que tu travailles trop, tu ne fais pas assez d'exercise et tu fumes trop.**	You see, my darling? I'm always telling you that you work too much, don't take enough exercise and smoke too much.

Retenez
Remember

(fyehvr)
la fièvre
fever

(vee-zeet)
la visite
visit

(ma-lad)

la gorge
throat

(or-do-nahns)
l'ordonnance
prescription

(spay-see-men) *(ew-reen)*
le spécimen d'urine
urine specimen

le malade
patient

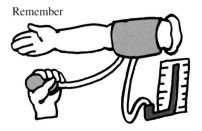

(tahn-syohn) *(ar-tay-ryel)*
la tension artérielle
blood pressure

(tahn-pay-ra-tewr)
la température
temperature
(an-feer-myehr)
l'infirmière
nurse

(zhay-nay-ra-leest)
le généraliste
general practitioner

(spay-sya-leest)
le spécialiste
specialist
(pwah)
le poids
weight

See if you can answer the following questions pertaining to the dialogues on the doctor, dentist, and hospital:

1. Pourquoi Marie va-t-elle chez le docteur? Parce qu'elle a
   A. mal à l'estomac
      (ma-la-dee)
   B. une maladie cardiaque
      illness
   C. mal à la gorge

2. Le docteur donne à Marie
   A. un conseil
   B. des comprimés
   C. une ordonnance

3. Marc va chez le dentiste
   A. parce qu'il a mal aux dents
   B. parce qu'il a besoin d'un dentier
   C. pour trouver une couronne

4. Qui est dans la salle d'attente du docteur Buisson?
   A. Jean
   B. beaucoup de monde
   C. un dentiste très patient

5. Qui a une petite crise?
   A. André
   B. Jean
   C. Agnès

Have fun with the following puzzle:

ACROSS
3. prescription
5. hand
6. throat
7. nose
8. illness

DOWN
1. arm
2. hospital
3. ear
4. pill
9. tooth

ANSWERS
DOWN 1. bras 2. hôpital 3. oreille 4. comprimé 9. dent
Puzzle ACROSS 3. ordonnance 5. main 6. gorge 7. nez 8. maladie

  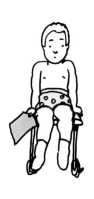 

Un jeune homme entre dans la salle	A young man walks into the waiting room of a
(say-lehbr)	
d'attente d'un célèbre spécialiste des	famous specialist of bone diseases. He tells the
(o-sūhz)	
maladies osseuses. Il dit à l'infirmière	nurse that he would like to talk with the doctor
qu'il voudrait parler au docteur en	in private. "Come in here," the nurse says, "get
(pree-vay)	
privé. "Entrez ici," dit l'infirmière,	undressed and wait."
(day-za-bee-yay)	
"déshabillez-vous et attendez."	
"Mais . . . ."	"But . . . ."
LE DOCTEUR **Qu'est-ce qui ne va pas?**	What's the matter with you?
"Je suis ici," répond le jeune homme,	"I am here," replies the young man, "to ask
"pour vous demander si vous voulez	you if you want to renew your subscription to
(ruh-noov-lay) *(a-bon-mahn)*	
renouveler votre abonnement	"Paris-Match."
à "Paris-Match."	

Can you remember? Just answer **vrai ou faux.**

1. _____ Le jeune homme voudrait parler au docteur et à l'infirmière.
2. _____ Le jeune homme est malade.
3. _____ Le docteur est un spécialiste du coeur.
4. _____ Le jeune homme demande au docteur s'il veut continuer son abonnement à
   "Paris-Match."

ANSWERS

Vrai ou faux   1. F   2. F   3. F   4. V

Here is a little courtroom drama. As in English the speakers use the present tense to give a sense of immediacy to their remarks.

(zhewzh)

LE JUGE   **Donc vous cassez votre**   So you break your
judge
(krahn)
    parapluie sur le crâne de votre mari.   umbrella over your husband's skull.

(ay-pooz)

L'ÉPOUSE   **Un accident, Monsieur le Juge.**   An accident, your honor.
the wife

LE JUGE   **Comment est-ce possible?**   How is that possible?

(an-tahn-syohn)

L'ÉPOUSE   **Je n'ai pas l'intention de**   I do not intend to

    casser le parapluie.   break the umbrella.

COMMENT APPELER UNE AMBULANCE
(ahn-bew-lahns)

How to Call an Ambulance

If you need an ambulance in Paris, you can call **S.O.S.** (707.77.77 or 336.03.86), the **Police** (17) or **Prompt Secours** (18). In small towns, emergency telephone numbers are listed on page 1 of the telephone directory. If you are near a pharmacy you'll find help there.

(At a party, Jack meets Dr. Henri Lasanté, a health officer of the French government.)

JACQUES   **Qu'est-ce que je dois faire si ma**   What should I do if my

    femme a une crise cardiaque?   wife has a heart attack?

LE DR. LASANTÉ **Pas de problème. Vous**

appelez ou demandez à quelqu'un

d'appeler Prompt Secours et une

ambulance va venir immédiatement.

Ne dites pas: ''Ma femme a mal au

coeur'' parce que ''avoir mal au
(noh-zay)
coeur'' veut dire ''avoir la nausée.''

Dites: *''Ma femme vient d'avoir une*

crise cardiaque.''

(ok-see-zhehn)
JACQUES **Les ambulances ont de l'oxygène et**
(ay-keep-mahn) *(nay-se-sehr)*
tout l'équipement nécessaire?

LE DR. LASANTÉ **Bien sûr.**

Ne vous inquiétez pas.

No problem. You

call or ask somebody

to call the **Prompt Secours** and an

ambulance will come immediately.

Do not say: ''My wife has mal au

coeur'' because this

means to be nauseated.

Say: ''My wife just had a

heart attack.''

The ambulances have oxygen and

all the necessary equipment?

Of course.

Don't worry.

(po-lees)
COMMENT APPELER LA POLICE
How to Call the Police

In case of emergency, ask the hotel's receptionist to call the police. If you are walking, ask a pedestrian or an **agent de police**:

Pouvez-vous me dire où est le

commissariat?

Can you tell me where the

police station is?

If you are traveling in the provinces, the number of the police is on the first page of the telephone book.

(At the same party, Jack meets a retired police official, Pierre Leflic.)

JACQUES **Quelle est la différence entre un**
(a-zhahn)   (zhahn-darm)
agent de police, un gendarme et un
(say-ehr-es)
C.R.S.?

What's the difference between an

''agent de police,'' a

''gendarme'' and a C.R.S.?

LEFLIC *L'agent de police* **dirige la**

circulation dans les villes. *Le*

gendarme **est sur les routes, en voiture**
(moh-toh)   (mee-lee-tehr)
ou à moto. Le *C.R.S.,* **un militaire,**
(mo-bee-lee-zay)
est mobilisé pour assurer l'ordre en
(ma-nee-fehs-ta-syohn)
cas de manifestation publique.

The *agent de police* regulates

traffic in the cities. The

gendarme is on the roads, in a car

or on a motorcycle. The *C.R.S.*, a military man,

is mobilized to keep order in

the case of public demonstrations.

(pyay-tohn)
JACQUES **Est-ce que les piétons traversent la**
(an-tehr-dee)
rue quand c'est interdit, comme en

Amérique?

Do pedestrians cross the

street illegally as in

America?

(ay-lahs) (tool)   (tahn)
LEFLIC **Hélas! Tout le temps. Mais vous**
(deek-tohn)
connaissez le dicton: À Rome, *ne*

faites *pas* **comme les Romains . . .''**

Alas! All the time. But you

know the saying: ''When in Rome, do *not*

do as the Romans do . . .''

BEFORE YOU LEAVE
Avant de partir

Now we have come to the final step in the learning process, and the most important one. What will you do in the following situations? It may be worthwhile to look over each unit to help you.

Situation 1: Faisons connaissance

1. It is day and you meet someone. What do you say in order to start a conversation?
   A. À bientôt
   B. Bonjour
   C. Au revoir

2. You have just run into a friend. What do you say?
   A. Merci
   B. Salut
   C. Au revoir

3. You introduce the friend to your wife. You say:
   A. Je te présente . . .
   B. Je vous en prie . . .
   C. Je vais bien merci . . .

4. Someone asks you how you are. Which of the following is *not* possible as an answer?
   A. Pas mal, merci
   B. Très bien, merci
   C. Bonjour, merci

Situation 2: L'arrivée

1. You do not have a reservation at the hotel. What do you say?
   A. Comment allez-vous, Monsieur?
   B. Excusez-moi, Monsieur, je n'ai pas de réservation.
   C. Bonjour, Monsieur, comment vous appelez-vous?

2. You want to say that you would like a room. You say:
   A. S'il vous plaît, je voudrais une chambre.
   B. S'il vous plaît, je ne veux pas de salle de bain.
   C. S'il vous plaît, je veux une fenêtre dans ma chambre.

3. You want to inquire about price and what is included. So you say . . .
   A. Pouvez-vous me dire où sont les toilettes?
   B. Pouvez-vous me dire combien coûte la chambre et si le service est compris?
   C. Pouvez-vous me dire comment vous vous appelez?

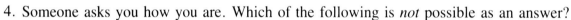

ANSWERS

Situation 1   1. B 2. B 3. A 4. C   **Situation 2**   1. B 2. A 3. B

244

Situation 3: Allons voir les curiosités

1. You are on foot and you want to find a certain street. You ask a passerby the following:
   A. Pardon, où allez-vous?
   B. Pardon, où est la rue du Cherche-Midi?
   C. Pardon, où habitez-vous?

2. The passerby might give you various directions such as . .
   A. À gauche, à droite, tout droit . . .
   B. Demain, hier, aujourd'hui . . .
   C. Le bureau de poste, la banque, le bureau de tabac . . .

3. Now you have just gotten onto a bus. You want to ask where to get off. You say . . .
   A. Excusez-moi, combien coûte le billet?
   B. Excusez-moi, où dois-je descendre pour la rue . . .
   C. Excusez-moi, comment vous appelez-vous?

4. You have flagged down a taxi, but before getting on you want to know how much it would cost to get to **la rue Molière.**
   A. Excusez-moi, est-ce que la rue Molière est loin?
   B. Excusez-moi, savez-vous où est la rue Molière?
   C. Excusez-moi, c'est combien pour aller à la rue Molière?

5. You have forgotten your watch. You stop a passerby to ask what time it is. You say . . .
   A. Pardon, quelle heure est-il?
   B. Pardon, j'ai une montre.
   C. Pardon, quel temps fait-il?

6. The passerby would *not* answer . . .
   A. Il est deux heures vingt-cinq.
   B. C'est demain.
   C. Il est une heure et demie.

7. You are at the train station and want to buy a ticket.
   A. Excusez-moi, combien coûte un billet pour Lyon?
   B. Excusez-moi, où est Lyon?
   C. Excusez-moi, quelle heure est-il?

8. The clerk answers that there is no room left on the train. He might say something like . . .
   A. Je suis désolé, mais vous êtes porteur.
   B. Je suis désolé, mais vous ne parlez pas français.
   C. Je suis désolé, mais il n'y a pas de place.

9. You want to say to someone that you are American and speak only a little French. You might say . . .
   A. Je suis américain, je parle un tout petit peu le français.
   B. Je parle américain, je ne suis pas français.
   C. Je ne suis pas français, je suis américain.

10. You want to rent a car cheaply. You might ask the clerk . . .
    A. Je voudrais une voiture pas trop chère.
    B. Je voudrais une voiture pas trop sale.
    C. Je voudrais une voiture pas trop bon marché.

11. You want to fill up your car. You might say . . .
    A. S'il vous plaît, une voiture jaune.
    B. S'il vous plaît, faites le plein.
    C. S'il vous plaît, c'est trop cher.

12. A service station attendant might tell you that your car needs repairs. He would *not* say…
    A. Votre voiture est belle.
    B. Votre voiture a besoin de nouveaux freins.
    C. Votre voiture a besoin d'un nouveau moteur.

13. You ask a ''camping employee'' if there are essential services. You would *not* say . . .
    A. Est-ce qu'il y a de l'eau?
    B. Est-ce qu'il y a des toilettes?
    C. Est-ce qu'il y a un cinéma?

14. As an answer to ''Quelle est la date d'aujourd'hui?'' (What's today's date?), you would not hear . . .
    A. C'est le trente mars.
    B. C'est le deuxième jour.
    C. C'est le trois mai.

15. To ask an airline employee at what time your flight leaves, you would say . . .
    A. Pardon, à quelle heure part mon vol?
    B. Pardon, quand arrive mon vol?
    C. Pardon, vous volez souvent?

16. With which statement does the picture go?
    A. Je voudrais louer une voiture pour une semaine.
    B. Je voudrais deux billets aller-retour pour Paris en deuxième classe.
    C. À quelle heure part le vol pour Zurich?

Situation 4: Les distractions

1. You are at a ticket agency. The clerk would *not* ask you . . .
    A. Vous voulez un billet d'opéra?
    B. Vous voulez un billet de cinéma?
    C. Vous voulez un billet d'avion?

2. If someone were to ask you what your favorite sport was (**Quel est votre sport préféré?**), you would *not* say . . .
    A. J'aime le tennis.
    B. J'aime la natation.
    C. J'aime le français.

ANSWERS

Situation 3   10. A   11. B   12. A   13. C   14. B   15. A   16. B   Situation 4   1. C   2. C

Situation 5: Comment commander un repas

1. You want to ask what the restaurants in France are like. You would ask . . .
   A. On mange bien en France?
   B. Comment sont les restaurants?
   C. Où sont les restaurants?

2. As a possible answer, you would *not* hear . . .
   A. Ils sont à Paris.
   B. Il y a beaucoup de restaurants.
   C. Ils sont bons.

3. When a waiter asks you to order, he might say .
   A. Vous désirez?
   B. Vous payez?
   C. Vous finissez?

4. To see the menu, you would say . . .
   A. Puis-je voir la cuisine?
   B. Puis-je voir la carte?
   C. Puis-je voir le directeur?

5. One of the following is not connected with eating . . .
   A. droguerie
   B. restaurant
   C. assiette

6. If you wanted to order some vegetables you would say . . .
   A. Une assiette de soupe chaude, s'il vous plaît.
   B. Un plat de légumes, s'il vous plaît.
   C. Des pamplemousses, s'il vous plaît.

7. After which course would you expect to be served your salad?
   A. l'entrée
   B. le fromage
   C. le dessert

8. An example of a dessert you might order is . . .
   A. du poisson
   B. de la glace
   C. de la confiture

9. At the end of a meal you say to the waiter/waitress . . .
   A. Le couteau, s'il vous plaît.
   B. Le pourboire, s'il vous plaît.
   C. L'addition, s'il vous plaît.

10. How would you ask if the tip is included on your bill?
    A. Le petit déjeuner est servi?
    B. La taxe est correcte?
    C. Le service est compris?

ANSWERS

Situation 5   1. B   2. A   3. A   4. B   5. A   6. B   7. A   8. B   9. C   10. C

Situation 6: Au magasin

1. Which of the following would you *not* say in a clothing store?
   - A. Pardon, combien coûte cette chemise?
   - B. Pardon, combien coûte ce pain?
   - C. Je voudrais des chaussures, des chaussettes et des cravates.

2. One of the following lists has nothing to do with clothing . . .
   - A. complet bleu, robe de laine, chemise blanche
   - B. gants de cuir, chaussures du soir, chemise de soie
   - C. légumes, viandes, fruits

3. You would *not* hear which of the following in a butcher's shop?
   - A. Combien coûtent les fruits?
   - B. La viande coûte 2.75 euros le kilo.
   - C. Le veau est frais.

4. You want to order a drug at the pharmacy. You might say . . .
   - A. Je voudrais ces légumes, s'il vous plaît.
   - B. Je voudrais ce médicament, s'il vous plaît.
   - C. Je voudrais ces fruits, s'il vous plaît.

5. A pharmacist would *not* ask you one of the following . . .
   - A. Voulez-vous une bouteille de vin?
   - B. Voulez-vous des aspirines?
   - C. Avez-vous une ordonnance?

6. You are at the laundry. You would *not* ask one of the following . . .
   - A. Pouvez-vous laver et repasser ces chemises pour demain?
   - B. Faites-vous aussi le nettoyage à sec?
   - C. Combien coûtent les chaussures?

7. You are at the barber's and want a haircut. You might say . . .
   - A. S'il vous plaît, donnez-moi un paquet de cigarettes.
   - B. S'il vous plaît, coupez-moi les cheveux très courts.
   - C. S'il vous plaît, donnez-moi un billet.

8. The hairdresser might ask you . . .
   - A. Voulez-vous une mise en plis?
   - B. Voulez-vous un biscuit?
   - C. Voulez-vous un journal?

ANSWERS

Situation 6   1. B 2. C 3. A 4. B 5. A 6. C 7. B 8. A

9. Choose the store for each question (match them up):

A. Combien coûte la réparation de mes chaussures?
B. Est-ce qu'il me faut une nouvelle montre?
C. Combien coûtent un journal et une revue?
D. Pouvez-vous développer les photos?
E. Combien coûtent ces disques?
F. Est-ce que vous vendez du papier à lettres?
G. Combien coûte cette robe?
H. Cette bague est magnifique.

1. cordonnerie
2. papeterie
3. magasin de photographie
4. magasin de disques
5. horlogerie
6. bureau de tabac
7. bijouterie
8. magasin de confection-dames

10. Each of these stores is selling an item which should be carried by another store. Can you correct the situation?

A. **PRÊT-À-PORTER**
1. **robes**
2. **collants**
3. **saucisson**
4. **jupes**

B. **SOUVENIRS**
1. **viande froide**
2. **reproductions**
3. **cartes postales**
4. **foulards**

C. **BOULANGERIE**
1. **croissants**
2. **pain**
3. **linge**
4. **petits fours**

D. **CHARCUTERIE**
1. **bagues**
2. **jambon**
3. **pâté**
4. **salami**

Situation 7: Services essentiels

1. You are at a bank and wish to exchange a traveler's check . . .
   A. Excusez-moi, pourriez-vous me dire l'heure?
   B. Excusez-moi, pourriez-vous me changer ce chèque de voyage?
   C. Excusez-moi, pourriez-vous me donner un cadeau?

2. A bank employee would *not* ask you . . .
   A. S'il vous plaît, remplissez cette formule.
   B. S'il vous plaît, signez ici.
   C. S'il vous plaît, mangez du pain.

3. You want to buy stamps at a post office. You would say . . .
   A. S'il vous plaît, je voudrais acheter du fromage.
   B. S'il vous plaît, je voudrais acheter des journaux.
   C. S'il vous plaît, je voudrais acheter des timbres.

4. Which of the following would you *not* say in a post office?
   A. Je voudrais envoyer cette lettre par avion.
   B. Je voudrais envoyer ce colis.
   C. Je voudrais écrire une lettre maintenant.

ANSWERS

Situation 7   1. B   2. C   3. C   4. C

Situation 6   **9.** A.1 B.5 C.6 D.3 E.4 F.2 G.8 H.7   **10.** A.3 B.1 C.3 D.1

5. You answer a phone call with . . .
   A. Allô
   B. Au revoir
   C. À bientôt

6. You want to make a long distance phone call. You would say . . .
   A. Excusez-moi, je voudrais payer la facture téléphonique.
   B. Excusez-moi, je voudrais faire un appel interurbain.
   C. Excusez-moi, je voudrais votre numéro de téléphone.

7. You want to ask someone how to dial a number. You would say . . .
   A. S'il vous plaît, comment faut-il composer le numéro?
   B. S'il vous plaît, où est le téléphone?
   C. S'il vous plaît, combien coûte la communication?

8. Which of the following would *not* be used to seek help in an emergency?
   A. S'il vous plaît, appelez une ambulance.
   B. S'il vous, plaît, appelez la police.
   C. S'il vous plaît, dites-moi où vous habitez.

9. You would *not* say one of the following to a doctor.
   A. Docteur, j'ai mal à la tête.
   B. Docteur, j'ai besoin d'un parapluie.
   C. Docteur, j'ai de la fièvre.

10. Can you match the questions in the left column with statements in the right column?

   A. Comment vous appelez-vous?
   B. Où descendons-nous pour aller au cinéma Broadway?
   C. Quelle heure est-il?
   D. Où puis-je acheter du lait?
   E. Pourriez-vous me couper les cheveux?
   F. Avez-vous des journaux en anglais?
   G. Il y a un trou dans ma chaussure. Pouvez-vous la réparer?
   H. Avez-vous des timbres?
   I. Combien coûte un billet aller-retour à Cannes pour quatre personnes?
   J. Est-ce qu'il y a un garage près d'ici?
   K. Quel temps fait-il?
   L. Qu-est-ce que tu veux faire ce soir?

   1. On pourrait aller au théâtre.
   2. Un temps magnifique!
   3. À la laiterie.
   4. Allez au guichet-timbres.
   5. Aimez-vous les cheveux courts?
   6. Je ne peux pas la réparer.
   7. Oui, nous avons un bon choix de journaux anglais et americains.
   8. À l'arrêt après la Concorde.
   9. Il est midi.
   10. Oui, au coin de la prochaine route.
   11. 125 euros par personne.
   12. Je m'appelle Marc Smith.

ANSWERS

Situation 7   5. A   6. B   7. A   8. C   9. B   10. A. 12   B. 8   C. 9   D. 3   E. 5   F. 7   G. 6   H. 4   I. 11   J. 10   K. 2   L. 1

Use the target word on top to answer the question. Then, check the answer on the back.

avoir

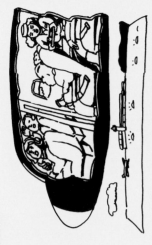

Est-ce que M. et Mme Smith ont des enfants?

être

Est-ce que le monsieur est content?

venir

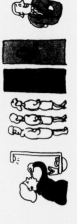

Qui vient avec le dîner des passagers?

aller

Où va Mme Dubois?

partir

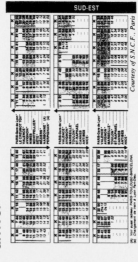

Pourriez-vous me dire à quelle heure le train part?

arriver

Courtesy of S.N.C.F., Paris

Et à quelle heure est-ce qu'il arrive à la Gare de Lyon? *(Answer, 19:50)*

faire

Est-ce que la dame s'amuse?

ouvrir

J'ouvre le coffre de la voiture?

fermer

Est-ce que la porte des toilettes est ouverte?

L'hôtesse de l'air **vient**.

Il **arrive** à dix-neuf heures cinquante.

Non, elle est **fermée**.

Non, il **est** fâché.

Il **part** à quinze heures.

Oui, **ouvre**-le pour le chien.

Oui, ils **ont** un fils et une fille.

Elle **va** aux Etats-Unis.

Non, elle **fait** ses courses.

demander

Que fait le père?

répondre

Que fait la jeune fille?

appeler

Que fait la jeune fille?

manger

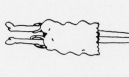

Que fait l'homme au veston noir?

boire

Qu'est-ce que le monsieur va faire?

mettre

Que fait la dame au magasin de prêt-à-porter?

enlever

Que fait le monsieur?

savoir

Pourquoi ces gens sont-ils surpris?

connaître

Est-ce que Jean Dubois connaît Marie Dubois?

Elle **appelle** son petit ami au téléphone.

Elle **met** une robe.

Il la **connaît** bien sûr, c'est sa femme!

Elle **répond**: "Il est trois heures, papa".

Il va **boire** du vin.

Parce qu'ils ne **savent** pas que les pharmacies américaines ne sont pas comme les "drugstores" américains.

Il **demande** à sa fille quelle heure il est.

Il **mange** de bon appétit.

Il **enlève** son veston.

beaucoup

Qu'est-ce que le pickpocket a dans sa veste?

grand

Vous êtes nombreux dans votre famille?

trop

Est-ce qu'il y a beaucoup de choses sur le terrain de camping?

assez

Le banquier a l'air content, pourquoi?

peu

Pourquoi le journaliste est-il fatigué?

quelques

Il y a des gens qui attendent le train?

bon, bonne

Le garçon: "Tout va bien, Monsieur"?

petit

Le garçon est grand?

tard

A quelle heure dînez-vous?

Il a **beaucoup** de montres.

Oui, nous avons une **grande** famille.

Il y a **trop** de choses.

Parce qu'il a **assez** d'argent.

Il est fatigué parce qu'il fait **peu** d'exercise.

Oui, il y a **quelques** passagers.

Le client: "Oui, merci, le poulet est très **bon**".

Non, il est **petit**.

En général vers huit heures, **tard** pour les américains.

la boulangerie

Où vend-on du pain et des croissants?

le marché

On achète les légumes et les fruits, à l'épicerie, au supermarché ou...

le tableau

Qu'est-ce que l'homme regarde?

l'agent de police

Qui est l'homme à droite?

entre

Où est la table?

aujourd'hui

Hier c'était dimanche.

la chaise

Il y a un fauteuil dans la chambre d'hôtel?

sur

Est-ce que le chat est sous la table?

l'église

Où va-t-on le dimanche matin si on est religieux?

A la **boulangerie**.

...au **marché**.

Il regarde un **tableau**.

C'est un **agent de police**.

Entre le réfrigérateur et la chaise.

Aujourd'hui c'est lundi.

Non, mais il y a une chaise.

Non, il est **sur** la chaise.

On va à la synagogue, à la mosquée ou à l'**église**.

dire

Que dit l'homme du kiosque au touriste?

sous

Que fait le garçon?

prendre

Et M. Lefèvre, qu'est-ce qu'il fait?

détester

Est-ce que cet homme est content?

vouloir

Qu'est-ce que le petit garçon veut faire?

donner

Que fait Mme Lefèvre?

aimer

Mme Dubois semble fâchée, pourquoi?

pleuvoir

Quel temps fait-il?

regarder

Qu'est-ce que le client au restaurant regarde?

Il lui **dit** où il peut acheter des cigarettes.

Il met une lettre **sous** la porte.

Il **prend** du fromage.

Non! Il **déteste** être chauve!

Il **veut** prendre quelque chose dans la boîte.

Elle **donne** du fromage à son mari.

Parce qu'elle n'**aime** pas avoir les cheveux blonds!

Il **pleut**.

Il **regarde** le menu.

le poisson

La sole est une viande?

le fromage

Aimez-vous le Brie?

la jupe

Qu'est-ce que tu vas mettre ce soir pour aller chez Jeanne?

la chaussure

Elles sont beaucoup trop grandes pour moi, ces...

la pâtisserie

Où trouve-t-on les meilleurs éclairs au chocolat?

le kilo

Deux livres américaines de sucre font...

le litre

Combien de "quarts" y a-t-il dans un litre?

la demi-douzaine

Donnez-moi six citrons, s'il vous plaît.

le panier

Qu'est-ce qu'il y a devant la fermière?

Je vais mettre ma **jupe** rouge et un chemisier beige.

...900 grammes de sucre en France, presque un **kilo**.

Il y a trois grands **paniers**.

Oui, c'est un excellent **fromage**.

A la **pâtisserie** Duroflet, là-bas.

Alors, une **demi-douzaine**?

Non, c'est un **poisson**.

...chaussures!

Un **litre** et un "quart", c'est presque la même chose.

désirer

Qu'est-ce que le jeune homme désire?

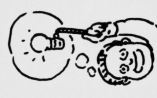

en

Où est Clermont-Ferrand?

toujours

Est-ce que Pierre est intelligent?

voir

Que voyez-vous sur le dessin?

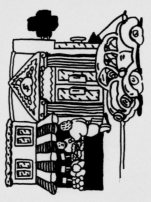

avec

Avec qui est-ce que la passante parle?

à droite

Est-ce que le Jardin du Luxembourg est à gauche du Boulevard Raspail?

dans

Est-ce que les passagers sont dans un avion?

sans

L'école a une porte, mais a-t-elle des fenêtres.

et

Qu'est-ce que le dessin représente?

Il **désire** téléphoner.

Clermond-Ferrand est **en** France.

Oui, il a **toujours** des idées intéressantes.

Je **vois** une maison.

Elle parle **avec** la marchande.

Non, il est **à droite**.

Non. Ils sont **dans** un train.

Non, c'est une école **sans** fenêtres.

Il représente un homme **et** sa femme qui s'amusent.

le guichet

Où est le caissier?

la monnaie

Excusez-moi, je n'ai qu'un billet de cent francs.

la bicyclette

Est-ce que le facteur apporte les lettres en voiture?

la bouche

Chez le dentiste, on doit …

les yeux

Ma sœur a les yeux bruns, mais moi, …

la main

Tu écris avec la main droite?

le cou

Les girafes ont une petite tête, mais . . .

la langue

Jean-Pierre, comme tu es impoli! Tu sais bien qu'on ne doit jamais …

le nez

Ce monsieur a un grand nez.

Non, il livre les lettres à **bicyclette**.

Non, j'écris avec la **main** gauche.

Moi, j'ai un petit **nez** en trompette.

Ça ne fait rien, voilà de la **monnaie**.

…J'ai les **yeux** bleus.

…tirer la **langue**!

Il est au **guichet** de la banque.

…ouvrir la **bouche**.

…un **cou** très long.

le chien

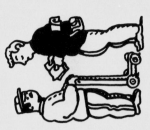

Est-ce que les Smith aiment les animaux?

montrer

Que fait le touriste?

le portefeuille

Où est l'argent?

entrer

Qu'est-ce que les touristes vont faire?

jouer

Qu'est-ce que les garçons font?

courir

Est-ce que l'homme marche?

écrire

Trois lettres dans mon courrier!

attendre

Que fait le piéton?

acheter

Vous désirez quelque chose, Monsieur?

Il **montre** son passeport à l'inspecteur.

Ils vont **entrer** dans le train.

Maintenant, je dois **écrire** à mes amis!

Dans le **portefeuille**.

Non, il **court**.

Oui, je voudrais **acheter** un rasoir électrique.

Oui, ils adorent les **chiens**.

Ils **jouent** au foot.

Il **attend** le feu vert pour traverser.

la brosse

A la droguerie, on vend des produits
de beauté, des peignes,...

la machine à laver

Quelle erreur est-ce que Susan fait?

se raser

Que fait l'homme?

le journal, les journaux

Au kiosque, on ne vend pas
de cigarettes mais on vend...

la papeterie

Où achète-t-on du papier
à lettres ou des enveloppes?

la bijouterie

Si vous voulez acheter
un bracelet, où allez-vous aller?

le disque

Je vais acheter des
cassettes françaises et...

le chanteur

Est-ce que cet homme chante
de la musique classique?

le reçu

Qu'est-ce que le vendeur donne au client?

Il **se rase**.

Elle met trop de lessive dans la **machine à laver**.

...des **brosses à cheveux** et beaucoup d'autres choses.

A la **bijouterie**.

A la **papeterie**.

...des **journaux**, des cartes postales, des magazines.

Il lui donne un **reçu**.

Non, c'est un **chanteur** folklorique.

...deux **disques** compacts pour David.